SURVIVAL

Religion, Theology, and the Holocaust
Alan L. Berger, *Series Editor*

SURVIVAL

THE STORY OF A
SIXTEEN-YEAR-OLD JEWISH BOY

Israel J. Rosengarten

Translated from the Dutch

SYRACUSE UNIVERSITY PRESS

First Edition 1999
99 00 01 02 03 04 05   7 6 5 4 3 2 1

This work was previously published in Dutch as *Overleven: Relaas van een Zestienjarige Joodse Antwerpenaar* by Uitgeverij C. de Vries-Brouwers, Antwerpen-Rotterdam, in 1996.

All photographs courtesy of the author.

The paper used in this publication meets the minimum requirements of American National Standard for Information Sciences—Permanence of Paper for Printed Library Materials, ANSI Z39.48-1984. ∞™

Library of Congress Cataloging-in-Publication Data

Rosengarten, Israel J., 1926–
[Overleven. English]
Survival : the story of a sixteen-year-old Jewish boy / Israel J. Rosengarten ; translated from the Dutch. — 1st ed.
p.   cm.—(Religion, theology, and the Holocaust)
ISBN 0-8156-0580-3 (cl. : alk. paper)
1. Rosengarten, Israel J., 1926– .   2. Jews—Belgium—Antwerp
Biography.   3. Holocaust, Jewish (1939–1945) Personal narratives.
4. Antwerp (Belgium) Biography.   I. Title.   II. Series.
DS135.B43R6713 1999
949.3'22004924'0092—dc21

[B]   99-25979

This book is dedicated to my close relatives:
to my father, my mother and my four brothers.
They were all killed by Nazism,
deported from the Dossin barracks at Mechelen.

My father, David Rosengarten, born in 1898, was deported as number 804 with the 18th transport, on January 15, 1943.

My mother, Grine Bruh, born in 1898, was deported as number 868 with the 7th transport, on September 1, 1942.

My brother Samuel Joachim Rosengarten, born in 1923, was deported as number 371 with the 17th transport, on October 31, 1942.

My brother Eliazar Leopold Rosengarten, born in 1935, was deported as number 870 with the 7th transport, on September 1, 1942.

My brother Isaak Rosengarten, born in 1936, was deported as number 871 with the 7th transport, on September 1, 1942.

My brother Henri Rosengarten, born in 1939, was deported as number 869 with the 7th transport, on September 1, 1942.

Berta Stempel, my grandmother; Feiwel Brie, my mother's brother; Golda Esther Hoch, the wife of Feiwel; their children, Isaac Brie and Sara Brie; Lea Brie, my mother's sister; Ire Zinger, my mother's uncle; his children, Debora Zinger and Reisel Zinger; Izak Weinfeld, the husband of Reisel; their children, Salomon Weinfeld and Nathan Weinfeld.

At the same time I wish, with this testimony, to honor
the six million Jews who no more live to tell the tale.

Israel J. Rosengarten was interned in Nazi concentration camps as a sixteen-year-old boy for 994 days before being liberated in Buchenwald by the Americans on April 11, 1945. He eventually married, raised two sons and a daughter, and became a successful businessman. In 1997, he was decorated by Albert II, King of Belgium, for his contributions to the community.

Contents

Illustrations

From a Son for His Father

The future had taken the upper hand over the past, or, more precisely, over that world of the past, of the time before my father's deportation. That world still echoed only in the past.

A past which had become blurred but which, nevertheless, was virulently present in his memory, in the memories. He speaks about it as if it had been yesterday. Yet I feel that it is now, more than ever, as if it were today. The irony of a life which can only be understood in its totality. The irony of a life which obliges one to think of tomorrow. That memory has become a luxury, a luxury which he has wanted to give to me in these few pages. To tell, but not just for the sake of telling, but simply to emphasize what has not been told, so as to bring me even closer to him into his world. To know better is a certain way of "loving better."

For this reason it is good that, in the simplicity and frugality of his tale, he allows me to fortify *our* history.

Steve Rosengarten

Foreword

PROFESSOR JULIEN KLENER

During the painful reading of the present work I suddenly thought about Nelly Sachs, a winner of the Nobel Prize for literature. She begins and concludes one of her wry poems with the following rhetorical question:

Warum die schwarze Antwort des Hasses auf dein Dasein, Israel?

[Why the black answer of hatred on your existence, Israel?]

The question remains open, like all questions that touch on the fundamentals of man's experience. It is one of the many paradoxes of life that the nearly unbearable burden of experience acts simultaneously as the main stimulant for human perseverance and activity. In the case of I. J. Rosengarten, this paradox applies in a very specific way. His urge to recount is aroused when the horror in human history reaches a cataclysmic depth. While millions died, a hesitant voice was born in him, a voice that wanted to testify to the suffering of millions of people in a direct, simple, and candid style. To say that for him life triumphed over death is but part of the truth. No more does there exist an answer to the above-mentioned question raised by the German-Jewish poet, no more does there exist a definite triumph on either side. There is the will to live, and there is the urge to destroy. This observation is, like any observation, relative. Opposite Man as a destroyer stands Man as the aware or unaware yearner for immortality. The uniqueness of each person makes his disappearance a complete loss for those who are dear to him. To save himself from this absolute void, to protect himself against this absurd disappearance, Man gropes for a supposed, hoped-for, and pretended absolute existence. Writing is an expression of this quest for immortality. How someone becomes immortalized is then of no virtual importance. We are dealing here with results, but also with the movements of thoughts and dreams. In other words, the concrete result can only be hoped for on the basis of successful empathic communication and continuous remembrance.

Being silent can, for some, be a means of doing justice to the remembrance and to the commemoration. It also can be used to suppress the subconscious—but not for I. J. Rosengarten. He would, must, and wanted to speak. It was his unavoidable duty because silence for him on the Holocaust was impermissible; it became a profanation. He had to sound it out by writing it down and transcribing it in his own way using his own simple rhythms and laconic language to put the unmentionable into words. He had to bring to life, just before the end of the century, those persons who were companions in his destiny and who had disappeared for a second time in the sinister anonymity of statistics. He had to give them eyes, faces, and voices again and return them to humanity through the greyness of the misty night. He did not abandon them to the empty greyness of oblivion but rather used their story to give better form to his and their enduring hope for a better tomorrow.

How shall he be read? With depression and sadness? With concern and anxiety? I do not know. It falls to many who, traumatized, survived the period of persecution or who, reflecting upon it, had difficulty in maintaining a sober outlook on the reality in which they are living at present. The general brutality and the general injustice have in no way disappeared. Because, as Prof. J. Presser writes in the first pages of *Ondergang* [Downfall], "not a single Jew, who consciously lived through the mentioned period, can react 'normally' to any treatment of this material, including the most businesslike, without intense, sometimes very intense, emotionality. . . . Nowhere has the reality been forgotten; nowhere does it seem to be compromised. It is unavoidable, therefore, not to speak of incurable wounds; all this will pass only when the generation that underwent it is no more, and not sooner".

And then? . . . and afterward? There remains a significant, unanswered question inspired by the evidence presented by I. J. Rosengarten and prompted by the reading of this poignant and distressing human tale about the aggression, cruelty, and perverse sadism directed against other human beings. How can we prevent a repetition of this near-annihilation through collective effort? Can we not come to understand that we must keep on fighting for individual, national, international projects using all modern methods of communication and using our present-day sophisticated knowledge of the human psyche—projects that have as their objective the rearing of children in a much-wished-for ethical-creative environment of activity and communication. By thinking it through, talking about it each day, or, like I. J. Rosengarten, writing about it, I hope we shall finally be able to honor suitably the memory of these victims of the Nazis and never permit any recurrence of the Nazi outrage. And here I think of a poetic voice, Paul Celan:

> speak as the last
> do your word . . .
> look around you
> see how everything comes to life
> where there is death! TO LIFE

University of Ghent

Preface

On March 13, 1995, I was asked to visit Auschwitz as a Dutch-speaking guide-witness on the occasion of the fiftieth anniversary of the liberation of the Nazi camps.

This trip was organized by the defense minister, Karel Pinxten, and the Jewish community of Belgium. The journey and its very positive reactions from many prominent people convinced me that it is certainly meaningful to continue talking about the atrocities of the past so that such things can be avoided in the future and that one might persist in achieving tolerance and understanding of his fellow man.

This visit to Auschwitz provided me an additional incentive to give this book shape—which I had proposed to do earlier and which I have been working on for years.

The book is about my personal experiences. It is not so much a historical document as my own testimony of well-defined, well-known historical happenings, situated in the context of the Second World War. What the "holocaust" was really like cannot be put into words.

Inspired by the eleventh-century poem in Aramaic, "Akda-mot," by the poet Rabbi Meïr, son of Rabbi Yitz'hak Nehoraï, the following can be said: "If the heavens were made of parchment and all the woods on the earth were wooden pens, the oceans and seas would be ink and all the inhabitants of the earth, writers and poets, all that would be insufficient for describing the 'holocaust'." Unfortunately, this testimony illuminates one of the darkest periods through which Jewish people have passed under Western civilization.

Nonetheless, I wish to end this introduction with a ray of hope.

In spite of all the horrors of the holocaust, there were also thousands of Belgians in Flanders and the Walloon provinces who, at the risk of their own lives, helped many Jewish people to go into hiding.

My wife, Rachel Kiper, when she was one and a half years old, was saved by the Vermeulen family: Joseph Vermeulen and Stephanie Geyskens. The daughter of the Vermeulen family, Maria Josepha (Mia), accepted my wife as if she were a little sister. The parents of my hidden wife, Jacob Kiper and Chana Perlmutter, were deported and murdered on August 2, 1942.

The heroic Vermeulen family kept my wife under their roof and protection in Ranst on 100 Schawijk Street. Even to this day we have maintained a close contact with Mia Vermeulen and her children. Courageous citizens like the Vermeulen family are called in Talmud "the righteous among the people."

I wish to thank the following persons for their help and support: my son David and daughter Mady, who for years have urged me to produce this testimony in book form; my youngest son Steve who in his message "From a Son for His Father" found the right words to justify the existence of the book; and I want especially to thank my wife Rachel who has so unfailingly stood by me and has accompanied me with patience and understanding during the years that I relived my memories and wrote them down. I also wish to thank Vital Baeken for his editorial collaboration.

January 1999

Israel J. Rosengarten
Antwerp, Belgium

SURVIVAL

Prologue

My family, the Rosengarten family, was of Polish origin. At the end of the nineteenth century, they settled in a region which, at that time, was called East Gallicia and was a part of the Austro-Hungarian monarchy. My grandmother on my father's side was called Ita Bruh-Babath. In a distant past the Bruhs came from a family of rabbis. But the Rosengartens were part of the ordinary, small-town middle class.

My grandfather lived some six kilometers from Belz, where the Hasidic Belzer dynasty originated. The Rabbi of Belz had many followers throughout Poland, Europe, and even overseas. People from everywhere came to his well-known synagogue to meet him and to ask his advice. There was even a popular song in Yiddish about someone's childhood years in Belz: "Belz, Mein Stetle Belz'. Once a month when the new month was consecrated on Saturday, my grandfather went to pray with the Belzer Rabbi.

It was in the little village of Krystinopel, Boratynie, in the region of Belz, that my grandfather ran a small, modest guest house with some twelve rooms. He owned a little plot of land where he kept some poultry and a garden with fruit trees. He had four children: David, my father; a younger son, Simon; two daughters, Tonka, the older, and Rosa, the younger.

At the outbreak of the First World War, my father, David Rosengarten, was sixteen years old. The Austro-Hungarian imperial army recruited him, and he was immediately sent to the front. He was wounded on two occasions, the first time, in 1915 or 1916, not so seriously, but the second time, shortly after, he sustained severe injuries. A piece of shrapnel struck his leg and a serious infection resulted. He remained bedridden for a long time.

The hospital where he landed was by chance in Rzeszow, a good two

My father as a sixteen years old recruit in the Austro-Hungarian army in Poland, 1914.

hundred kilometers from Krakau. One of David's second cousins, Grine Bruh, lived in Rzeszow. Grine was related to David through her father, Meilech Bruh; Meilech was a nephew of David's mother, Bruh-Babath.

When Grine had received news that a distant member of her family lay in the military hospital, she went there to visit him, but this was not to be her only visit. She returned regularly, and quickly these young people developed a fondness for each other. According to the custom in orthodox circles, Grine's parents called in a sort of matchmaker, and soon David and Grine became husband and wife. My parents had found each other.

My mother, Grine Bruh, had a different background than my father.

My mother's brother, Feiwel Bruh, in Poland, 1925.

My father had at least been able to complete lower school education, quite an achievement, in the small, rural Krystynopel. My mother, on the other hand, lived as a West Gallician under the more advanced Austrian system. After eight years at the lower school, she attended Gymnasium for an additional two-and-a-half years. Her family was also well known in Poland. On her father's side, Bruh, there were great rabbis in her family. Her great-grandfather on her father's side was the well-known rabbi, Menachem Mendel Lezer. He was a rabbi in Stryzow and later in Tarnow. He wrote commentaries on two tracts from the Talmud: Kidusjin and Ketoebot. In 1848 and 1849 he published these com-

The two late sisters of my father in Poland.

mentaries under the title *Sova Semachot** These writings are still being consulted by prominent rabbis and Talmudists.

Grine's mother had the family name of Stempel. The Stempels were a name of much importance in West Gallicia. Feiwel Stempel, a nephew of my grandmother, was a deputy in the Chamber of People's Representatives for the administration of Krakau.

When my father's father died, he did not leave much for his descendants. His guest house never brought in more than just enough to maintain his family. For this reason, my father decided to take a chance on city life. Together with Grine, he stayed in Rseszow and sent for his mother, Ita, and his two youngest, still unmarried sisters, Tonka and Rosa. The younger brother of my father, Simon, was somewhat more ambitious. After the First World War, he went to America to study. Since then, he has been called "Uncle Sy." Due to the crisis, he had difficulty establishing his law practice and, consequently, took up the printing profession, building a printing company worthy of mention. In August 1994 Uncle Sy turned ninety-one, and his children and

---

"Sova Semachot" means "joy in happiness," and was the leitmotiv of the rabbi. The descendants of Rabbi Menachem Mendel Lezer are called the grandsons and granddaughters of the "Sova Semachot."

grandchildren gave him an intimate birthday party. My youngest son, Steve, who at that time was twenty and working a summer job in the United States, attended the party. After all these years and despite the great distance, our family remained tied to each other.

The first child born to David and Grine was called Samuel. He came into the world on December 23, 1923. I myself was born two years and two months later on February 27, 1926. At that time, i.e., between the wars, an enormous economic crisis raged in Poland. It was especially difficult for the Jewish people, who numbered about three-and-a-half million. As an unschooled worker, my father had difficulty earning a living. He tried to build a wholesale business in textiles but had to give up because of the competition. By the end of 1928, completely defeated, he decided to leave the country. He would seek out opportunities in Belgium. The rest of his young family would follow him later.

The fact that he chose Belgium was no accident. Several of Grine's relatives had gone there earlier: at first her parents and afterward her brother Feiwel and her two sisters, Lea and Ruchka. It seemed as if they, with the necessary effort, could indeed earn their daily bread in Belgium. Moreover, anti-Semitism in Belgium was still insignificant compared to Poland. The life of Jewish people in Poland had already become sufficiently hard.

My father found work in the diamond industry in Antwerp. The lowest paid professions were those of diamond girdler and polisher, which one could master largely in three months. More prestigious was the profession of diamond sawer, for which one had to work in a factory. It was, most desirable to be a diamond cleaver, which required a very long and difficult apprenticeship. My father became a diamond girdler. A diamond polisher had to have access to a studio or workshop, while a girdler could have his machine at home.

A good two years later, at the end of 1930, my mother, Samuel, and I followed him. Although I was then not yet five, I still have some impressions of this move; I remember the day when we said farewell to the Stempels, the brothers of my grandmother Berta Stempel. We came to Benjamin Stempel, the youngest brother of my grandmother. He lived in Zolinya and had six children. We also went to bid farewell to a somewhat richer great-uncle of mine, Jacob Reich. He lived in Lancut, a bigger town in the region. I saw a telephone for the first time in my life in his house. I took the receiver in my hand to look at it and suddenly a voice came out. "Hello? Hello?" Obviously, the voice came from the exchange, but as a child I was terrified! I threw the receiver

My father's brother, Uncle Sy, in New York at his graduation as a lawyer, 1926. He is my father's only surviving brother and emigrated to the United States after World War I.

back and ran away. What had I done? I felt as if I had received a rebuke, as if I had been caught red-handed.

On the return journey from Zolinya to Rzeszow, a trip of about one hour, something further awaited me. We took the bus. It was jammed full and there was no seat left for me. Close by sat a policeman guarding a shackled prisoner. The policeman could see that I was about to fall, and suddenly he picked me up. He set me on the lap of the prisoner! I sat for the rest of the trip stiff with fright, staring ahead, as still as a mouse, praying that this trip would soon be over.

Finally, our train journey to Belgium began. The trip took us through Rzeszow, Krakau, Katowice, and finally Brussels. For me this was an amazing experience. As a special treat, my mother had taken with us a couple of bottles of cocoa, actually a homemade mixture of cocoa, water, and sugar. For the entire trip, I held the bottle in my hands. Whereever we stopped, we could see people exiting the train,

*My mother in 1926, with my older brother Samuel
and me on her lap in Poland.*

walking along the platform, passing our coach, and chatting. At each
station, I could see and hear that the people were different, with different clothes and different dialects.

In Katowice, we were met by Uncle Douchek, the husband of Aunt
Rosa. They lived in Katowice. When I saw Uncle Douchek with his
long, closely buttoned coat, standing near a train coach, I became so
uncontrollably excited that the bottle of cocoa, which I had cherished
throughout, slipped through my fingers and fell to smithereens on the
ground. I was inconsolable until my uncle appeared with a surprise; he
had brought with him a bunch of bananas. What sort of things were
these? I had never seen anything like them before. They tasted deli-
cious, really special. It was already a little bit of the taste of the West, of
the whole new world that awaited me.

On the second night, we reached Brussels. Here, at the change of

Some family members and friends from Lancut, c. 1929.

trains, we were met by grandfather, my mother's father. By chance, he also had bananas with him, but they were not so wonderful as those of Uncle Douchek.

My grandparents lived in the Bloemstraat 53 in Borgerhout. My father lived with them. He had a little room there where he ate and slept, which also served as his workshop, holding his diamond girdling machine. In other words, I could hardly step there without knocking something over. Everything stood stacked on top of each other! Yet we all had to live there together for a couple of months: my father, my mother, Samuel, and me. We lived like sardines in a tin, without the slightest kind of luxury.

As soon as we could pay for it, we began to look for something better. We moved to an attic on the Plantin and Moretuslei 137, still in Borgerhout. It was the attic of a house with four floors, a small, low-vaulted room that was normally only used for storage. We now had two rooms, one of which had been converted into a kitchen. And, at least, we also had running water (not yet hot water—that was still something exceptional for those times).

Here, on the Plantin and Moretuslei, my mother bore another two children, Eliazar Leopold in 1935 and Isaac in 1936. Actually, the name Leopold came from Lipe. When naming a child according to Jewish tradition, one can only use the names of family members who have passed away. The grandfather of my grandmother was called Lipe. But my parents always wanted to let it be known that they favored the Flemish and their king, and for this reason they called him Leopold instead of Lipe.

Since the birth of the most recent children, our home again became too small and the steps too high. One year after the birth of Isaac we moved for the third and final time, this time just around the corner. The address where I spent most of my childhood days is in Borgerhout, in Kroonstraat 200, on the third floor. My grandparents had already come to that house. They lived on the first floor, and we lived on the third. We now had the use of a kitchen, two living rooms, and a washing place. My father had his work place on the second floor. Bathrooms in general were not common. To wash ourselves we would go to the public shower baths on Zegepraal Street—half a frank for twenty minutes of undressing, showering, and dressing.

In 1939, my youngest brother Henri was born, the only one not born at home. Our midwife had become an independent practioner in a small obstetric clinic in our district on the Brialmontlei.

Our standard of living left much to be desired. In my sixth year, I received a splendidly fashionable sailor suit, but this was an exception to the rule. According to Jewish tradition, until I attained my thirteenth year (my bar mitzvah) I had either to take over the outgrown clothes of my brother Samuel or to wear a suit made by a so-called "reparateur": somebody who could make something new of an old, worn-out suit, usually by turning it inside out. But even in the best of circumstances, such suits could easily be recognized; on the other side of the front pocket there was always a stitch visible showing where the previous pocket had been. Oh, well! Nearly everybody was in the same position. Most of my little friends were certainly not better off than we were. We bore our existence, with seven persons in the house, and lived together harmoniously enough. We laughed a lot, and there was always something going on.

I received my lower school studies at the Israelite boys' school, the Jesode Hatorah, on Lange Van Ruusbroeck Street. Because I was born so early in the year, on February 27, I was allowed to begin my first year of study one year early. I already could read and write well

Wedding party on the Plantin Moretuslei 137, Borgerhout, in 1933. Included in the photograph are the Rosengarten family (with two children); grandparents Bruh with son, Feiwel; the Zingers, aunt and uncle of my mother, and their children; the bride Devora; Herschl Zinger, the Zinger's son (with whom my brother Samuel fled to Roeselaere; and Sonja Zinger, who took care of me like a sister after the war.

enough, and I could say my prayers, which were in Biblical Hebrew. After a comprehensive interview with the director of the Jesode Hatorah, I was allowed to skip the last year of pre-school!

As a child, this did not entirely appeal to me. I was especially not very keen about acquiring perfect handwriting. One afternoon, I received a little rebuke from the form mistress and ran out of the class. I went back to the pre-school. I thought, why don't you all leave me in peace! None of the staff had any idea where I had gone.

In the end, it was the school director in person who, after searching for me for a whole hour, found me where I sat playing with the beads. In his two gigantic arms, he carried me back to the little class. I struggled like a devil in holy water, crying and roaring, but I could no longer stay with the babies of the pre-school; the director made that perfectly clear to me. From now on to be a diligent student!

At the time I attended the Jesode Hatorah, there was both a Flemish and a French section. I was with the Flemish section. After third grade, the Flemish and the French sections merged. Cliqués sought out new members, and new friendships were forged. From here on-

My parents in 1934, Borgerhout/Antwerp.

ward began the joint preparations for the final exam in the eighth class (for the fourth and last grade), but also preparations for the notorious state exam.

The Jesode Hatorah was a school with a very heavy curriculum. In addition to the state curriculum, we were given seventeen to eighteen hours of religious teaching. This religious portion, to which the state made no financial contribution, had to be paid for separately as if it was a private school. I remember that the money for the religious part amounted to some twenty franks per month. At that time this was a very large (and, for some, problematic) amount of money.

On Sundays we also received lessons, in the beginning only two hours at a time but in the later years up to five hours. During the two months that were theoretically set aside as a holiday, we still studied for some time. After only three weeks, preparatory religious lessons were offered. Legally, these lessons were not obligatory, but morally they were: if you lived in the town and did not turn up for these supplementary lessons you were soon viewed as an idler and a good-for-nothing. In Jewish tradition, learning is an important precept.

On the playground, our games were the traditional ones. At that time diabolo was popular (you had to make sure that you had a dia-

My brothers Samuel and Leopold with me in an Antwerp park, 1938.

bolo) and everybody had to have a yo-yo. I remember that I was very good at leapfrog and sometimes could dive over five or six boys together—but there was always a boy who could beat me.

After school we played in the street. The places where we could go were limited. We usually met in the town park. Two places called the Dageraadplaats and the Koxpleintje were also close by, but there was more fun to be had in the town park.

Also, we often played farther off at the viaduct of the Cogels-Osylei, where we could play soccer with rubber balls or with homemade balls of sewn-together socks, which we always had in our pockets. As soon as we had five minutes to ourselves, we took them out and started to play.

The Boelaer Park, the Nachtegalen Park, and the Rivierenhof were too far away for us, certainly when we were still younger.

On Saturday afternoons I went to the youth movement, which conformed to the level of Jewish orthodoxy of the Jesode Hatorah, Agoedath Israel. After we had studied a few hours, we were rewarded with a story. The youth leader then read adapted chapters from Jewish history about the medieval inquisition, about how people at that time already wanted to convert the Jews, or even to exterminate them. They were breathtaking, bloodcurdling histories. Each one of us sat on the edge of his chair. The youth leader who told these stories was Moshe Schiff, the father of Tobias Schiff. Tobias Schiff would later be one of the few who survived the holocaust. In the media he was not an unknown.

Again, on Sunday afternoon we had the so-called "activities." Afterwards, we went to play soccer or made our way to the forts by Uitbreiding Street. If it rained, we would stay at the youth organization. We played checkers, chess, or "hang man." Our favorite time was when a film was scheduled. We used a sheet for a screen, laughing heartily at Charlie Chaplin or Laurel and Hardy. But thinking back, quite often something went wrong with the projector, and always at the most exciting moment. Now *there* was a problem that caused a fuss.

On some weekends and every day during the holidays, I had to take care of my small brothers. This was my personal cross to bear. I had become an adolescent, and so I began, just like my contemporaries, to take some interest in girls. I then saw how my friends sometimes had short, secretive dates with them, and while I heard stories about how they, somewhat further up in the neighborhood, had been able to make contact with each other, had been able to whisper a few words, had even been able to touch a hand, while *I* had to take care of the children the whole time—a block on my leg! That lasted until my thirteenth birthday, until Henri arrived. Then my mother had to make herself available at least. My parents understood also that I, as a young man, also had to have my freedom.

Nevertheless, the most important opportunities, however small, for making contact with girls occurred in the youth movement. Girls and boys were separated into adjacent buildings. But when we went to play on the Dageraadplaats, the boys found themselves on the one side and the girls on the other. Each group walked around in its own direction: the girls clockwise, the boys counterclockwise, crossing paths at certain points. These were the ideal moments to say a few hasty words or to make eye contact rather shyly. It never went further than this for us. Just the smallest look or word kept us blissfully waiting for the following Saturday.

For our family, the older the children became the more difficult it was to make ends meet. My father alone could no longer support the family. The financial pressure became so great that Samuel had to be taken from school, after he had completed middle school. This was not entirely legal. Children were required to stay in school until their fourteenth year. In September, Samuel was not quite fourteen, but we had no other choice. My father taught him diamond girdling, and already after a couple of months he had mastered the profession. Soon after, he even overtook my father. That was no surprise. My father was approaching the age of forty and had often known fourteen-hour work days. He no longer had the same stamina. But our income was now larger, almost double. From now on, we could afford a little more. Once, we even bought a second-hand set of bedroom furniture.

In order to catch up on his interrupted studies, Samuel took extra private lessons in French and Hebrew. He also studied the Talmud as was the custom in our family (we were practicing orthodox). Although my parents set great store by such studies and were very pleased by his endeavors, Samuel was under no obligation to do it. But Samuel was simply an intelligent, eager-to-learn fellow who wanted to move mountains of work.

In 1933, the German-Jewish refugees began joining our class. These were some of the families who were forced out by Nazism. In March 1938, immediately after the Anschluss, the Austrian-Jewish refugees left Austria in full panic. In very clear language they talked with us about the conflict between Jews and the Nazis in their country and the incomprehensible proportions it assumed.

Already during the second half of the thirties, with the ratification of the Neurenberg laws, the Jews in Germany were systematically intimidated by Nazism. Jews were no longer permitted to practice the free professions, and they could not have their own shops. They were forbidden to court non-Jewish partners, and universities were no longer accessible to them. The boys who had fled from Germany told us of the very first German concentration camps, Dachau and Buchenwald. Some children told of a member of their family who had been captured and sent there. Some of them later returned, but with a very severe writ against speaking publically. Others came back home a few weeks later by post in a little box their bodies incinerated! When we heard this, we felt hot and cold. These reports must be exaggerated! No, we knew well that it was true, but we could not imagine it. It was simply beyond our comprehension.

At the end of my last year at the Jesode Hatorah, in 1939, all the students of our class had passed the state exams. The level of our class was, therefore, very high. For my own past, my achievements were outstanding. I was always the first in the class, and in this same manner I finished all my studies. I was especially good in mathematics.

I still remember how, while awaiting our examination results, we found the girls who had taken their exams with us. The relation between us were good and relaxed. We chatted somewhat about the possible solutions for this or that question.

In September 1939, I began my secondary school education. The greater part of my class transferred to the Talmudic High School Jesjivah, in Heide Kalmthout. But I went together with twenty others of the Jesode Hatorah to the Commercial School, on the Grote Steenweg in Berchem, right next to the Symposium. It was a good twenty-five minute walk from home. I only went there by tram in the winter.

The Commercial School was a state school. The days passed here differently than in the Jesode Hatorah. Each class consisted of some twenty students but, because of a shortage of teachers, different classes were brought together in a single classroom. Here and there, there were somewhat older louts, beanpoles of a meter-eighty high, footballers who played with the Seniors of Berchem Sport and who often bragged more or less shamelessly. In addition, I was, for the first time in my life, in a truly mixed group with all sorts of different religions and political outlooks, each person possessing his own distinctive views.

One problem for the Jewish students was that here lessons were also given on Saturdays. But because we were some twenty in number, a separate class for Israelites could be established to make up the Saturday classes.

In the evenings, I took private lessons in religion, Hebrew, French, and the Talmud, just as Samuel had done. Religion was taught us for free by volunteers. Private language lessons were mostly given to us by ex-professors who had fled from Germany or Austria. Their pay was much lower than normal. They did their work for five franks per hour, but they were happy enough to be able to earn something.

In the Commercial School, personnel were mobilized from the beginning of the year. Our director was a reserve officer, so he had to depart quickly. Our English-German lecturer, Van Kauwenberg, took his place. Several other lecturers also had to leave us to serve the fatherland. Female teachers were sent to replace them.

We called one of them "Little Snow White." I did not like Snow White, but the big louts of our class had their eyes on her and even tried to flirt with her. One female teacher with whom I got on exceptionally well was Miss De Fraiteur.

On September 1, 1939, my first month at the Commercial School, the Nazis invaded Poland. Even though France and England had now declared war on Germany, both countries remained completely passive. In Antwerp all kinds of ideas were hurriedly being considered to bring help to the Polish victims. Our own relatives in Poland were affected in the most appalling way: poverty stricken, desperate, agitated. By railway, we sent them old, second-hand clothes, sewn into a jute bag, and we also sent them a hundred grams of tea through the post. They were small things, drops on a glowing plate, but we were completely helpless to support them any further. On a hundred grams of tea, it seemed, one could last a whole week in Poland.

The first months at the Commercial School passed very quickly. A good mutual relationship existed among the boys. My good friends included Bram Fischler, Salomon Wackstok, Jacob Wiederkehr, Joske Blitz, Oscar Spira, Jacki Seisman, and Radoschitski. We lived a five-minute walk from each other and went to school together. During that first six-month term in the Commercial School, I remained the first in the class; Bram Fischler was second.

Still others in our class included Van Aelst, a good footballer; Goossens, who was one meter and ninety centimeters tall; Velloza; and Bal, who sometimes came to school with a shaving brush and shaved his lower legs during the class.

Exceptionally close to me was my friend and class companion Hersch Fink (called Herschl Fink by everybody). His father, Chaim Fink, was an official in the Israeli orthodox community of Antwerp, where its chief synagogue, which was called the Great Synagogue, was located at Oostenstraat 43. Through this official capacity, Fink was granted an official residence in the Lamorinièrestraat 60. In that same house was the ritual bath of the community. The man responsible for the bath was a certain Klein, who also lived in this house. On the evening before Yom Kippur 1936, the boiler of the bath exploded unexpectedly, and Klein fell unconscious. After the emergency call of his wife, Hersch's father ran to him with the hope of rescuing him. It was heroic fight against death, but the results were catastrophic. Klein's condition was already hopeless; he died the day after the accident. But in his attempt to rescue Klein, Chaim Fink's lungs were burnt by the steam and other hot gases. He fought for his life, but three weeks after the tragedy, he too died. It was a harrowing incident that depressed the whole Jewish community. I remember how his sons recited the Kaddish for the whole year, three times a day. When I saw Hersch reciting the Kaddish, I could hardly bear it. His heartfelt emotion overwhelmed me. To lose your father in such a tragic way at the age of eleven seemed to me so unthinkable, unthinkable because, until that moment, I had never experienced a death or mourning in my family.

Thanks to my continuing good performance in school, I had many friends who invited me to join them. It was even an honor to be allowed to sit next to me. Then at exam time, they would try to copy from me!

I had a rather sour relationship with my mathematics teacher. He liked me because I was such a star pupil in his subject; on one occasion, he called me the "mathematician of the century." But he certainly got irritated if I caught him making a mistake, and, in general, I was also somewhat of a babbler. For this he took points off.

On Wednesday, April 10, 1940, we discussed current affairs with one of our teachers called Dillen. He told us how the Germans had invaded Denmark and Norway the day before, and with how much violence, barbarity, and sadism it was conducted. The earnestness in his voice betrayed how real it all was. We felt that we were also being threatened. Even though on that day we were allowed to go home at eleven o'clock, we left in a dejected, anxious mood.

Gradually, we became accustomed to the ever-growing presence of the army in the streets of Antwerp. Parading soldiers and armed vehicles were everywhere. And then, on Friday, May 10, 1940, the war broke out.

War and German Occupation

It began at about four or five o'clock in the morning. We were awoken by a strange, protracted sound. Could it be the droning of engines? We did not immediately know what it was, but at about five-thirty, when everybody, filled with curiosity, had run outside, we could see it: whole squadrons of airplanes flew low and slowly over us. No shots were fired, which certainly seemed odd. They flew neatly in rows, as if it were an exercise. It looked just like a flying match or competition. Earlier we first thought that it was our own airplanes, that the Belgian airforce wanted to show us what they had. Gradually, they flew lower and lower. After a while we could distinguish with our own eyes on the fuselages and wings of the planes: swastikas! The Germans had invaded our country! We stood there, totally stunned.

The announcement of the attack was broadcast on the radio. By midday everybody had understood what was going on. Jewish people who were a bit affluent now immediately fled with everything hastily scraped together. Some of them had a tradesman's van; others drove away in taxis. Whatever the cast, there was almost a psychotic urge to flee via de Panne to southern France, or to try to cross to England. This did not only apply to Jewish Belgians. Other Belgians still remembered the Germans from the First World War. They knew the kind of trouble and misery they could expect.

Our family did not immediately think of taking flight. With three young children, we did not have the means to undertake anything. And, besides, there was the sister of my grandfather, Amalia Zinger, who had just been operated on for breast cancer. Traveling with her was out of the question. Escaping the war seemed impossible for us.

In the course of time, so many of those around us began to run like hares that my parents also began to panic. This one had left, and that one had left, and then another one! The town was emptying itself! Finally, we decided also to go: my mother, my father, my three little brothers, and I.

At that time, Samuel was no longer with us. On Saturday, May 11, immediately after the German invasion, he and his cousin Herschl Zinger, Amalia Zinger's son, were called up and ordered by radio to leave by train to Roeselare, ostensibly "for further instruction by the ministry of defense." The call-up was for young men between the ages of sixteen and thirty who had still not been recruited for military service. I stayed behind, as the oldest of the children, with a great responsibility.

By Monday, May 13, we had gathered together our most valued possessions, especially our bedding. We took it to the Central Station to send it ahead with the train (to de Panne, but in reality to Adinkerke). The station was bursting with chaos. Rows and rows of people were already standing in Pelikaan Street alongside the railway station, impatiently waiting to also be able to send their baggage. There was enormous tension: everywhere there were trunks, suitcases, jute sacks, bedding. It took six or seven hours before we finally could be served.

The next day, we again went to Central Station, this time to leave Antwerp ourselves. We took another five suitcases with us as hand luggage. We had 8,000 franks in cash, of which my mother had sewn 2,000 franks into the leg of my trousers, as a precaution. Apart from the 8,000 franks, there was nothing else. That was all that we had.

The train was jammed full, mostly with Jews, because they knew what awaited them. They were pulling and pushing. Our father could not even get into the same coach as ours: it was already too crowded. Separated from him, we left, shaken and buffeted by people.

The journey lasted forever. It was already three in the afternoon when we arrived in Brussels. Here, the train stopped. What I still remember clearly from that moment is our panic, our fit of anxiety, when we realized that our father's coach was being detached from our own. Our part of the train rolled on. What was happening? We were here alone. What of him? Where was he? A train guard reassured us: these coaches were only being reorganized, and that after a few minutes, they would again be coupled together.

But could he be trusted? Ten minutes passed, then fifteen; after three-quarters of an hour our father's coach was still nowhere to be seen! And I sat here, as the only grown-up boy, with my mother, with the little children, and all the luggage!

Finally, at about seven in the evening, the train was again made ready. The train in which my father was sitting reappeared and was coupled with our train. What a relief! With starts and stops, with halts, pauses, and other obstacles, we continued on.

It took the entire night to get to the coast. Throughout the trip there were bombardments and the terrifying sounds of noisy airplanes skimming closely over us. It was not until the morning that things calmed down a bit and became a little more peaceful. At about five in the morning, we arrived in Ostend in the half-light of the morning. We were parched with thirst.

We did not even know where the destination of our journey, de Panne, lay. After asking around, we were told that, at about two in the afternoon, a little local tram would pass which could take refugees to that place. The suffocating, chaotic tension everywhere still prevailed over us. A mass of hysteria.

It was already late in the afternoon when we arrived in the Panne. At last! But, what now? We heard from passers-by that the border with France was closed. Not a single exception was made; nobody could pass. Totally without hope and completely exhausted, we sat down on our suitcases. Little Henri had begun to cry miserably. We saw a shop opposite us; it was a seasonal shop for seaside holiday makers. My father took the chance of entering to ask for advice. And the shopkeeper seemed to be a very sympathetic, peace-loving person. She was also from Antwerp, but from May on she always began to prepare her shop for the season. Perhaps she weakened when she saw the children, who were looking in with large, exhausted eyes. In any case, she knew of a lady opposite her shop who ran a pub and who had an empty room above her pub on the third floor. The shop lady would have a word with her on our behalf . . . and yes, after a few words, she got her agreement! We could spend the night there free of charge in condition that, tomorrow morning early, we would immediately collect all our belongings and leave. We were overjoyed; it was an immense relief!

The room where we installed ourselves had just been painted with a view to receiving the new season's tourists. The floor was covered with canvas sheets, giving the room a chilly, miserable appearance. In the end, we did not stick to the agreement. It turned out that we spent three nights there instead. It was not our intention to be a nuisance to this stranger, but we simply had no choice. We could not get a hotel room, and left outside we would be at the mercy of the rain and the cold of the night.

The streets were thronged with tens of thousands of refugees. I still remember that I was sent to the baker every day; that meant routinely waiting in line for half an hour or more. The retailers made a fortune.

The landlady, meanwhile, became aware that, through her generosity, she had made trouble for herself. She now threatened to call the police if we stayed one day longer, and so on Sunday morning, May 19, we left. We had heard that we could go to Adinkerke, that there was a possibility of still being able to cross the border. We asked the lady to forgive us, and we moved on.

We were brought to Adinkerke in a pushcart for 150 franks. But once there, after walking for one-and-a-half hours, we ran into more problems. We were not allowed to cross the border because we were considered to be not Belgian but Polish. But hardly any foreigner had been naturalized during the period between the wars. The cost of applying for Belgian nationality was exorbitantly high. It also involved much time and difficulty; one was examined as if under a microscope before becoming eligible for naturalization. While we watched the Belgian refugees leaving the country without much delay, we ourselves had to turn back and retrace our steps.

When we had arrived at the coast four days earlier, we had met with Tonka Blander-Babath, a cousin of my father's. For practical reasons, she had stayed with us to help with the care of the children and to share her food. She was thirty years old and unmarried. But now, at the border, she decided to go ahead on her own. Without children, she was more mobile and had a better chance of getting across. Without interruption, she ran back and forth alongside the border guards. After a while, on Monday, May 20, we noticed that she did not return. She must have succeeded in slipping past the guards and over the border.

Many years later, just after the war, I heard what had happened to Tonka. She made it to the place which, at that time, we had all dreamed of reaching, Calais. It was from Calais, and also from Dunkirk, that the British army was retreating. Many civilians had already been able to escape on sloops, which had been placed at their disposal by the English.

We spent Sunday night under the stars on a thin layer of straw. We could hear the fighting throughout the night, the Germans who were bombarding the English were firing back with their anti-aircraft guns. Grenade fragments fell continuously in front of us. I was as scared as a rabbit.

I still remember how, on the following day, Monday, I was sent on my own to the center of Adinkerke to once again see if I could find some bread. As a fourteen-year-old boy, it was a true odyssey. I had to make my way through the endless throng of pushing people. There were so many adults through which I had to make my way all by myself. It took me three-quarters of an hour of struggling before I reached the first bakery. I had to stand in line for ages, and just when it would have been my turn, the doors were closed; the bread had been sold out. At the next bakery, I had to stand waiting for another three hours. After a half-day, I returned to my parents in the early evening with a fresh, warm loaf. It was our only meal that day.

On Monday night we again slept under the open skies. It was only on the third night after we were in Adinkerke, Tuesday, May 23, that we heard an announcement that, we could finally, cross the border; this included people with a Polish passport. At about three-thirty in the afternoon we left Belgium in the direction of Dunkirk.

But, how far can one get with three children, the youngest not even one year old, and with impossibly heavy suitcases? After six or seven tiring kilometers, we finally had to stop to spend the night. We slept on the floor in a miserable, empty house. The next morning we met pedestrians coming from the opposite direction, thousands of them. "Give up all hope!" they cried. "Calais is already surrounded! Not a chance of getting there!" In other words, German troops were already moving in our direction.

We had nothing else to do but to turn around and retrace our steps with the rest of the herd. It was a terribly demoralizing blow for us. All these attempts to escape from the Nazis had been in vain. And nobody knew what was now in store for us.

This useless flight had an unpleasant ending. On the way, Belgian gendarmes came riding past along the coastline. They halted by our forlorn caravan. All non-Belgian Jewish women and children had to accompany them. We were loaded up onto trucks. We were to be taken to a military camp in Oost-Duinkerken, a sort of internment camp. We were not told what would happen to us there. The men would follow us on foot.

The camp in Oost-Duinkerken was a military barracks camp. There was no nourishing food other than stone-hard sea biscuits, which seamen in earlier times used to take with them on long sea journeys. Regularly, more women and children arrived and the place was soon overpopulated.

Throughout Wednesday, Thursday, and Friday, we awaited the arrival of our father. We could not understand why it was taking him so long to come. The distance to here from the place where we had been picked up was, at most, only twenty-five kilometers. And between Thursday evening and Friday morning, all the other men had arrived to rejoin their families. Father's baggage was also already here. Something strange was going on. Every half-hour, we went on the lookout to see where he could be. I wanted to cheer my mother up, to try to give her courage, but I could not. I was uneasy myself. Had he met with an accident? Had they taken him to a hospital? In a state of panic, we considered all these possibilities.

In the meantime I, as the oldest boy, had become the unofficial head of the family. I was somewhat proud of this role, which I performed to the best of my ability. On Friday, I was sent to a shop to buy a few necessities, some food and drink. Of the two thousand franks that had been sewn into my trouser leg, there only remained a little more than nine hundred. In the shop where I came I was suddenly tempted by everything that I saw. After all, the deprivations that I had experienced the small child in me came to the surface! I bought all sorts of things: confectioneries, chocolates, cheese . . . I nearly squandered two hundred franks!

On the way back to the camp, I was overcome with feelings of guilt. What had I done? *what* had I done! My mother's rebuke would be awaiting me, of *that* I could be sure!

On the same day, our father finally turned up, at about five o'clock in the afternoon. We saw in the distance, in the twilight, a silhouette approaching us. Was it he? In any case, it was his way of walking. And then we suddenly recognized his face! Our hearts revived!

Apparently, my father had been arrested as a possible spy, because he did not have a Belgian passport and because he only spoke broken Dutch. Gendarmes had taken him to somewhere in the region of Eeklo for a cross-examination. Later, they had simply released him without much explanation and even without any questioning. He got here on foot—my father showed the soles of his shoes. They were worn out by the walking. He told us that he had spent the night in a castle. Because the invaders were already so close, the woman of the house there had very nicely tidied up the building, in expectation of the German officers.

Soon, the Germans surrounded us. From northern France, from Ghent, from Eeklo. The gendarmes hastily released everybody from the internment camp before it became too late. The reason for the camp's creation and its purpose was a mystery to us. But on the day that we were allowed to leave, there was artillery fire all around us. We could no longer advance or retreat. We were trapped between the wolves.

For the umpteenth time, we sought a place to spend the night. For a whole week we slept in a beach hotel cellar with other fleeing families. By chance, another family from Antwerp had also landed here. I had vaguely known the eldest son at the Commercial School. He had been a couple of years ahead of me.

Our stay in this cellar was simply atrocious. Apart from a little butter and a few sweets, we had absolutely no more food with us. Every second day, we went out in search of bread. At the two bakers' shops here, there was invariably a mob of people standing in line for hours and hours. Sometimes bread was available but then suddenly, there was none left. It was impossible to predict. And at night, throughout the entire night, more and more bombardments occurred.

Exactly one week later, on Saturday, June 1, we awoke to an unusual, suspicious silence. We could hear each other breathing. It seemed as if everyone had been swept off the face of the earth. After a while, I left the cellar and went to have a look around in the hotel. In front of the door, which was wide open, I saw a young German soldier. Everywhere on the driveway of the hotel, I saw cars, motorbikes, and sidecars. I knew we were lost.

When the Germans saw that this place was teeming with refugees, they behaved with perfect courtesy toward us. They were even on their best behavior with their favorite victims, Jews wearing the typical beard. "Who wants to go to Ghent?" they asked. "Who wants to go to Liège? Who wants to go to Antwerp?" They would help us to find transport, they said.

We could not believe our ears. The Germans about whom we had heard nothing but beastliness for years! They behaved like liberators, extremely considerate and well-mannered.

However, my father remained skeptical. He wanted to have as little to do with the Nazis as possible. Rather than accepting a so-called offer of help, he tried to find a way to get home on his own.

Below, near the hotel, stood a couple of empty peddler's carts of the type used by market vendors—carts with wooden wheels and a shoulder band to make the pulling easier. In such a cart, my father decided, we would return to Antwerp.

My mother and my three little brothers sat in the cart. My father and I, each in turn, pulled it for a couple of kilometers. The route which we followed was one fraught with obstacles. Especially when we came to slopes, we barely progressed. Every day, we advance some fifteen kilometers, but the distance from the coast to home was 130 to 140 kilometers! But it was altogether better than the transportation supplied by the Germans, my father repeated. Naturally, he particularly had in mind the appalling, merciless terror that his family had suffered at the hands of the Germans in Poland.

On the first day of our return journey, we came upon a mass of people who stood crowded together in front of a small cheese factory. What was going on? It was a cheese factory being plundered. Here, enormous balls of cheese were being distributed to the people by the Germans. It was taking place in a disorderly fashion. He who was lucky could get two cheeses at once, he who was unlucky, not even one! But even so, I managed to grab one. A gigantic round of cheese of eleven or thirteen kilos heavy as lead—that was something unforgettable.

At night we mostly stayed in barracks, barns, or empty farm houses. On Wednesday, June 5, we got within fifteen kilometers of Ghent, and we slept in a barrack that was organized as a refugee camp. And on Thursday evening, June 6, we arrived in Ghent. But that was the end; we could not manage anymore.

The people who allowed us to pass the night in Ghent saw how pitiful we were. They were really kind to us. The following morning they prepared a breakfast for us with bread, butter, jam, and very strong coffee. My father asked them if they had any idea how we could get some transportation, and they were also able to help us with this. They knew somebody who could drive us to Antwerp for 150 franks—all the way to our home. That was a considerable amount of money, but we had no other choice. My father agreed.

The vehicle was rather like a small motor van. With baggage and all, we drove through the streets at an enormous speed in contrast to the snail's pace of the previous days. By midday we were standing with keys in our hands in front of our old house in the Kroonstraat. We were jolly lucky that in the interim nobody had broken in to plunder!

We were the only ones of the whole family who had tried to escape. Now that our grandparents and our cousins saw us back again, their "correct choice" was proven in a way. Did not Germans behave courteously here? They were not going to get involved with the population; the Jews in Belgium formed a purely domestic concern. Our panic had been unjustified.

During mealtimes around the family table we resumed our life as Antwerpers. "Welcome home!" But my poor mother wept from exhaustion and disillusionment—and from worry about Samuel. Where was he exactly? What was he doing? Nobody knew.

Henceforth, the entire neighborhood lived soberly and unassumingly, from one day to the next. It *was* war, and everyone in the neighborhood was in the same boat.

Initially, we did not suffer excessive burdens from the occupation. The Germans continued to behave in a friendly manner toward us. In Belgium, we Jewish people were by far not so plentiful as in Poland. Therefore, as citizens of occupied Belgium we would probably be left in peace.

Diamond workers still had considerable work during the early period of the occupation. Certainly, new diamonds were no longer being imported, but there was still a adequate supply available in the home country. The big bosses allowed work on the existing inventory of diamonds.

But, how was my brother getting on in the meantime? What had happened to him? Apparently he had arrived in Roeselare with Herschl Zinger on May 11. Total chaos reigned. Where did he now have to go? What did they want of him? Without much explanation, he was included with Herschl in a convoy which would be sent by train to the south of France. What had to be done there remained a mystery. But on the way, in the region of Calais, they encountered a bombardment. The train stopped. Once again a confusion arose, obscure running here and there. Everybody was in a panic; nobody knew where to go. Samuel and Herschl lost sight of each other and from there on went separate ways.

My brother had reached a refugee camp in Toulouse in the south of France. But we, in Antwerp, knew nothing of this. We did not have the slightest idea where in the world he had gone. He was still only seventeen years old; would he be able to save himself? Silently, we even feared for his life. In July and August, most of the youngsters from Antwerp who had disappeared during the invasion began to return. In the beginning, we regularly came across people who had seen Samuel. "Don't worry," they said. "One of these days, perhaps tomorrow, you will see him back home again!" But still later practically everyone had come back, and we heard nothing more of Samuel. It seemed as if he had disappeared off the face of the earth.

It was only at the end of September that he suddenly appeared at our door. He was as thin as a pin. He looked like a vagrant with hollow cheeks, large, empty eyes, and disheveled hair. The reason why he had returned so late was horrifying. In the camp where he had been, it was customary that the refugees, when they went home, sometimes took a thing or two with them—a piece of soap, a flannel, a towel. Samuel also had stuffed such a towel in his bag. As he was leaving, a guard grabbed him by the collar. Without any investigation or trial, the commissioner's office sent him away to prison. There he landed among the worst rabble imaginable: murderers, bandits, hardened criminals. He was so completely ignored and neglected that after a few days he got scurvy. They held him in jail for six long weeks. Only then was he brought before a judge. The judge was very surprised; my brother had no criminal record. The judge apologized and immediately had him released.

My brother opened his gigantic eyes while he was telling us this. The songs that they sang in the jail, the terror, the loneliness, and the anxiety that he had suffered—the brutalities of his fellow prisoners had made another person of him.

It was only after the war that I discovered what had become of

Herschl Zinger. Following the bombardment, he remained on the train that was sent to the harbor of Calais, and from there, he was taken to England. Just like Blander, he had escaped the clutches of the Nazis.

In September 1940, when the oppressive atmosphere of the war seemed to have diminished somewhat, I returned once again to the Commercial School, ready to begin a new year. In my previous year, I had only been able to take one exam, but the director knew what I had already accomplished and was willing to let me advance. As the war progressed, there were fewer and fewer teachers and students at the school. The school had lost its drive. After a month, I decided that it was not for me.

For another two months, I went to the Jesjivah, the Jewish Talmud high school in Heide Kalmthout, which had been transferred to Antwerp at the outbreak of war. But, after that experience, I simply stayed at home. It was simply too discouraging to continue going to school, under these circumstances. And at home a great responsibility awaited me.

The first time that I was tested personally by the Germans was on a Saturday. Together with other Jewish people, I was on the way from the synagogue to St. Erasmus Street in Borgerhout, where we had to go to receive our welfare benefits. But there we were, probably on the orders of the Germans, taken by the arm and brought to the harbor. We were forced to unload completely a ship that was docked there. It was a ship full of coal. When I got home, on this holy day for Jews (the Sabbath), I was as black as a miner. Something had broken in me. I had been unjustly treated and degraded.

This brief intimidation was but a forerunner of a more strongly organized form of forced labor which the Nazis had in store for us. That same year, in November 1940, they enacted a law requiring certain foreigners in Antwerp to leave the town and go to Limburg to work for the Third Reich. My father became a victim of this opportunistic measure. He was forced to go to Alken, where he had to do work as a kind of farm laborer for a big rich gentleman farmer. He was not that badly off there. He did his work more than adequately, and it seemed that he was respected by his neighbors. But he was, nevertheless, away from home where his family, and certainly the little children, now had to do without him. I visited him twice, each time getting a lift from a truck driver who drove back and forth between the beer brewery in Alken and a depot in Antwerp.

Thus, gradually, the so-called courtesy of the invaders evaporated.

My grandfather David Meilech Bruh who passed away in Borgerhout in 1941 before the deportations.

More and more, the anti-Semitism began to impose itself. In April 1941, a signal was given for a whole series of harassments. Some twenty Flemish S.S. and a few German officers made some disturbances on Langekievit and Quellin Streets. They plundered diamond shops and destroyed shop windows. Later, in April, it became even more barbaric: synagogues were set on fire in the Van den Nestlei and on Oosten Street. I remember how, as an inquisitive child, I went to look in the Van den Nestlei at the scorching, roaring, terrifying flames, as I stood in the middle of a shocked and desperate crowd. I became aware that this was a very delicate situation and that we all had to be careful. This was no longer normal. The fire brigade was forbidden to

My grandfather's gravestone at Putte-Holland with inscriptions about the family roots and origins of my grandfather, 1874–1941.

intervene. They had to stand as motionless as us, watching the whole building collapse and become a heap of ashes.

In the same month of April we were forbidden to enter the public parks. This was a very restrictive measure against the Jewish population. Where could the many young mothers with small children go?

In the meantime, the measure which had directed that my father go into forced labor in Limburg was rescinded. But, he was forbidden to return to Antwerp all the same. He had to settle in Anderlecht. From now on this was "officially" his place of residence. However, in practice, he came secretly back to us.

In May 1941, Jewish entrepreneurs were obliged to hang a notice on the entrances of their offices on which the following words were written: "Jüdisches Unternehmen—Joodse onderneming—Entreprise Juive" ["Jewish Business," written in German, Flemish, and French].

During the following month, in August, a curfew was introduced. Between eight P.M. and seven A.M., we were required to stay inside our own homes.

November 1941 brought us the "Judenrat" or Jewish Council. On orders from the Nazis, the Jews founded an organization that all other Jewish organizations had to join. If the Germans could be believed, this umbrella organization called the Judenrat was initiated for our own benefit. Through the Judenrat, we, who now would be completely excluded socially could mutually support each other. However, it would soon be apparent that the Judenrat was none other than an instrument of the nazis. The Judenrat became the go-between between the Gestapo and the Jews.

In May 1942, in our neighborhood, demands began to be distributed by the Arbeitseinsatz, Organization TODT. All Jewish men between the ages of eighteen and forty received a letter sent to their homes by a district police officer. They were called up to go and work on the fortifications in northern France, on the Atlantic Wall. It was a call for straight slave labor.

As soon as we became aware that these letters were being circulated, my parents, Samuel, and I discussed how best we should react to this situation. Samuel was eighteen and a half; he could expect one of those letters at any moment. Finally, we decided to try to stay ahead of the TODT. To keep him safe, we chose the simplest solution that we could devise and which lay within our power. Samuel would leave on his own for Charleroi to go there illegally in search of work.

And so our family on Kroon Street was thus thinned to six: my father, my mother, my three little brothers, and me.

Steadily, the discriminatory laws began to strangle us like a noose. Even earlier, all the Jews from the age of six were obliged to wear a Jew-

My brother Samuel at seventeen in Antwerp, 1941, before the deportation.

ish star: a six-pointed star made of yellow material the size of the palm of a hand with a black background and with a black letter *J* in the middle. After this, the Jews were forbidden to practice in the medical profession or to be pharmacists, hospital nurses, or midwives (although many German soldiers consulted Jewish doctors). A bit later, we were not allowed to frequent cinemas, theaters, or public establishments.

We found ourselves on the threshold of the very first raids (or "round-ups") for the concentration camps. In spite of it all, we still did not have the slightest suspicion of what was in store for us.

Breendonk

Thursday, July 23, 1942, was a Jewish mourning and fasting day, Tisj'a b'av (which means "the ninth day of the month *av*"). On Tisj'a b'av, the devastation of the holy temple in Jerusalem is remembered, the temple of which the wailing wall still exists. According to tradition, this temple was taken and destroyed by the Assyrians in the year 701 B.C. Later, in 609 B.C., the heroic Jewish Maccabees recaptured the temple, and finally, in 586 B.C. it was destroyed by Nebuchadnezzar whence the Diaspora of the Jewish people began for good.

The day before Tisj'a b'av, Erev Tisj'a b'av, I had to leave the house. After long consideration, it was decided in our family that I, on that day, as the oldest of the remaining children, would be sent to Charlerloi. Samuel would have urgent need of food, clothing, and laundry articles, and I was to bring him this. A really daunting prospect. I screwed up my courage and promised my parents to do what I had been asked.

Very early in the morning, I took the train. It was to be one of the last days when Jews were to be permitted to travel. I said farewell to my mother and hugged her but, thinking back, certainly not tightly enough. If, at that moment, I would have known what fate was hanging over my head, I would probably never had loosened my hold on her.

During my outward journey, nothing special happened. About midday, I arrived at Charlerloi. My brother worked there in a big factory making washtubs. When we saw each other, he explained to me what his responsibilities were. He showed me his place of work and led me around a bit of the factory. Only now did it begin to penetrate my mind how much his life had changed. Earlier he had been a diamond worker who had just begun a promising future. After his day's work Samuel could be an intellectual. He read English and Hebrew; he studied the Talmud and, at the same time, deepened his knowledge of ortho-dox and modern philosophical theories. Now he was a laborer. He was occupied with things completely unknown to me. But we were happy to see each other again and spent nearly the entire night chatting. We hardly had time to sleep. In the morning, we each had to return to our respective places and we said goodbye to each other. It had been a short but very memorable visit.

Until Brussels, the return journey went quite normally. In Brussels South, I took a tram to connect with the train in Brussels North, ready to continue my journey to Antwerp. After a short time in this train there occurred a strange disturbance. Germans in civilian clothes, with long overcoats and hats with broad brims, stepped onto the train. They were members of the Gestapo, the plainclothes security police. All the Jews who were on the train and who were identified by their "Jew star" (or, if need be, by their passports) were driven together into sepa-rate compartments. The action was not carried out roughly. The Gestapo addressed us normally, with subdued voices, and even tried to calm us with a little smile. But why we trembled with anxiety need not be explained.

Later, I learned from others that news of this raid had traveled rapidly through the train. Jewish travelers who were in the rear most coaches had tried to protect themselves. They pulled the Jew stars off their coats and, in the chaos that raged, tried to squeeze themselves in among other travelers. Some of them were actually able to slip out of the strings of the Gestapo net.

When we reached the station of Mechelen, we were all forced to get out the train. Once we had gotten out of the train, the Gestapo became more brutal. They brought up two trucks and pushed us into them with much ruckus. They screamed at us and pulled our hair. None of us could say what was happening or why. Before we knew anything, we were locked in, and the truck drove away.

We drove over a normal road. Through the screens of the truck we could see that we were driving among military vehicles, motorbikes with sidecars and, now and then a heavy truck. Outside, people were peacefully going about their daily routines, blissfully unaware of our plight. The soldiers who could see us speechless and terrified and pressed together in the truck continued totally unconcerned, looking in front of themselves, as if nothing unusual was going on. After a while, we were driving along a more rural road, and there we could see cyclists. Peacefully tranquil, they rode along in the pleasant sunshine, not aware of anything evil going on. In any case, bad things always happen to others! But ahead of us the road led to the Fortress of Breendonk. For us the world was collapsing in all around us.

Before coming to the Fortress, I had already heard something of its existence. I knew that it was a camp where, in particular, political prisoners were locked up, including members of the underground resistance, whether or not alleged agitators. Because some people still managed to return from that place, it was known that at so-called "interrogations" people were tortured severely.

After driving along for about a half-hour, we came to a stop. With much violence, the S.S. pulled us out of the trucks. They dragged us up the concrete ramp, right in front of the gate of the Fort. This was the first time that I came into contact with the S.S. They wore long shiny boots and flared riding breeches. They could immediately be recognized as S.S. by their caps. These caps bore a grotesque image of a skull. A hard leather truncheon and a revolver, which they always kept within reach, were their favorite weapons.

The S.S. did not seem to be in such a hurry, but their behavior was severely militant, brutal, and noisy. With physical blows and shoves, they drove us into the building. I can still very well remember the moment at which we went in through the first heavy door. Welcome to camp life! In a damp, echoing passage way we passed by a skinny man with a shaven head. This man stared at us with a dull, snuffed-out look in his eyes. He wore a neglected, tattered, Belgian army uniform. This stranger looked so miserable that, at a first glance, I took him to be a corpse, but a living corpse that moved slowly forward. But later I came to realize that this man actually held a privileged position in Breendonk. He was the tailor of the security men, the commander and the other highly placed gentlemen. Compared with the other prisoners, he was somewhat better off.

Totally bewildered, we moved deeper into the passage. The intervening door squeaked and groaned. We were brought to a kind of desk, to the right of the entrance, and there began a cross-examination. It would last throughout the entire day and night and into the next morning. We were all made to stand in a row, with our noses against the wall. We had to keep our hands up. Not for one, not for two, but for eighteen hours altogether! It was impossible. After a short time it felt as if your shoulder joints were about to burst. But if someone was caught letting his arms drop to his sides, even for a second, he was immediately shoved with his face forced against the wall.

The man who took the notes was a Belgian member of the S.S. He looked much too sweet-natured for the brutal work that he did. He was a young man with delicate features, his mouth looked so innocent. The way in which he sat at his little table and diligently wrote everything down made one think rather of a student or a bank clerk. But while he addressed us softly and in a friendly manner, as if dealing with routine questions, he administered spiteful slaps from time to time when he got the impression that the truth was being kept from him. He then struck unexpectedly and each time very hard.

The S.S. wanted to know everything about us. They questioned us about our dwelling places, our work, our families. They wanted to know if we had relatives in Palestine or America, acting as if they already had things in hand over there. And although they were now already torturing us psychologically, they still tried to win us over. They were almost friendly to us—sweetly natured—as if this were no more than an interview, as if this were for our own good. We were told that we would be able to write a letter to our family and to keep in touch with them. They said we had nothing, absolutely nothing, to fear.

To the questions asked of me (but about which I had the impression that they already knew the answers) I answered truthfully. But, bit by bit, I began to understand that they were really busy working on a file, an enormous puzzle of information down to the smallest details. I did, indeed, speak about my parents, my home, and my close family, but I was silent about my other relatives. I perceived that, with further questions, they were turning things upside-down, that it was pure intimidation. I was also silent about my father's address. I said that he had left our family in the lurch and that we had no idea where he was. Nor did I let anything out about my brother's work in Charlerloi. Should they ask me a question about the reasons for my train journey, I would have had to invent a lie. I had already thought about what I should say. I would try to let them think that I was going to seek advice from a doctor about my mother. Foreseeing that this subject would come up for discussion, I was worried to death. But luckily the S.S. did not return to the subject of the train journey.

It was not until the following morning that everybody had been "interviewed." At last, we were allowed to drop our arms. We had nearly fainted from the pain. We still had to fill in some information on a form, and then we were led somewhere else.

The interrogation was conducted entirely in German, although most of the S.S. who were Flemish could barely express themselves in that language. Except for the young clerk, the Flemish S.S. spoke such broken German that we could hardly understand them.

With about ten of the other prisoners, I was driven further through the chilly, dark corridors to a room, Room 5. It was a cold, stone cell. On the walls, thick chalk-white walls, mildew grew. Even though it was July, a noticeable chill hung about the place. This space was cut off from the outside world by a high, heavily barred frame that looked out on an inner yard. There were sets of wooden bunk beds for three persons, each with a straw bag covered with a grey horse blanket.

The prisoners who were already in the room, looked at us forlornly as we entered. They were Jewish people who had also been caught on the train the day before. The room, a small chamber, could accommodate forty-eight people, and we were the last ones to be added to the group.

Who were these unhappy people with whom I was to remain locked up in this sickly oppressive room? History would make them anonymous. Their personal story, their personal agony remains untold. There was Jacob Willner, a couple of years older than I. He had been snatched away from his two brothers and two sisters. He was to die later in the concentration camps. I had known him at home, his parents had a kosher poultry shop on Magdalena Street. I must also not forget the friendly Simon Beller, the father of Arthur Beller, whom I knew from the synagogue when I was still a little boy. His family would be able to avoid the camps. Further, there was Rafael Mendel Gutwirth, with his round, rose-red cheeks. I still remembered him from school; he was the same age as I. In Breendonk, he now slept in the bunk above mine. Also there, were the Bader brothers, one of whom had been a lively tailor, and there was Rosenberg, their brother-in-law. Videtski, the engineer—a fine, grey-haired, somewhat timid Luxemburger who walked slowly between our beds. Also, Weinstock, a small, lively, broad-backed fellow, a representative of the baking trade, and Ingber, a tailor, slender and about thirty, were Luxemburgers. Further, I remember the Fessel brothers from Brussels, and Pitel, also from Brussels, and the barber Grajewski. And let me also mention Gruft, a thirty-five-year-old athletic fellow. He could imitate bird songs and could whistle like a nightingale. Sometimes, lying on his bed with his hands behind his head, he whistled a little tune for us to give us courage.

We were all different people. We were of different ages and carried a different past along with us. But what we all shared with each other was our inutterable grief. We only had to look at each other to be able to understand that we each felt himself just as shocked, scared, and uncertain.

The chief commander of the fort was S.S. Sturmbannführer Philip Johann Adolf Schmitt. When he came to the camp on inspections, he behaved like a so-called "gentleman." He was a well-built fellow, but under his eyes he had heavy, sinister pouches. It seemed that Schmitt felt himself too good to dirty his hands in this fort. The only thing he did was now and then look around somewhat to see if everything was still running smoothly. He showed off a bit with his clothes, his very "chic" new dress-uniforms. But he was not like that every day. Sometimes his wife came to pick him up from work. Through the window, we could see how they went back outside like a young pair in love.

My recollection of him, however, is very limited. Seeing that he was the leader of the fort, he also oversaw the running of the torture chamber; it was there that he showed what he could do. After the war, in August 1949, Schmitt was summoned before the war council at Antwerp. One day, I myself was present among the public at the trial. The ex-commander was found guilty of eighty-three murders. In November of that year he was sentenced to death and executed.

The lieutenant of the fort was more active in the daily course of affairs. He was a scoundrel and a drunk, and a compulsive murderer. His red, pockmarked face was invariably flushed with alcohol, and his voice alone, a strangling, screeching barking voice, made us shrink with fear. He always carried a cudgel in his hand, as well as a revolver, always ready to shoot down a prisoner, without a second thought.

On one occasion, when we were in the square, a Jewish boy from our room tried to approach the lieutenant. He clicked his heels together and greeted him. "Herr Luitenant!" he said as quietly and humbly as possible. The lieutenant nearly had a stroke. "What??" he yelled. "What?? You lout?? You dare to speak to me??" He grabbed his whip and gave the boy a couple of blows. "I am by profession a saddler!" said the boy, who wouldn't give up. "Do you perhaps have some work for me!" "I can do anything you want!" Only now did the lieutenant listen to him a bit. He doubtfully scratched his chin. "Listen," he then said, "I have this old whip, come to think of it. The foreman will bring it to you. I want to see what you can make of it. But heaven help you if I do not like the result! In that case, I will kill you!"

On the same day still, the whip was handed over to the boy. He saw his chance and did his very best to make a showpiece out of it. He braided the unraveled end together again, and then he added little knife-sharp bits of lead.

The lieutenant was ecstatic with this achievement. That day, out of gratefulness, he gave the prisoner an extra portion of bread. But now the lieutenant would always have the whip with him, from morning to night. He intimidated everybody he met with it. If need be, he would beat somebody to death with it. The lieutenant was a total maniac.

Furthermore, there were the S.S. They were S.S. specially trained for the camps, and the Flemish were the most dangerous. Even we, who seldom came into contact with them, had to watch out very carefully for them. Every word that we spoke, every sign that we made could be one too many. Among the Flemish S.S. were Wijss and De Bodt, two seriously psychopathic sadists. Their chief activity was torturing. They too were caught after the war and tried. (Wijss was shot, De Bodt got a life sentence.)

The final members of the leadership consisted of two foremen. They were also prisoners, but they had a certain authority over their fellow captives. One of these foremen was called Obler. It seems that Obler's father was Jewish and his mother non-Jewish. In earlier days, he had been a part of the Hitler Youth where he had taken up an important leadership position. But later, when the Neurenberger laws came into force, he was removed from the Hitler Youth. Now that he had landed in Breendonk, he gave free rein to all his frustrations on his fellow captives. Whatever the S.S. gave him to do—the dirtiest, most bestial tasks—he carried them out with visible pleasure. He also took over the musters with great pleasure from the S.S. Like most of the traitors, Obler was one of the worst sadists with whom we came in contact.

Even though I have stood eye to eye with all these Nazi tyrants, I can only supply a limited account of Breendonk's regime of general terror. Breendonk consisted largely of political, non-Jewish prisoners. We, the Jewish people who had been picked up in the train, only saw a part of what was going on. For nearly the entire day we sat in our room, passively, vegetatively, awaiting whatever might happen to us. As to how the other prisoners were being bullied, we only learned by glimpses through the railings of our window or from what we heard in the corridors.

The political prisoners had to be ready for roll call at five o'clock in the morning. It was a roll call that could last for an hour and a half. First of all, they left the prisoners standing around waiting, for nothing. Only then did the overseer come along, all neatly dressed up, bloodthirsty as ever. "Turn left!!" they shouted. "Turn right!!" "Pull in your bellies!!" The clothes, the shoes, the haircut, everything was inspected. Head butting, thumping with the elbows, torturing—everything that these overseers could devise to harass their prisoners was used.

Only then did the lieutenant come along, clearly under the influence of alcohol. He shrieked, kicked, thumped, and bashed.

Each prisoner was observed continuously. The slightest movement, a small, inappropriate glance or an accidental little cough could be a sufficient reason to be knocked to pieces. All the frustrations that these leaders felt were unleashed on these skinny, defenseless people. They flogged us as much as they could. There was constant noise and the barbarous shrieking and screeching echoing along the walls!

When the lieutenant had had enough of it, the prisoners could leave. "Marsch!! Los!! Los!!" A line in rows of three was formed, and everybody cleared out.

During their exit march, the prisoners were forced to sing heartily a song. Those who did not sing loud enough were knocked down. I have never forgotten the gruesome lyrics of that song. It was in German and, literally translated, goes as follows:

> When the day dawns
> And the sun laughs
> We carry in the knapsack
> A bit of bread
> In hearts, in hearts which ache.

> O Breendonk,
> I shall not forget you
> While you are my fortune
> He who leaves you
> Can only appreciate
> O how beautiful freedom is.

> O Breendonk,
> We have nothing to complain about
> About what shall our future be
> Nevertheless, we say "yes" to life
> When the day comes
> When we are free.

The work place lay only four or five hundred meters further up. We could hardly discern through the window what exactly went on there.

We saw the prisoners resembling walking skeletons plodding past with small trolleys—from left to right, from right to left. For as far as we could make out, their work consisted of moving sand with this trolley (sometimes they used a wheelbarrow), sand which in the course of the years had blown down into the old barrack. We could not see from here where it had to be taken.

Now and then, a trolley came off the tracks and tipped over. That provided a perfect opportunity for the S.S. to beat up the workers. Each day, some of them died on the job of exhaustion or from torture and agony, or by the bullet. We could see their corpses being carried away.

The work went on until nightfall.

As previously mentioned, our own routine for the day was completely different. Around five o'clock we had to get up. Every day we had to be out of the room in five minutes to run outside in a circle on the inner courtyard. For the rest of the time we could do nothing other than sit inside and wait. Some chatted a bit; others remained sorrowful. Still others said absolutely nothing but sat with their backs to the wall, staring straight ahead with great, glassy eyes.

After a while the people became resigned to their situation. There was nothing else one could do about it. But worst of all was the unfathomable, ever-threatening future. No one could predict what was going to happen to us. Of course, speculations were attempted: we would be released to freedom; we would remain here; we would be taken to a labor camp. That we, in contrast to the political prisoners, were still in our civilian clothing seemed to indicate that our stay here would be only temporary. This useless chattering got us nowhere, but at least it kept us busy.

Everyone felt so isolated that it was difficult to actually make friends. But real quarreling was rare. Everybody was too depressed for such things.

There was nearly always someone who stood looking through the window to keep an eye on what was happening outside. I was able to observe that ten postmen, still in their professional uniforms, were being brought in. Perhaps they had been arrested because of some political dissidence. They disappeared into the building while the guards stood by, yelling at, and bludgeoning, them. A couple of hours later, the postmen were forced to change into the Breendonk uniforms, the old, washed-out, Belgian soldier's uniform, loose at all the seams. And throughout these nights we could hear from their blood-curdling cries how they were being tortured incessantly. All of the prisoners' rooms, including airs, looked out onto the inner courtyard. What happened outside the camp was seen and heard by no one. Only when it rained or the wind blew did we hear the dreary shuddering of the windows.

The most important moments of the day were those when we received something to eat. In the corridor we could hear the guard coming, accompanied by an S.S. man. Our door was thrown open with a loud grating sound. It was a substantial barred gate with heavy iron locks. The guard with a white apron pushed his cart up to the entrance. He had large, metal cans like those used by milk farmers. Our room representative had appointed two of us to bring our can into the room under strict surveillance. They distributed small tin plates, which were full of scratches and dents, and then zinc spoons. Then, the door was slammed shut again.

In the mornings we received ersatz burnt barley. The warmth of the drink which spread through my body was really pleasant and gave me a little strength again. At midday we received a thin, nearly worthless soup and in the evening we got a small portion of bread. The political prisoners might have received a bit more bread than us, but precisely how much I cannot say.

The youngest prisoner in our group was a pale, fragile lad of fourteen. But this boy was in the good graces of Obler, the sadistic foreman who had crossed over to the Nazis. While he snarled at, and knocked about, the other prisoners (and even killed them as if the experience were nothing), he became a little gentler when he saw the youngster. Sometimes he even pushed an extra portion of bread to him through the railings.

The first time that I saw my soup, after my interminably long, nocturnal interrogation in the "reception area", I felt a nausea rising up in me. The smell alone made me feel like vomiting. Also because I felt so depressed, I was psychologically unable to eat what was served to me. Two sips were enough to put me off. I gave my soup to somebody else. The next day, however, I ate everything as if it were a delicacy.

After a brief period to allow us to eat, the eating implements were taken back in the same sequence: first the plates, then the spoons. Finally, the guards came and went and we were again left alone.

The sanitary facilities in Breendonk, as impossible as it may seem, were even more miserable. There was no toilet. In its place, there was placed on one side, in a corner, a large cylindrical tin with a capacity of about twenty or twenty-five liters. A wire was soldered onto the top, with which the bucket could be lifted up. If the bucket was full, you could not lift it with the wire, whether you wanted to or not; you had to grab the tin with your hands. The unspeakable shame of using that bucket! You could get used to it. But carrying it remained disgusting! And I could never overcome the stench that it spread. Still, I was lucky in that I slept near the window. The clean air that filtered in from the inner courtyard made the stench a little more bearable.

We had two water pumps for washing ourselves, but no towels. If we wanted, we could dry ourselves with our blankets.

What I remember about Breendonk more than anything else were the endless, sleepless evenings in which we heard fellow prisoners being tortured. Because nearly every day new prisoners were brought in, there was seldom an evening that remained quiet. And the tortures were not limited to one evening; they often lasted two or three evenings in a row. You then heard how they were performed in stages. Before the interrogation, the prisoners had their feet chained and were taken out of the room. The permanent, icy silence of our prison contrasted sharply with the sound of the chain-dragging feet, the crackling of unoiled locks, and the opening and closing of the doors. Breendonk was a heavy, archaic fort, more than a hundred years old. Everywhere things creaked and groaned. Each step that one took echoed; the echo following in a gruesome and ghostly way. And then one heard the torturing itself. The groaning growing louder and louder, hysterical, animal-like, and after that, the pauses, the icy silence. Then, once again, the screams that penetrated to the marrow of one's bones, and once again the silence. After an hour or two, the prisoner would finally be brought back. Usually he was unconscious and was dragged along the ground. His chains clattered continuously over the concrete floor.

In a room next to us was an opera singer, whose last name was Koplowitz. Because he was arrested with his wife, he was taken to the room for couples. Often Koplowitz, at any time of the day, would begin to sing an aria at full throat. At such moments in the evenings, when there was torturing going on, he sang at full volume. One heard then, from the one side, that insane, frenzied wailing and groaning of the victim and, from the other side right next to us, that heart-rending singing of a beautiful aria. I cannot find words to describe how, at such times, I shrank from the horror and the pathos of it under my blanket in the darkness of the night.

My stay in Breendonk lasted for a month and a half, but all my days were spent the same way. The monotony, the motionlessness in our room, and the slow passage of time were the most unbearable.

The one moment that broke this monotony was the arrival of any parcel for us. Upon our arrival at the fort, we were indeed allowed to write a letter, as we had been promised. Only now, some four weeks later, did some of us finally get something back. When the list of the twelve happy chosen ones was being read aloud, the tension that hovered in that room could have been cut with a knife. Each prisoner who received something clapped his hands with joy. But when the list was folded up, our disappointment became immense. For me, there was nothing. I could not understand it—until there seemed to be a parcel left over. The parcel had been sent by a certain Hoch. A married aunt of mine was called Hoch. As cautiously as possible, I explained this to an S.S. man, as my teeth chattered with fear. My aunt had been caught with her whole family, but a sister of hers lived in Holland. Perhaps it was she who had wanted to send a parcel to my aunt. But had it arrived here too late for her? I begged now: would it not be possible to receive the parcel in her stead? Still somebody else claimed it with a very complicated explanation, but because I continued to plead, beg, and insist for a long time, the S.S. man finally gave it to me. The S.S. man was only vaguely interested in my statements; he had better things to do.

In the parcel, there was a gingerbread and a kilo of sugar cubes of the Tirlemont brand. Not much, but it was heartwarming. After having eaten a bit of it myself, I shared some sugar cubes, two to each prisoner. It seemed to me only fair. I also gave some gingerbread to my neighbors who slept in the bunks near me. But when I observed that the others who had received parcels only shared with their immediate neighbors and not with all members of the room, it was a blow to my morale. I had not wanted to exchange anything, but I had been too naïve; I had wanted to be good to everyone. For me, that moment meant the beginning of survival.

On another occasion, the Nazis were looking for women who could type. They would be called in to assist in the administration. The women in Breendonk were either in rooms with couples or in rooms with just women. But the message that they had received also circulated with us in Room 5. Of the many women who presented themselves, only ten were finally selected. Included in this group, I learned from someone, was Lunia Schiff. Lunia was a nineteen-year-old girl whom I knew from our neighborhood. Her brother, Tobias, had been in my class. In the opinion of many of us, Lunia was one of the prettiest girls of Antwerp. She had splendid, long, dark hair and an impressive character that commanded everyone's respect. That she was here with us I considered to be remarkable. I thought again about the early days, about my normal life with its freedoms. My friends, my family . . . how far all that was removed from our present misery!

Although we were still being kept desperately in ignorance about our future, I believed that perhaps this call-up of typists might be a portent of a change in our lifestyle. Shortly after we had arrived in Breendonk, I was able to talk surreptitiously and hastily with someone from the outside world, a carpenter. He worked somewhere on the side of the inner yard. He had walked past me with a few tools and then had spoken to me—as inconspicuously as possible while he looked at the ground. He had comrades who were working on the barracks in Mechelen and that, as far as was known, those barracks were to be rebuilt to become a large camp. Thus, perhaps, our imprisonment in Breendonk was only temporary? Possibly we were only here waiting for further transportation and that the administration, which the S.S. was busy organizing, was ready for imminent transfer. Actually, we were groping in the dark; nothing was certain.

But indeed. From the second half of August, prisoners were called out of from our rooms of despair. They were pulled out by heavily armed S.S. and driven away. To where? Nobody knew. Gradually, our room became emptier and emptier. Towards the end of the month, only about twelve of us were left behind. On September 4, our turn came.

It happened one morning. We could hear from a distance as the S.S. came charging at us through the echoing corridor with their heavy, clamping boots. They bashed the door open. "Raus, Raus!!" they screamed, "Raus!! Los!! Los!!". Because there were only twelve of us, a roll call was no longer necessary. With a couple of other prisoners from other rooms, we were brought outside precisely along the same route that we had followed when we came in, a month and a half ago. Through the dark corridors and the cheerless gates. In front of the exit, an army truck drove up: "Einsteigen!! Einsteigen!!" [Climb in!]. We were now being handled by S.S. that we did not know. They grinned with satisfaction. They made us stand up straight on the platform of the truck, and joltingly, jerkingly, they started the vehicle.

After forty-three days of useless, pointless, suffering, we could see the fort disappearing from our field of vision. But what was awaiting us? The unknown could be still worse and more cruel than that which we were now leaving behind.

Mechelen

When I think back to the Dossinkazerne of Mechelen, I have before me only a few confused, chaotic images. The Dossinkazerne was a transit camp. The prisoners were driven in there in great groups, and a few days later they were immediately sent on again to other camps. One group came, another group went at a pace that was difficult to follow. Because of these constant hasty exchanges, any type of infrastructure or regularity was totally unimaginable. The S.S. beat up people with cudgels and rifle butts, as if it had become a sort of addiction, but they did not bring order.

The groups of prisoners who were brought in to the Dossinkazerne mingled among themselves. For those of us who had come from Breendonk there were no more registrations or interrogations. From now on our imprisonment, or at least the security used to confine us, had become something we completely took for granted.

When we arrived in the Dossinkazerne, there was no system of supervision that could have contained, for a little while at least, the disorder which was rampant and reigned supreme. Men, women, and children—everybody ran around in confusion. If we wanted to sleep at night, we had to lie pressed against each other on the straw, which was spread untidily over the floor. It smelled as if it were a horse stable. Hygiene was nonexistent, as if it had not yet been discovered. Now and then, prisoners were appointed to do chores. The toilets, the floors, the walls, everything needed to be scrubbed. But at this point the sanitary measures that the S.S. could provide stopped. The Dossinkazerne was a disgusting, sickening, loathsome nightmare.

The main reason why I describe so little about Mechelen, so much less than about the other camps which I have experienced, is that it was there I encountered one of my greatest traumas. I experienced a shock which, during the days that I spent there, devastated me completely. The groups of captives who were assembled together in Mechelen had mostly been picked up during the same neighborhood "razzia" or raid, which automatically created a situation where most people knew each other. Neighbors, family members, and friends were all thrown together with each other. They could still make plans among themselves; should they ever be separated from each other, they made plans to keep in contact. Did they know someone who could be a courier for them? Moreover they could, if it was required, say farewell to each other. That was then a horrendous, heartbreaking task, yet it was still something. For me such a farewell was not even possible. Immediately after my arrival in the Dossinkazerne, even before I could adapt myself to this place, I encountered a few friends of mine who brought me news about my mother. Only four days ago, on Monday, September 1, they had seen my mother and my three little brothers, Leopold, Isaac, and Henri, being carried away from Mechelen. I felt that I would collapse when I heard that. Six weeks had already passed since I last saw my mother. And from now on, without respite, the feeling kept murmuring through my being like an unpleasant, chilling breeze sighing through some trees on a cruel winter's night. What a terrible lottery ticket I had drawn in the game of fate! Had they sent me from Breendonk to Mechelen a couple of days sooner, we would have, at least, been together again. We then could have traveled together on the transport, and I would have been able to carry out my responsibilities within the family. There had also been prisoners in Breendonk who had been transferred a couple of days before me. They had indeed been able to go with the transport that took away my mother and my little brothers. But I had arrived just a little too late. I was left behind alone, not even being able to know what had become of my family. The environment in which I now found myself looked totally surrealistic. "How *could* this be?" I kept asking myself. "It could simply not be true!" I became nearly crazy with anxiety and grief. Nobody could console me.

My acquaintances told me that they still had something special for me. Without exactly understanding what was happening, something was secretly, quietly, given to me. A small piece of khaki-colored material. I asked them what it was. It seemed a modest, home-made little rucksack that my mother had specially left behind for me in the Dossinkazerne. My mother knew that I was in Breendonk. I had, at least, been able to write her a letter. Probably, she had also come to know that people were regularly transferred from Breendonk to Mechelen. For this reason, she had especially kept that little rucksack apart for me. It contained a couple of shirts and some underclothes, a pair of wooden clogs and a pair of beautiful strong shoes which were worn for the Sabbath. It is difficult to explain how rich it made me feel! Although the S.S. had, from the beginning, regularly plundered their captives, most of us could, here and there, still keep something for ourselves. Something small that did not readily come into view. But I had not, until now, any baggage. I had been caught unexpectedly en route on a train. I now grasped tightly to these new possessions, as if my future depended on it.

A few days after our arrival the next transport was already beginning to be formed. How long it would take depended on the speed with which the prisoners streamed into the barracks. The only thing that was important to the Nazis in assembling a transport was the roundup of a thousand persons. If somebody within the thousand was not transportable, he was replaced by another. It was all the same to the Nazis. They regarded us as numbers.

I have never been able to forget that evening before our departure from the Dossinkazerne. The camp was really still like a building site. The carpenters transforming the old barracks into a transit camp had, here and there, left lying around some planks, boxes, and plates. A kind of podium was made with these things. By nightfall, a couple of short, simple skits were put together in which we all had to participate to raise our spirits. Perhaps the mentality of the Jewish people has always been thus: the strength of will would never, even under the most wretched circumstances imaginable, let their heads hang low.

The high point of the performance was Koplowitz, the opera singer who had been with us in Breendonk and who came again to be among us with the next transport. He stood like a noble, patient, resigned man on the shabby, rickety planks and gave us a song (one of his best) that made us tremble. Everybody wept. Every now and then an S.S. agent came along to see how things were going. His attitude was like that of an executioner who was granting one more cigarette to the prisoners condemned under the death penalty.

The following day, September 8, 1942, we got up at three o'clock in the morning. We prepared ourselves for the transport. A short two hours later we were brought in trucks to the railway station of Mechelen.

Saccrau

mood: tone (handwritten marginalia)

Imagery / Figurative language (handwritten marginalia)

The trains in the station of Mechelen were those long commonplace passenger trains. But we were driven into the coaches like cattle on the way to the slaughterhouse. On the roofs of the coaches we could see S.S. men, who had positioned themselves behind machine guns. They pointed their weapons deliberately in our direction. It looked as if, at any moment, they would shoot us to pieces.

We were violently pressed backward into the coaches with great force, like sardines in a tin. The S.S. men who were guarding us sat in the front part of the coaches. They had enough space; they walked about, chatting and laughing among themselves. We had no idea what they wanted to do with us. Where were they taking us? What did they want of us? The wheels grated, the floor began to shudder, and we all left Mechelen on the way to another unknown destination.

Pretty soon we could see that we were traveling in an easterly direction, although we moved very slowly and experienced many detours through smaller, insignificant stations. We had left at about six o'clock in the morning and about two o'clock in the afternoon we crossed the border. We read the word "Deutschland"! It was enemy country! The lion's den where everybody could be a Nazi! But we couldn't really believe it. It had to be a nightmare from which we would soon awaken!

The most crazy moments occurred when the train stopped for a while. Peering through the damp, clouded glass of the windows, we saw a pair of S.S. men who were walking along the platform in search of a cup of ersatz coffee or a glass of beer. They strolled along among unsuspecting civilians. They stopped at a newspaper kiosk to buy a lottery ticket or to thumb through a magazine. A soldier was saying good-bye to his girl friend, and somebody else stood waiting on the platform with a suitcase and tied his shoelaces. We were cut off from

48

everything. People glanced at us from time to time, but there was no one who seemed to care about what was going on. Our suffering was solely for us alone. Nobody would help us.

The journey lasted two days and two nights, from September 8 to September 10, 1942. We had nothing to eat. Some of the prisoners who had left from Mechelen had been able to bring some provisions with them from home as a last reserve. Those of us who had come from Breendonk were already famished. As hungry as wolves!

The trip ended abruptly. Late into the night, at about four o'clock in the morning, the train suddenly braked and screeched to a halt. I woke up in the dark. "Alle Männer raus!!" [All men out!!] somebody shouted. S.S. men barged into our coach. They came in unexpectedly, grabbed us by the shoulders, and dragged us out. A man I knew, Leibisch Wahl, was sitting diagonally in front of me. He sat with his wife and two children. An S.S. man dragged him brutally by the collar of his coat. Before he knew or realized what was happening, and without even being able to glance back at his family, he was pulled into the mob. He had no baggage or anything with him. It seemed as if they had specifically targeted him.

"So, they are calling in the men." This was the thought that flashed through my mind. But was I actually a man? Did I have to go with them? Or was I still a youngster? I had no time to reflect on these questions. I grabbed my few things and went with the rest, compelled along by shoves and physical blows. Still completely confused, I struggled out. Then suddenly, while I was standing on that platform among all these adults, I realized that, from one moment to the next, I had changed completely and had become once and for all a grown-up. I was still only sixteen, but I would no longer be able to return to that age. I had, in full awareness, chosen to face up to my future and my responsibilities as an adult.

After a few minutes—in fact, we were still not completely awake—the train proceeded on. Very quickly, it disappeared from view.

In retrospect, I can state that the decision which I had so hastily made at that moment—to go outside with the rest—was the only correct one. That decision was the first of several miracles that would save my life. As far as I know, the train, which I had left behind, went straight on to Auschwitz and to the gas chambers and incineration ovens. Leibisch Wahl never again saw his wife and children. Not even the slightest farewell gesture was granted him. The drama took place in a few quick and totally chaotic seconds.

The platform on which we now stood was that of a small transit station. From a signpost, we could see where we were: Kozel. We were driven together in rows. This presented some difficulty because we had not yet acquired the necessary discipline. We were still not accustomed to the behavior of the S.S. They ran among us with dogs—enormous, impressive, Alsatian sheepdogs that had been specially trained for this kind of work. These barking and panting dogs made such a frightening and infernal row that you felt your body weakening with fear. They were on leashes, but they held us in their bloodthirsty gaze, ready at any moment to spring into attack.

The S.S. began to count us. A thousand or so of us had left Mechelen with the so-called Eighth Transport. Among these thousand were about four hundred men. Within a half-hour after the counting we were loaded into truck and driven away. The destination, once again, was unknown to us. We feared the worst.

The camp to which we had now been brought was called Saccrau. It was situated just near Kozel. It was a so-called Jewish forced labor camp. It also served as a transit camp, just like the Dossin barracks in Mechelen, but with the difference that the prisoners here, in anticipation of a further transportation to other camps, were already being put to work.

S.A. staff ran the camp. A kind of "Blue Police" assisted them. In addition, there was the surveillance by the Wehrmacht or German Army. The number of captives (or, in German terminology, "Häftlinge") varied between 2,500 to 3,500. They were exclusively Jewish.

Saccrau was a typical barracks camp. It was situated not far from a wood and away from all civilization. Here and there the walls were illuminated by strong searchlights, and in each of the towers on the sides were posted two marksmen.

We were given a cup of ersatz coffee and were immediately subdivided into rooms. We were not allowed to establish ourselves properly and could only lay our belongings on the bed and have a quick look around. Immediately afterward, we were again called into the inner courtyard. It was still morning. We were nearly dead from hunger and fatigue. But instead of getting something to eat, as we had hoped, we were divided into work details, small randomly assembled groups of fifty people. And then immediately after our arrival, "Quick march!" "Straight to work!"

The place where we had to work was at a distance of two kilometers from the camp. We had to prepare the construction of a new motorway.

Before the German specialists could arrive to build the road themselves we had to ensure that the whole terrain was leveled. We had to eliminate all the bumpy spots with a spade and a mattock. The removal of bits of rock was done by hand. Holes which became an obstacle had to be filled in with these fragments. In order to be able to transport the larger pieces of rock, stone, and sand, we had at our disposal a small locomotive with about a dozen trolleys. The locomotive was driven by a native German, a Silesian. The moving of the rails with the help of crowbars was also one of our tasks.

What made this sudden work so burdensome was not so much the scorching heat, which prevailed throughout the day, but the attitude of the S.A. and the inhuman pace demanded of us. We had removed our shirts and worked with naked torsos. "Los, los!" they screamed. We could not work fast enough for them. "Los, los!" The next skip was there again! The S.A. continually administered blows with the butts of their rifles, or with cudgels, or with anything that they could lay their hands on, all the time ceaselessly cursing, screaming, and barking orders. They wanted to show us what we could expect—the hellish and beastly life to which we had become accustomed. Also, the building contractors and foremen, who themselves had little to do with the S.A.s, took pleasure in beating us up. For them it was a competition in sadism.

Road construction was something completely new to me. I was only a boy. Until now, I had never done physical work. Suddenly, a pace was demanded of me that even an adult in the peak of physical condition could not achieve. In the evening, after a day's work, I was completely overwhelmed and completely exhausted.

At last, they gave us something to eat, potatoes boiled in their skins, the sort of food that is meant only for animals. But in my entire camp life, it was the only delicate morsel that I ever received. I ate like one possessed. My salivary glands burned, my stomach turned.

After eating, at last, we were allowed to go to our barracks. Exhausted, the captives flung themselves onto their beds. Here and there, there was some discussion going on about the situation. But we were not allowed the tranquillity of being in our barracks for long. We heard a noise descending upon us. "What now?" Our bedrooms were surrounded: a raid was taking place. The leaders who came to pull us out of our rooms during every "roundup" were "kapos," Jewish detainees who were appointed by the S.A. to occupy a kind of an in-between position. They served as intermediaries between the S.A. and the prisoners with their work requirements. They drove us outside, pulling and pushing us with their blows. They also checked us to ensure that nothing had been left behind. Corners were searched and straw mattresses turned over.

The raid was designed to make pillaging possible. The S.A. wanted to grab all our possessions forever. Theoretically, we owned nothing more at that moment; no watches, no money, no books or anything else. The only thing that most of us still had was a minimum of baggage, a suitcase with a few clothes, and perhaps some sweets. Others, though, had been able to scrape together some tools from their homes. The prisoners who had arrived before us in Saccrau had been able to hide something here and there. But we from Mechelen were still carrying everything with us. And then we were pulled outside.

The plundering took place, it was said, on orders from the German government. The profits arising from this would go to German families who had been affected by the war and who had clothing and other needs, orphans, for example. In reality, what happened was that the S.A. put everything into their own pockets. They tried to take everything, even if it was only a spool of sewing thread—merely to take what they could.

The S.A. waited for us in an empty barrack between rows of tables. Each one of us had, in turn, to pass and show what we still owned. The S.A.s made their choice. We were allowed to keep this or that, and the rest—everything else—was taken and thrown on the tables. Suitcases, shirts, trousers, bathrobes, shoes, everything that looked the least bit valuable lay in heaps.

I experienced a stroke of luck; my only possession, the rucksack, did not look very attractive. In fact, it could hardly be called a rucksack. It was only a poor little sewn-together piece of material containing bits of rubbish. The S.A.s just let me pass without handling it. An unparalleled relief. I still had my shoes and my clogs.

Finally returning to our barrack, I climbed, fully clothed, onto my bed. I could not even take off my shoes. I still wanted to think over what had happened, about where my family had gone, about where I found myself and what I had to do. But my head was so full of worries that it was ready to burst. The babbling voices of the prisoners around me sounded empty and unintelligible. Immediately, I sank into bottomless sleep.

At the next roll call, early in the morning, something strange happened. From among the people of our transport from Mechelen, about one hundred were designated and taken aside in a separate line without any reason or explanation. Among them were the Fessel brothers and the young sixteen-year-old Gutwirth, whom I already knew from schooldays. All three had been together with me in Breendonk. When we marched off to work, they remained behind. Nobody knew why. We were afraid and uncertain for them. The prisoners themselves stood shivering and immobile. We all lived our situation so intensely from one minute to the next that the slightest unexpected turn of events struck panic in our hearts. What was going on? What were we to expect? Were we going to be murdered? Were we going to be tortured?

On that day at work, I was beaten for the first time in my life. I was working with my heavy, uncomfortable clogs on because I did not want to wear out my good shoes. I had perhaps worked a little less hard than the peak of my powers would have permitted. It was necessary; if I had used up my strength during the work, I would have immediately collapsed. They demanded maximum effort from us, but food and hygiene were never offered in exchange. To work less hard was, therefore, of vital importance if we were to stay alive—as long as it was not at the expense of fellow captives! But at a certain moment a guard passed. He had spotted me immediately. Sparing your strength required a certain expertise, which I had not yet acquired. And so I was discovered. The guard took his gun. I heard him coming towards me. Howling with rage, he prodded me in the ribs with his rifle butt. I doubled over with pain. He shouted at me and accused me of being an idler, a swine. A piece of vermin.

I had received only routine blows, but because it was the first punishment of my life, it seemed very hard. The blows were also very humiliating. A complete stranger could now beat me to pieces, and nobody would do anything about it. I tried not to think about it. I had to humbly bow my head and apply myself to the work.

Only when we had arrived back in the camp—once again completely exhausted—did we hear from others about what had happened to the hundred prisoners after they had been taken aside in the yard. They were sent to another labor camp. They had remained waiting for a while and then were loaded into truck and, without much fuss, were driven away to somewhere else.

Of the Fessel brothers, I now know that one of them died in the camps. The other survived the Holocaust. Gutwirth, the young boy, also died in the camps.

The Jewish New Year, Rosh Hashanah, fell in 1942 on Saturday and

Sunday, September 12 and 13. However, we never worked full days on Saturday not because we were being granted a rest-break but because the non-Jewish people who supervised us in the yard were off-duty at that time, so there was nobody to keep an eye on us. At about three o'-clock in the afternoon, we returned from work on Saturday. Prisoners who were interested could assemble in strict secrecy in a room to perform a very brief prayer service. We were about thirty in number (should we be caught, a punishment would follow).

Our stay in Saccrau lasted only three days. During those three nights I slept fully clothed. In any other camp this would have been impossible, but actually Saccrau was only a transit camp. It was fairly chaotic there. The roll calls received relatively little attention, and the discipline, which we had to observe, was by far not so strict as that which we would experience later on. Also little attention was paid to hygiene. Except for Breendonk and Mechelen, I never washed myself during these days! Saccrau was a prologue for me, an initiation into the limitless insanity that further awaited me.

Laurahütte

On the fourth day of my stay in Saccrau, September 13, 1942, the roll call only lasted a short time, because it was a Sunday. After a few minutes it was explained to us that no work had to be done on that day. They announced it to us with a little laugh as if they were doing us a favor. But what was really planned for us was unknown. The S.A.-ers walked with a superior, judgmental air. Here and there, someone was beaten. Afterward, we were sent back to our barracks. We were given five minutes of time to pack our things and then report to the parade ground. I took my little rucksack out from behind my straw bag, closed it up more firmly than before, and hurried out with the crowd. Once again we stood for the roll call, as quiet as mice. We stood staring ahead, stiffened with fright. What was happening today was beyond our comprehension. After a little while, we were startled by a threatening, growling sound that built to a crescendo, and under the brown, rising clouds at the entrance of the camp, we saw some twenty army trucks being driven in. They drove in a curve up to the front of the roll area call. We would again be transported away, that much was clear! Thus, we thought, "farewell, Saccrau." But we were not without mixed feelings; fear of the unknown could be worse than the terror that we had already experienced.

Each truck was filled to capacity with prisoners, and its gate was banged shut. Not only those of us who had come from Mechelen but also others from Saccrau were being transported, altogether about one thousand men. At the exit from the loading area stood a heavily armed S.A. who watched us closely.

The trip lasted for about one hour. When about midday were allowed to get out, our bones creaked.

The concentration camp to which we had been driven was that of

Laurahütte, or, according to the Polish name, Semianowice. It was another Jewish forced labor camp and was situated about ten kilometers above Katowice. Thus it was not too far from Auschwitz.

Laurahütte was actually a gigantic bare factory building. Under the most primitive circumstances imaginable, somewhat less than a thousand men were kept captive. There were no rooms as such. The wooden bunk beds, always three tiers high, were arranged in such a way that they, in each unit, gave separate shelter to thirty-six prisoners with well-defined, dividing corridors in between. Each unit had its own overseer who was responsible for order, hygiene, and the distribution of the rations. Here too, the person overseeing was called the Stubenälteste. Thus structurally, it was as if there were rooms here.

In the middle of the hall, tables had been placed in a long continuous row. Outside, there was a courtyard, but beyond, there was but little to be seen in Laurahütte. The stone walls, which encircled the concentration camp, were four metres high with barbed wire on top and a guard placed here and there. Because we often heard trolley buses driving past the outside walls (we could even see the electric cables of these vehicles), the presence of normal, everyday life always seemed to be very close by. Such sounds made the experience of our imprisonment all the more harrowing.

One advantage that we enjoyed came from the pair of large zinc pipes which ran the length of the factory hall. During the winter months we were able to experience the full benefit of this. The steam contained in the pipes spread a certain warmth throughout the space and created a somewhat erratic central heating system. Without this, the single blanket, which we had, would certainly not have been sufficient to help us through the nights.

The hierarchy of Laurahütte was similar to that of Saccrau. The Stubenälteste of my group was called Smuliver, a real bruiser, who had been a sailor. I had known him from the time at Saccrau. He had been picked up in France.

A Stubenälteste enjoyed the benefit of sometimes getting extra food, for example, a layer on the bottom of the jam pots or an extra cup of ersatz coffee. And he did not even have to take a turn in the cleaning of the unit. But the disadvantage was that all the responsibilities of his section fell upon him. If problems arose, there was no guarantee that he would not be subject to the same blows. He also had to go to work like everyone else, and therefore, he could not really be called a privileged person.

Above all the other prisoners stood a Judenälteste. He worked as an intermediary between the Jews and the Nazis. If he dropped out, there was usually a deputy Judenälteste who could replace him.

In the camp, there was a certain Schlein, who we had actually expected would be promoted to Judenälteste. He was a German Jew who had emigrated to Belgium and was a natural leader. Over the months, we had more or less become accustomed to the idea that he was our spokesman, the leader of our group. The lieutenant of Breendonk, a pockmarked, cruel murderer, had designated him for this particular position, and in Mechelen and in Saccrau, he kept this function. In Laurahütte he was, however, disenfranchised because of internal politics. The S.A.-ers of Laurahütte got along better with Polish Jews; S.A.-ers were themselves mostly from Polish Silesia. In Schlein's place, they gave preference to a Polish Jew.

The Judenälteste was a political instrument for Nazi camp command. The immediate boss of the Judenälteste was the Nazi camp commander. From him, the Judenälteste got orders that he had to pass on to his Kapos. He had to provide reports to the Nazi camp commander about all the orders which the Judenälteste had carried out.

Further, there were policemen, the so-called Polizisten. Their number varied with the size of the camp. In Laurahütte there were two. The Polizisten were the tyrants of the camp, the bullies, hangmen, and executioners. They worked without consulting the Judenälteste because they were also a direct instrument of the Leitung or leadership. If the Nazis sometimes did not want to be bothered with the punishment of the detainees, the Polizisten were sent in their place. The rank of the these Polizisten was that of Kapo or overseer (in military language, a noncommissioned officer). In a smaller camp, like Laurahütte, they went out daily with the prisoners to work.

One of our Polizisten in Laurahütte was named Kampf, a German Jew who had been deported from France. He was an extremely brutal, callous bastard. He had already been active in camps for three years. His favorite weapon was the whip. When we saw him in our vicinity, we shivered with fear. His sadism exceeded the tolerances that were established by higher authority.

At work again, apart from the civilian Meisters, it was the Kapos whom we had to obey. Each Kapo had his own work detail and, depending on the size of that detail, one or two Vorarbeiters, also called Unterkapos.

If the Stubenälteste was lucky, he had at work a Kapo over him who

made up part of his own Stube or barrack room. Then it could sometimes happen that the Kapo at the work might give him some small,
practical advantages. For the Stubenälteste it was entirely a question of
luck because to offer something in return was not possible for him. A
Stubenälteste was merely an insignificant nobody, whereas Kapo
nearly meant "God Almighty".

We were still running around in our own old civilian clothes. The
only difference was that our clothes were affixed with Jewish stars.
Häftlinge or detainees whose work coincidentally brought them into
contact with civilian, non-Jewish people tried to sell any surplus items
of clothing that they still had. The paint of the Jewish star, a watercolor,
was then carefully scratched off. But one day the Leitung or management noticed this practice. They organized a raid, and all clothes and
other textiles were provided with new stars. No longer with paint but
with scissors. Everything made of material was cut into and snipped.
From then on, nothing was marketable.

Those who owned leather shoes could occasionally get fat from the
Stübenalteste with which to coat and protect them.

Sunday, September 13, 1942, the day of our arrival in Laurahütte,
was the second day of Rosh Hashanah. On that day we were truly fully
preoccupied by our new living conditions. We had to orient and establish ourselves. Because of this, the religious service could not be carried out. Upon our arrival at Laurahütte, we were immediately driven
into the factory building and, no sooner had we gotten out of the vehicle, then we were assembled into long, conveniently arranged rows.
We were to be divided into work details. There was work at Laurahütte itself, but there were also work areas somewhat further away,
in Königshütte and Bismarckhütte.

The division of the work force was almost completely arbitrary. The
overseers watched from a distance how the S.A. counted us off and
sent us to a certain job. Our specific situation was not taken into account. But by chance, I saw an overseer who did indeed actually make
certain selections. It was clear that he wanted to keep his best men together. When he came past, I took quite a large risk. I asked him
straight off, with a fixed, expressionless face, of what precisely his
work consisted. He offered a short explanation, which I did not understand very well, about having to handle a type of tongs. In the work
that I had earlier performed, there was never a pair of tongs available,
only heavier tools. Working with a pair of tongs seemed to me to be
not so difficult. Thus, I offered myself as a volunteer. I went to stand in

the row that I was sure would join his little group. I was placed apart with ten or twelve people. The detail would be called the Mader detail after the name of the Kapo for whom we worked. We would begin the next day. Among the prisoners who would be working for Mader was a certain Sam Kummel. He had been with me in Breendonk and Saccrau. He came from Antwerp and would survive the camps.

The people who worked for Köningshütte or Bismarckhütte were worse off than I. While our work for Mader was not even a five-minute walk from the camp, the others had to travel a considerable distance each day. From the camp they had to go to a tram stop near Katowice; that trip alone took a whole hour and a quarter. After that, they had to ride another half-hour to the shipyard. For the return journey, again a half-hour ride and again an hour and a quarter of walking. Altogether, they were en route three and a half hours each day. They had to get up an hour earlier than us and, in the evenings, they returned an hour later.

While we had to work for about ten hours each day, the workers of Köningshütte and Bismarckhütte only did eight. But their work was also much heavier. It consisted mainly of unskilled work, really bruising stuff: loading and unloading gravel with a shovel or moving heavy cement blocks in trolleys, all at an inhuman pace. Weakened physical conditions developed quite soon in these details. The prisoners easily developed edema; they became emaciated and lost their mental resistance. As in all the hard-work details, most of the prisoners entered a kind of vicious circle that led to death in a short time. The weaker one became the less accomplished one, and the one more chastised, bawled out, and beaten. The more people were brutalized, the worse the results became and the more beatings were dealt out. The details of Köningshütte and Bismarckhütte in fact looked like punishment details. After a short time, many of their unhappy participants left this life.

The work that I did for Mader in Laurahütte itself was not so heavy. There were about forty-five people working there. Those of us in that group of twelve which had been taken aside did a kind of plaiting or weaving job. We had to take iron wires and braid them into "ropes," which were needed to make a kind of iron skeleton for the concrete workers to use. As soon as the skeleton was ready, the carpenters boxed it in with wooden planks, and into these boxes a concrete mix was poured. When the concrete had set, the planks were removed, and the result was a series of iron and concrete pillars. The disposal of the planks after they had been removed was also one of our tasks.

To be able to complete our weaving work, we were each given a pair of pliers but no protective gloves. The result was that, after a few days, our hands were in a terrible mess, full of blisters and cuts.

After some ten days, I had gained some confidence in this work. So I tried to start a conversation with my work boss. He was a calm, intelligent, forty year old from Dresden. He was certainly not among the worst. On one occasion when he was standing next to me, I asked him very cautiously—because you always needed to watch your step—what his view of the war was and what he thought would happen to the Jews. The work boss answered: "I shall tell it to you honestly. If we win the war, I assume that somewhere in Siberia a sort of colony will be established where you will all be able to go on living." Then he looked at me. "But if it should end differently and we lose the war, I cannot vouch for anything. The consequences are incalculable. All hell will break loose!"

In 1942, Yom Kippur, the day of forgiveness and the most important feast on the Jewish calendar, fell on Monday, September 21. The evening before, we tried to get a few people together to organize a service, but we were not successful. On the day of Yom Kippur itself, I, with a few other prisoners, fasted in accordance with the Jewish custom. It was a difficult observance in our condition, but I persevered.

I had now been in captivity for nearly two months. Everything in that short space of time had changed so fast and so drastically that I did not even have time to think about it. Only now did I have the small opportunity to reflect about myself and my circumstance.

I had already "written off" my mother and my three younger brothers in Mechelen. I understood that they did not have a single chance of surviving because of reports that I had heard about the general policy of the Nazis and because of what I had personally experienced in the meantime. Whatever may have happened to them, they would be lost. But I still had hope for my brother Samuel. He had gone underground and his chances seemed to me to be good. Would he be able to get away? I had not yet given up hope for my father either.

The fact that I could now so broadly consider these things all at once was truly exceptional. The struggle to survive in the concentration camp was so formidable and demanded so much attention from us all, second after second for twenty-four hours a day, to such an extent that we simply could not find the time nor the energy for such important worries.

The most important thoughts that *always* occupied our attention concerned food. That subject was our one great, overwhelming obsession. Should I eat now, or should I wait a little bit, or should I keep a little bit on the side? The act of eating was the focal point of the day around which everything revolved. Every day, the kitchen staff brought in gigantic cans of soup under strict guard. These were set on the table and opened. Each barrack room or Stube could, under the strict supervision of the senior soldier or Stubenälteste, come and get its soup. The Stubenälteste knew his men and saw to it that nobody went more than once to get a helping of food.

Because of the heavy work and because the food was so meager, you were always plagued by personal doubts and worries, always the same compulsive thoughts. Will I get enough? Will the prisoner standing in front of me get a bit more soup than I? Has perhaps a thicker portion been kept apart for him, with less water and more substance to it? You watched like a hungry vulture as the ladle disappeared and came up with your ration. As soon as you had received something, the reactions were always the same. First, you tried to guess what it was that you had received. Once discovered that what had been dished out to you was O.K., that they had done their best to serve you well, you then began to spoon it in like a lunatic and after a few seconds you swallowed the whole plateful. All was finished. Once again you began to feel cheated. Was it only that much? Almost immediately you began to crave the food for the following day.

The bread rations in Laurahütte were a little bit larger than before. But here again the worry: is my bit of bread perhaps less than advantageous? Has it been cut somewhat more at an angle? The question about whether you were more disadvantaged than the others was the most penetrating of all of camp life.

Besides the meals, besides eating, there were other sources of distress. While at work, you always had to be on your guard against accidents. There was absolutely no protection; there were no safety devices. Each day, prisoners received wounds or died before your eyes. Also you always had to keep an eye on the team boss and to make sure that you were creating a good impression. If he should happen to look in your direction, you should be observed to be working diligently, like a beaver, even if the nature of the work seemed to be less than urgent. And when it came to surveillance done by the S.A., you had to be even more on your toes—that was simply a matter of life or death.

After work, you had to watch out for the Stubenälteste. He was your boss from 6 P.M. until 5 A.M. Therefore, you had to ensure that you always pleased him, if only by flattery. After all, he was only a human being with his own feelings. If you antagonized him, he could still give you extra work inside the camp after hours!

And, finally, you also had to think about, and watch out for, your fellow prisoners, your neighbors. The Nazis had brought us to such a severe state of deprivation that few of us could still think rationally. Certain prisoners had become so antisocial that they would steal from their best friends, even knowing that they could be beaten to death for it on the next day.

Because of this, you had to be on your toes and wide awake for every minute of the day. You could hardly concern yourself about less immediate problems than those which directly surrounded you. The only time at which you could relax even a little was at night. The evening was the great moment for which you had been waiting all day. The warmth of the blanket and sleep—that experience was the most beautiful and the best that could happen to you. The evening passed by rapidly. Before everybody from the construction site had returned, it was already a quarter past six. By half past six most people had washed a bit and were able to start to relax, waiting for the meal. The lights were put out in the great hall around nine o'clock, a short hour after everybody had finished eating. The Kapos and the Stubenälteste mostly chatted until ten o'clock. They discussed the work coordination and the schedule. They chatted about various things. Except for food, the most important topics of conversation were about how the day had gone, especially about the day's death toll. How was this one or that one getting on? Who was on the edge of death? Would this one or that one still be able to go to the construction site tomorrow? Or would he be found dead in his bed in the morning? Or, in the throes of death, like a living corpse, would he need to be taken to the camp hospital?

Usually, I fell asleep quickly, before the lights went out. But the anxiety of having to go to work so soon, of having to start another atrocious, hideous day so preoccupied my sleep that frequently after only a half-hour of sleep I became awake again. I saw the lights burning while other prisoners, still dressed, sat on their beds talking a bit to each other. The immediate impression I got was that another horrid day had already dawned. What a shock! But then I gradually realized that the night had not yet begun. A pleasant surprise! Still a night's rest ahead! Sleeping once more—that was the only relief.

For three weeks I worked on the concrete irons. After that, the assignments for my detail began to diminish. The stronger workers were still kept in Laurahütte, but all the others were sent elsewhere. The prospect of some new, as yet unknown, work inspired me with so much anxiety that for a few more days I tried to give the impression that I was still hard at work in the hope of not having to be transferred. But a while later, on Wednesday, October 7, 1942, I was transferred to a work detail in Königshütte. This transfer meant that, from now on, I would have to get up one hour earlier, around five o'clock, and that every day I would be traveling for three-and-a-half hours on foot and by tram.

The new work involved pulling electric cables. Under the supervision of an S.A. man (instead of someone from the Wehrmacht, as was customary), we had to supply firms who asked for it with electricity. We dug trenches and laid big electric cables measuring eight to ten centimeters in diameter inside them. Because everything had to be done so quickly, the treaches were hardly wide enough for us. We couldn't even move properly through them.

Often we were also called upon to load and unload stones and cement at an impossible speed from the trucks as they arrived. We alternated the pulling of cables and the loading and unloading of the trucks with yet another task: breaking up old rocks. For this purpose, pickaxes were made available to us. One of the prisoners even received a rock drill. The stone fragments had to be loaded into trolleys, which stood on rails.

The entire work detail of Königshütte consisted of older or weaker people. They were prisoners who actually were earmarked to die. They were obliged to work until they literally collapsed. The work became even more onerous because, in the meantime, winter had arrived with a vengeance. Piles of snow had accumulated everywhere. The air was bitterly cold; it cut into our faces and through our flimsy clothes. When I had been arrested, it was the middle of July. At that time I was wearing summer clothes, but since then I had not yet been able to get other, warmer clothes.

My shoes were another problem. I had put aside my better pair of shoes from home for as long as possible, hiding them under my straw bag. In the meantime, I was still using my wooden clogs. But, in the time that I was in Köngshütte, I had qualified for a new pair of shoes. The idea that I could exchange these wooden clogs was a delightful prospect. I looked forward to it for days. But when finally the moment arrived, it was to be a disappointment. The top of the shoes were not made of leather but of a thin, useless piece of material. The soles were made of wood. When I marched to and from the yard, the snow stuck to the soles at each step, so that I soon lost my balance. Every fifty meters of this grim march, I tried to stand still for a while, without being observed, to scrape the snow off with a piece of wood or iron. I was worn out and stressed even before arriving at Königshütte. My toes seemed to be frozen solid with the cold. I also had boils on my left cheek and on my neck which were so severe that my eye was nearly closed. Because of the lack of nutrition, these boils could not heal, and they became bigger and bigger. My face was a mass of pus and blood.

My hands were also severely hurt by the tools that were given to us, tools which were difficult to handle. On one occasion, I had to work with a rock drill. The implement vibrated so much that it simply tore my fingers open.

Finally, I was simply unable to continue this work at Königshütte with all the additional traumas it caused. On one particular day, I was again pulling a long, very heavy cable through one of the trenches. But the pain was so intense that I could no longer keep up with the work. An S.A. man yelled at me: "Los!! Los!! Tempo!! Tempo!!" he screamed! But, still being naïve, I showed him my wounded hands as humbly as possible. I told him, carefully, that for the moment the work was too heavy for me. I was still only sixteen, I said.

"What!?" screamed the S.A. man, even before I had finished speaking, "What must the oldies and the sick ones then say!? You are sixteen!! You must therefore work twice as hard!!"

He gave me such a hard slap that blood and pus spattered into his face. He looked at me as if I were a lump of mud. My legs turned to jelly in my fright. He pulled me up by my clothes and pushed me with his gun into his room, his lair at the work site. Inside, behind the door, in the musty, overheated atmosphere of the stove that stood there, I had to bend over a little table. He gave me five cuts with the whip on my bare buttocks. It was my first total humiliation, a severely traumatic experience. I had now learned my lesson for good. I would in the future never, *never* show myself as a weakling again. From now on, I would present myself as a strong prisoner, a man who knew how to take on all the assignments that he received without difficulty.

Everyday there were prisoners who could no longer do their work. They collapsed on the job or dragged themselves up to a guard to say that they could go on no longer. Such prisoners actually should have been in the camp hospital. They could no longer get out of their beds, but by means of a cudgel and whip they were forced to stand for the roll call. They had to be supported by fellow prisoners during the march to work. They arrived in a kind of apathetic trance. They could no longer follow what was going on. If they were still able to dress themselves, it was done only mechanically. Spiritually, they were no longer there.

When such a nearly vegetative person collapsed during work, he was grabbed by one of the guards and dragged away. On one side of the yard stood a cask full of ice-cold water. The prisoner was thrown into it up to his shoulders. He struggled against it for a few seconds, but the guard held onto him until he stopped struggling. The prisoner was drowned while everybody else watched from a distance. Other prisoners were ordered to carry the dead body away. In the camp he was thrown among the corpses.

The drowning of prisoners was one of the most traumatic, animalistic happenings that I have ever seen. I have never been able to drive it out of my memory.

Not all the Jews had been deported during this period toward the end of 1942 in the part of Poland called Upper Silesia. It was chiefly in Bendin and Sosnowice (now called Sosnowies) that Jews still lived at home. During the day, these free Jews had to do forced labor under the guardianship of the S.A. and the Blue Police. It was only in the evening that they were allowed to go home. In Katowice we occasionally came across these "free" Jews when we were entering or exiting the trams. They stood at a tram stop a bit further on. It was a very strange experience, almost incomprehensible. These free Jews looked better off than us. They wore boots of cheap leather, but at least it was leather, and some of them even wore gloves. They were also less underfed and less bashed about than us. Because the guards could not be everywhere at the same time, one of us was sometimes able to speak to these free people. Especially for the imprisoned Jews of this region it was an unbelievably important interaction. The free Jews were in solidary with them. On a few occasions, it was possible for a prisoner who had lived in the region to send a small letter to his family and, a somewhat later, to receive a reply. But one had to be extremely careful, and a dose of good luck was needed. Anybody caught during such a contact was a lost man!

The difference between the Jews from this region and other Jews could be seen within the camp. The Jews who originated from Katowice and other regions within a perimeter of two hundred kilometers

from Laurahütte were called the Ostjuden or Eastern Jews. In Laurahütte there was a total of only twelve Ostjuden. Before they had been
brought here, they had been in an Osteinsatzlager behind the Russian
front. They followed the German army. These Ostjuden were much
more hardened than the Westjuden. They knew the cracking of the
whip. The twelve Ostjuden who found themselves among us were the
sole remaining members of a convoy of five hundred. Most of them
were workers, probably not builders, but shoemakers, electricians, or
carpenters.

One of the Ostjuden was called Lederberg. He was a blond fellow
with fat, red cheeks. I can also remember Czute, Goldi, and Elias. All
twelve of the Ostjuden originally came from the region of Bendin.

We heard from the Ostjuden about the existence of Auschwitz for
the first time. They told us of it down to the smallest details. They told
us about the "Brausebad," the shower bath where prisoners were not
washed but gassed. We knew that they told the truth. But it was so terrible that we had difficulty comprehending it. Despite the beastly circumstances in which we lived, the thought of a gas chamber remained
incomprehensible. It was simply too insane, too sick.

When compared with the Ostjuden, the Westjuden or Western Jews
were still novices dealing with camp life. The Western Jews came
chiefly from Belgium, Holland, and France and had not, by far, the
long-lasting experience of captivity behind them.

Among the Western Jews, the Dutch Jews were tormented most
strenuously by the Nazis. Before the war, the Dutch Jews were not so
much workmen as middle-class folk, intellectuals, teachers, lawyers;
they were not acquainted in the least with heavy manual labor. For the
Nazis, this was sufficient reason to make them the biggest scapegoats.

One day in Königshütte a Dutch prisoner was standing next to me.
We were busy breaking stones with all our strength, with no time to
look up or around. But the S.A. man who was guarding us came to
stand between us both. "Tell me," he asked the Dutch man in an apparently friendly way, as if he wanted to have a little chat with him. "What
was your father's occupation, really?" The Dutch man, alarmed,
looked down at the ground and answered as stiffly as possible: "My father was a bank employee." "What!?" screamed the S.A. man. "A rotten Jew who is a bank employee? That is absolutely impossible!! I'll
show you what that is, a Jewish bank employee! You shall work for me
until you drop!" He produced his gun. He bashed him on the back
with the rifle butt. He continued to hit him until he collapsed in a heap.

"And you?" the S.A. man now asked. He had turned to me. My knees trembled. "What was your Jew father's job?" "An electrician," I promptly lied. I assumed that this was a job more respected by the Nazis. "Ach, ja?" said the S.A. man. "That I did not know—that there are Jews who were electrical fitters. This is the first time I've heard of that." He turned around and went away. Without being able to say anything more to each other, the Dutch man and I went on with our work. But the Dutch man could hardly stand; he sobbed and bled.

At the end of a workday at Königshütte, we were once again up for roll calls at five o'clock to return to the camp. These roll calls were not the same as those held in the camp. In the yard we amounted to no more than one hundred and fifty prisoners. Each detail consisted of about thirty prisoners. The S.A. counted the men of their respective teams and checked to see if each team was in order. After that, we could depart. The end of a working day was always accompanied by unbelievable relief. It was simply a miracle that one was still alive.

It was the middle of October when, immediately after the roll call, we were pushed directly into the trucks. We were driven away in the opposite direction of the tram stop in Katowice. We did not have the faintest idea about what was now awaiting us. We feared for our lives again. After traveling for five minutes we stopped again; we now understood even less about all this! Surely we could have covered this distance quite easily on foot. We arrived at a miserable concrete building, and there we had to get out again. We found ourselves in a no-man's land. In the distance, we saw several stone barracks and some little private houses surrounded by walls. A bit further on, there was even a cow grazing. For half an hour, we stood about looking around, bewildered. Then out of the concrete building came a couple of Blue Assistants of the S.A. walking towards us, accompanied by a somewhat older, corpulent member of the S.A. They approached us with much military pomp and circumstance. The S.A. man stood in front of us and launched into a sermon:

"From now on you are in a completely new camp! I am your Lagercommandant! Here, strict order and discipline shall reign! I shall teach you all that! Here, in this new camp, there shall be so much hygiene that one will be able to eat off the ground! Nobody shall try to conserve his energy! You will all work your hardest for the well-being of the Third Reich! Whoever cooperates will have nothing to be sorry about!"

So he really came to play the Big Boss. While he continued to scream and promise us everything, food, work, hygiene, and discipline, it began to "sink in" what exactly was happening. We had simply, from one day to the next, been transferred to a totally new concentration camp. The few possessions that some of us had still been able to keep had been left behind in Laurahütte, a cloth, a toothbrush, a little photo from home. There I still had the shoes and some underclothing. Here we had absolutely nothing, only the cold, tattered work clothes that we were still wearing. We were standing in an utterly desolate place. The cold wind blew in our faces. We shivered with dismay.

After the Commandant had satisfied himself fully with his pompous, sick speech, we were led to our rooms. But there were no rooms. The camp at which we had arrived was not even a camp. It was a little dump that had been chosen haphazardly by the Nazis. It still had to be completely developed. There were no provisions anywhere, no structure, no space, no beds even. Only a straw bag lay here and there on the ground. And what was the value of a camp of a hundred and fifty prisoners? What could they achieve? The majority of prisoners had been a part of a punishment detail in Königshütte: pitiful old people, emaciated invalids, and lame people who the other Kapos wanted to get rid of. What could be done with them? Nobody would be able to keep up with the work; after a very short time we would all be in a state of collapse.

We had also already learned that in smaller camps the corrupt nature of the Nazis emerged more forcefully. The people of the camp administration were paid by higher authorities. The amount of food rations, provisions, and necessities depended directly on the number of prisoners. With all they received, the Nazis could start a small business. They could hold back our bread and sell it. And the smaller the number of prisoners, the more directly one experienced the shortage of food. Yet the S.A. tried to steal as much from a small group as from a large one. They grabbed what they could until everybody was plucked naked.

For that matter, that evening there was absolutely no distribution of food. The soup, which under normal circumstances was dished out to us after the day's work and which we were always ready for, did not appear. We had to go to bed on an empty stomach.

Still wearing my clothes and my shoes, I crept on the floor under a straw mattress. I sank away in misery. In Laurahütte, I had had acquaintances, prisoners who had been with me since Breendonk, such as the Luxemburgers, Brachfeld, and Stern. In the meantime, I became also friendly with the twelve Eastern Jews who were in my Stube. I had a nucleus of people with whom I had come to feel an affinity, either because of the work that we did, or because we passed the nights in the same barrack. They were my talking partners. Now, however, I was alone again, hopelessly alone, among a bunch of strangers, whom at best I had only met slightly. I knew practically nobody here.

Around midnight we were awakened by loud screaming. What was happening? A new day of work? A punishment? An unpleasant surprise? No, finally we understood! We were going to get a bowl of soup! At last! There were some among us who could no longer stand up straight because of their great hunger; they had to be supported and carried into the inner chamber.

While the soup was being distributed, I came to stand in front of Bienenstock. Bienenstock was a prisoner from Brussels, whom I already knew from Breendonk. Apparently, he had made use of the opportunity to be appointed as the new chef. That was a clever move on his part; he who worked in the kitchen could fill his belly. The chef had access to bread and other food. In general, the cooks suffered the least among all the prisoners.

All of a sudden, Bienenstock did not recognize me, or at least, he could not let it be seen that he did. But, anyhow, it was useful that I had bumped into an acquaintance here.

After the soup, we were allowed to return to the rooms. Again, I kept my clothes on. I was so tired I could do nothing else; I was at the end of my tether. Through the sudden warmth of the soup and the effects of my rags and the straw mattress which covered me, I suddenly became very hot. I began to shiver and sweat feverishly as if I were boiling. And thus I finally got to sleep. As soon as you felt warmer and could sleep, you subconsciously ceased being so fatalistic. You then thought: come what may, but for now I am O.K.! For a little while, the worries slid away, and I could give in to my tiredness.

The next morning we received a little piece of bread. We stood in roll call for a long time. Again an endless speech from the flabby, sadistic Lagercommandant! After that we were taken by foot to the construction site in Königshütte. Perhaps this was the only reason why we had been brought over to a new camp; we now lived closer to the work, a short half-hour's walk.

We worked through the entire day. We feared for our future; what, for goodness sake, was their plan for us? Where would it all end? After the work there was a roll call, like always, and then we marched out again. We noticed that we took the road we had always taken, the long, snow-filled path in the direction of Katowice. How could this be? We remained suspicious. But then, once again, we arrived at the tram stop. Finally, we were told what the plans were. We were going to Laurahütte, our original quarters!

In other words, the Nazis had themselves not known precisely what they wanted. The idea of the new camp was again conveyed the next day. Nazism was not seamless or perfect, as was sometimes supposed. None of the Nazis knew exactly what one had to do. Everybody there got conflicting assignments, and none of these assignments were constructive.

When we returned to Laurahütte we felt so elated that our hearts nearly rejoiced. Although it was a morbid triumph. But we again got some hold on the situation. We returned to our friends, our fellow sufferers and, compared with the hell of that anonymous, one-day camp, Laurahütte was still bearable. There was at least space, some structure, and a regular food distribution. Also the other prisoners who had all remained behind in Laurahütte were delighted to see us again. They had not been able to guess what had happened to us. They had feared that we had been murdered. So, in spite of everything, solidarity still reigned. Furthermore, what happened today with another group could happen the next day with their own group.

Our sleeping facilities in Laurahütte had remained unchanged. When I came to my bed, I saw that my little parcel with my shoes and shirts was still there—an enormous relief!

The history of the one-day camp was completely crazy, completely surreal, but precisely for that reason so dramatic. From now on we all lived with still more fear that, sooner or later, our situation was going to get worse. For us, certainty had ceased to exist. Each minute we lived was only a single minute more of life.

The work at Königshütte went on as usual. Pulling cables, loading and unloading, breaking stones, moving rails. The early rising and the heavy tasks, together with the meager rations, the ill-treatment, the torture, and the anxiety all began to weigh heavily on me. My right hand was now very much inflamed. It was so swollen that I could touch nothing with it. Tuesday, October 24, 1942, was the day when I collapsed. On the return trip to the camp there were always prisoners who could no longer walk; they had to be supported. Now I, too, had to be dragged along between two prisoners. At the same time, they had to watch out that the guards did not notice us. Had they noticed us we would have run the risk of being punished on the spot. That had already happened often with other victims.

I was half-unconscious. In the camp, I had to be brought to the field hospital, a small compartment next to the entrance of the hall where there was a small, improvised hospital. The head surgeon, Dr. Kornreich from Paris, was a very competent man. However, he could help but little under the atrocious conditions in which he had to work. He treated about two hundred patients daily and was obliged to give priority to those patients who had the best chance of recovering, not to the most severely affected or hopeless cases. When he saw me struggling in, more dead than alive, he immediately saw how serious my situation was. For my inflammation, he gave me sort of dressing, an elastic piece of material that looked more like a piece of paper than anything else. He wrapped it carefully around my hand. In addition, he wrote a prescription in which he declared that I should not work for one day. Anything more he could not do. Getting one day off was already phenomenal, really a rare piece of luck.

Normally, invalids who could not go out to work were kept together in the field hospital. In this severe winter period the field hospital was more than fully occupied. Because of this, I stayed in my normal room. I slept the whole night. On the following day, Wednesday, October 25, I was again allowed to go to the doctor. My sick leave was extended to include the week-end!

I wanted to do something. If I simply remained lying down, certain death awaited me. I had to make use of this opportunity to get something done.

Elie Kanner, one of my neighbors, was an acquaintance of mine. He had been with me since Breendonk. He had also been allowed to stay behind in the camp because he was even worse off than I. We sought each other out, and Kanner told me that now was the right moment: in his yard, he was in contact with a Pole who was interested in my good pair of shoes. He suggested that he should show them to this Pole and sell them.

The shoes were in really good condition, so I would not exchange them for less than three breads—that was my demand. But I took the risk and agreed with his plan. With the hope of benefiting from this deal, I had to hand these shoes over. The following day, Elie slipped past me. I got the impression that he was avoiding me. When, finally, we could talk to each other, Kanner explained to me, with much erasion, that the Pole with whom he wanted to barter had looked at my shoes and taken them but without giving anything in exchange. While I heard Kanner explaining so hastily, I got the impression that it was none other than he who was cheating me—that he had most certainly received the breads, or at least a part of them, and that he kept them for himself. Although I understood that there was no sense in arguing about it, the whole experience left ill. But I had to consider it a dead issue.

During all those months, I had saved my shoes to no avail. My shoes, for which my dear mother had cared with so much love, in her very last attempt to do something worthwhile for her child! I had simply walked my feet to shreds in those wooden clogs. And now I had to manage with those "planks," the useless ersatz shoes which I had received from the Germans.

To make things worse, there was a plague of lice in the camp. I had already seen my roommates searching in their clothes, without knowing the reason why at first. A bit later it became clear to me. I slept on the lowest bed. The prisoners who lay in the beds above me spent the whole night scratching and tossing about. The lice, which they had, fell with a rattling sound onto the floor alongside my bed. In the meantime, I had become scared to death of these insects. The thought alone of these creatures made me itch. By now, a full louse epidemic threatened. We now had second and third generation lice.

Precisely during the weekend when I was bedridden, a delousing throughout the whole camp was being organized. All people who could still walk that far (everyone except those in the camp hospital) were to report on Saturday to public disinfection showers. There the lice would be flushed out with a high pressure shower and then immediately disinfested with an insecticide. The prisoners had to have the hair of their heads shaved off. The pubic hair was also to be shaved away. During the absence of the prisoners, the barracks were also to be disinfested, the floor, the clothes, the beds, and the bedding. I was sent the day before, a Friday, to the camp hospital. Here, the delousing was only partially done, in a slovenly and ineffective manner. I had seen so much misery experienced by the victims of lice that I was afraid they might attack me at any moment. For this reason, I regretted that I had been left behind in the hospital barracks.

The swelling of my hand did not show any sign of getting better. Nevertheless, I was sent back to work, and everything that I had to do there gave me so much pain that everybody who knew me began to fear for my life.

I was desperate and at the end of my tether. I tried to make contacts. I went everywhere and explained my plight in the hope of being able to change my work. I wanted to get back to the Mader detail in Laurahütte. Although it was nearly impossible to arrange a transfer by oneself, a miracle occurred after a day or two! A place for me had become free in Laurahütte! I did not understand how it came about, but come about it did!

Changing jobs always carried an enormous risk. One never knew beforehand how hard the new job was going to be. One was especially ignorant of how the guards were going to behave, especially the German-Polish foremen. Would they push us around? Would they hit us? Would they shoot us down for the slightest trifle? Or would they be kinder and leave us in peace now and then? But I seized this opportunity Königshütte would mean my ruin in any case.

Back in Laurahütte, I worked for the same group as before. The concrete and wire twisting work was finished. I was transferred to the transport detail where we had to drag big concrete blocks. The concrete blocks lay on wooden planks under which had been placed big cylindrical iron rollers. As soon as the last roller became free it had to be carried forward to be placed again as the first roller under the plank, and so on, to move the concrete block along. Compared to Königshütte, it was hardly an improvement, but I did not dare to complain any more; my situation was hopeless. I would succumb here. But there was one good thing—the march to the work was not as far, only a ten-minute walk from the sleeping quarters.

The thought of an escape was entirely fantastic, yet I always had it at the back of my mind. I secretly speculated about it, and even more secretly dreamed about it. In the middle of December 1942, there were four prisoners in Laurahütte who would have given anything to get away from here, even their life. In the days before their internment they had been rather rich. It was said that they had been able to buy their freedom from the camp. They had promised the S.A. men diamonds, which they had hidden away somewhere at home. In exchange for these diamonds, they were to be allowed to escape to freedom by the Nazis. For the prisoners who stayed behind, it was outrageous to see those four leaving. Of course, we did not begrudge them their freedom, but why could they leave and we couldn't? Would a day also dawn for us when we, just like they were now doing, would be able to turn our backs on this death camp? Their sudden freedom emphasized our sense of captivity. Again, our noses were pressed against the bitter reality of the camp's inequity.

It was only after the war was over that I learned from one of the survivors among these four prisoners how they had managed it. In fact, they had been rather daring. They did not possess anything of value. They were then sent at once to Sosnowitze, to one of the transit camps for Silesian Jews. One of the four was shot dead. Two survived the camps; the fourth also died. But the Germans had never had any intention of giving them their freedom under any circumstance. The Germans would first of all have robbed them under the best of conditions.

A few weeks later, at the time of the 1943 New Year, we did not go to work: the non-Jewish workers had a holiday. The day before, December 31, a real attempt at escape took place. During work, two prisoners had simply tried to run away. Their attempt had failed, and the punishment followed on New Years' Day.

One of these unlucky prisoners was a certain Hauser, a prisoner whom I knew because he belonged to our very own room. Hauser was a German refugee. He belonged to the many hunted Jews who had grown up in Germany but who had fled to Belgium between 1933 and 1939. He had sought shelter in Brussels, and his nationality was Polish.

We learned on New Year's Day that Hauser and his friend had tried to escape. They had run away but without being in possession of documents, without having decent clothing, and without the prospect of a place of refuge. Anybody could tell by seeing their thin faces that they were not ordinary citizens. During their flight they were arrested in a tram by the Nazis and brought back to Laurahütte.

Even before the roll call, the rumor spread that the whole camp would be disbanded and sent to Auschwitz. That morning a macabre atmosphere pervaded the camp. Everybody had to come forward in the hall under the leadership of the Stubenälteste. Nobody of the Leitung gave us any explanation about what was awaiting us. The S.A. men were all there, they paraded up and down in dashing uniforms. For them, it was a day of celebration.

At about eleven o'clock in the morning they began their act of retaliation. The front gate opened. A naked person, white as a sheet, was carried in. It was Hauser. Normally, he was a strong, impressive man, but the S.A. had done everything possible to display him as negatively as possible. He looked so ghastly, so horrendous, that I had hardly recognized him. He was tossed onto a table, and shortly after that, the other, equally miserable prisoner was carried in.

The Camp Commander started shrieking. "Jewish Schweinhunde! We shall show you what it means to try to escape from a German camp! *That* does not succeed! Nobody has ever succeeded, and in the future nobody will ever succeed! You are the trash, the shit of the world! And we are the elite, the Knights of the Order! We shall show you what we do with retarded swines who want to escape from this marvelous camp! Let this be an example for you!"

On each side of the table stood a policemen. One of them was Kampf, the sturdy heartless sadist. They placed a wet cloth on the buttocks of the victim, and each policeman in turn whipped him with the regularity of a metronome. Every blow was counted. The number of blows would not be announced in advance. At the tenth lash, I already had the impression that Hauser would collapse. How he stood it, I did not know. It was simply unimaginable. Twenty, thirty, forty, whiplashes—they simply kept going, and there seem to be no end to it. After a while, the whiplashes of these brutes became totally mechanical, although they were using the extreme of their strength. Fifty, sixty, seventy . . . Hauser looked like a piece of dead meat; there was no reaction from his body anymore. Only upon reaching the count of one hundred did they stop. Only at a hundred! With a kick of a boot, he was rolled off the table, and the other prisoner was made ready. They also laid a damp cloth on him. This made the lashes more painful and enabled the victims to endure the torture for a while longer. Yesterday he had been sitting in a tram in town; now he lay here. He got precisely the same punishment as Hauser: one hundred fierce lashes.

The Nazis had chosen this brutal punishment to intimidate us to the depths of our being. They wanted to suppress any dream of escaping, any thought of possible freedom. That we should be sent to Auschwitz, after this event, had indeed been a groundless fear; this practice would have run counter to the economic principles of the camp. To evacuate a camp like Laurahütte would have meant an enormous and laborious undertaking, and the work in the yards, in any case, had to continue. But at that time, we were not so acquainted with the policy of the camps.

But all that personal punishment was not enough. The Nazis still carried out collective punishment. Because Hauser was from our room, we also had to share in the punishment. Each one of his roommates had to come forward. We were laid on the table, one after the other, in the blood of our predecessors. We each got twenty-five very severe whiplashes, without a cloth. This beating could have been fatal for the weaker ones among us. We were already quite accustomed to beatings, but this punishment was something new to us because it was so systematic. There seemed to be no end to it. Fourteen! Fifteen! Sixteen! The fear and pain that I suffered were indescribable.

For weeks, I had physical problems because of that punishment. I simply felt paralyzed, numb. When I lay in bed on my back, I could not possibly move. And each time I bent over during work, it felt as if my skin were being torn apart. How Hauser survived four times as many whiplashes, I cannot understand.

But that was our New Year's Day in Laurahütte.

Rumors started to circulate during the second half of December 1942 that the camp would be split up. Parts of Laurahütte would be transferred to another camp. Auschwitz was not mentioned; the new location would be another Jewish forced labor camp. The number of prisoners needed by the camp leadership did not amount to more than three hundred. Naturally, the prospect of being deported to such a small camp made me very fearful. The smaller the camp, the smaller one's chances of survival. The unfortunate ones selected for the new camp were identified only after the necessary number of prisoners had been decided. It was customary that each work section attempt to discard only its weakest men, its most emaciated, powerless victims. They were not of much use anyway. But then this practice resulted in a newly constituted camp completely compose of invalids, which could never thrive as a work camp.

Their names were read out during the roll call. My name was also mentioned. The work in the transport detail had left such severe traces on me that I was counted among the useless recruits without any future, someone nobody wanted. When I heard the S.A. man calling out my name, it made me feel faint. We were to leave a few days later, on Sunday, January 3, 1943. I saw that I would soon be a part of a camp of which 85 percent of its prisoners would be condemned to death.

Bismarckhütte

We were taken to the next camp, Bismarckhütte, in trucks. Immediately, it became clear to us that we had arrived in a sort of a desert. As always, there was a kind of a roll call and, as always, we were addressed by a Lagercommandant who presented himself to us as the great hero. He demanded extreme obedience and discipline of us. Those prisoners who obeyed the rules would have no problems, but heaven help those, he screamed, who did not obey the rules! They would immediately be taken away!

Where to? That he did not tell us.

In sharp contrast to the extravagant and bombastic promises of the commandant were the utterly miserable and shabby conditions of his camp. Not a single one of the barracks there had been completed. These buildings were small skeletons of roughly assembled buildings, and here and there several of them stood crookedly, as if at any moment they would collapse. We could hardly wade through the paths between the barracks because of the deep mud, filthy and overgrown with weeds. Places to wash oneself and other hygienic facilities were nowhere to be found. The camp was a catastrophe.

The hierarchy in Bismarckütte was the same as before. At the head stood the Lagercommandant, and he was supported by German S.A.-ers on the one hand, and on the other hand by the Judenälteste, the Kapo's, the Stubenälteste and the Lagerpolizist. The Lagerpolizist of Bismarckhütte was Goldi, one of the twelve Eastern Jews from Laurahütte. During the day, he worked with us as foreman. Fichel Horowitz from Antwerp and Breendonk was a Stubenälteste here, but not of my Stube. Yet I maintained some contact with him.

As already mentioned, the greatest disadvantage of Bismarckhütte was that we were only three hundred men here and continually under the watchful eyes of the Nazis. Absolutely nothing escaped their itchy fingers; nothing approached their corrupt and pilfering natures. Even the commandant, like a great emperor, was not above regularly sniffing around the camp hoping to be able to steal something. As if that weren't enough, much sadism existed among the Nazis. The Nazis of the smaller camps were ridiculed by those of the bigger camps and considered to be inferior. As a result, all the frustrations, jealousies, and resentments of the smaller camp Nazis were released on us. We could expect yet more punishment, more harassment, and torture than normal. Especially if a prisoner had done something that was not permitted, he had to prepare himself for the worst of the worst. Our chances of survival were extremely small. Most of us were, at the time of our arrival, in such a pitiful physical condition. The health of the prisoners in our group was already precarious. We were terribly emaciated, ill, physically wounded, and psychologically broken. There was not even a doctor in the sick bay. We would have to build the entire infrastructure of Bismarckhütte singlehandedly *after* the daily work schedule.

During the first roll call, the division of the work forces took place. One of the bosses came to stand in front of us and shouted that he needed twelve strong men. He said that he had a very difficult task in store for us. What that task involved we could only guess at. But because I had already experienced how dangerous it was to creep out of a corner like a weakling, I immediately volunteered. I still felt terrible pain from the twenty-five whiplashes I had received. During the journey in the truck those wounds had become worse. But I still had to be counted among the strong ones, that was my only chance of surviving. Together with some ten other volunteers, I was moved aside to a corner of the compound. I could see that we formed a team of which about half were young men still possessing relatively good morale. A weak or passive group would have caused more uncertainty among us.

The team which we formed was to work with blast furnaces in the vicinity of the camp. The work was to give shape to the red-hot, glowing, molten iron that came out of a furnace on rollers. It was pushed forward past several groups of workers. We had to seize the iron with tongs and, wearing gloves, move it to one side where a guillotine-like shears hung. The iron, which in the meantime had cooled a little, was cut into several well-formed rectangular plates. The plates then moved further along the conveyer to the following team, which continued to work with the material. Each time, we had to pull the left-over fragments to one side with two or three men.

This furnace work was indeed heavier labor than average; yet, there were some advantages attached to it. First, we had practically no guards apart from the Germans with whom we worked. Even the fore-man, who also participated in most of the work (we were only his helpers), stood to the right of me in the row. It was from him that I took over. He kept a close watch on me, but he was a capable, reasonable, and lenient man. As long as we did our best, we were not bothered by him or anybody else. Secondly, the rhythm could easily be maintained. Thirdly, it was warm there, too warm in fact. But more than anything else, during the winter, we did not run the risk of freezing to death in the cold at work.

Twelve of us composed the team for the night shift. We worked from seven o'clock in the evening until three o'clock in the morning. In the camp, this divergent work schedule gave us a slightly different sta-tus. We certainly did not enjoy any privileges but we *were* left in peace somewhat more than the average prisoner. After a day's work the rest of them were still obliged to help with creating an infrastructure for the camp. We could still be pulled out of bed at times but, on the whole, they left us alone.

Winter weather was very severe during the time spent in Bismarck-hütte. The snows came much earlier, and it froze—-10 to -23° Celsius. The death toll rose with grim regularity because about 80 percent of the prisoners were already at the end of their tether upon arrival at the camp. We were a camp of emaciated living corpses who walked along with dragging feet. The number of the sick rose so high that, after a short time, it became essential to create some kind of hospital. A gallery at the side of the entrance to the camp was put to use for this purpose. Here, some twenty beds were installed. But every day more than a hundred prisoners lined up for medical attention until past mid-night. Those who were diagnosed seriously ill were given a day or sometimes even two days of sick-leave and had to drag themselves back to their beds. There was no other space available for them. No real doctors were available, only male nurses. One of these was called Fuchs, a man who had once run a chemist's shop in Antwerp. Another male nurse was named Jakubovic. Jakubovic survived the camp. After the war, he became a doctor in Brussels.

The greatest plagues in the camp were diarrhea, dysentery, and ty-phus fever (also known as European, classic, or jail fever, or louse-borne typhus). Cases of typhus were immediately eliminated from the camp for fear of an epidemic. Their fate was unknown to us. We thought that they were taken to Auschwitz, but at that time there was no corroboration of this. In the best of circumstances victims of edema, recognizable by their swollen legs and faces, were allowed to stay in their room for a day or two. Otherwise, they were obliged to accompany us to their work and to go on working until they collapsed. After a week or so, such a victim could no longer manage the return journey from the building site, and he had to be carried by his fellow workers. Either he was unconscious or he was dead.

Many prisoners also got wounded at work. No safety precautions were ever provided. Due to a shortage of adequate shoes, many prisoners also had ripped-open or frozen feet or feet with blisters and inflammations. Gloves were never distributed and, as a result, hands were mostly frozen and full of cuts. No remedies were available for such victims; they had to try to protect themselves as best they could. A wound on my right hand caused me unremitting pain.

The very worst invalids were sent away to an Erholungslager or convalescent camp. It was a place some fifty or sixty kilometers outside the camp. Prisoners from all the camps of the region were received there. To my knowledge, there were two such places: Annaberg and Gogolin. Here some were chosen to go to Auschwitz. Only very few people returned from an Erholungslager. They were not necessarily those who had been sent from our camp, but persons who had come from other camps. From what these people told us, we became aware of what was going on. The stories were so gruesome, so horrifying, that bit by bit it began to penetrate our minds how unendingly hellish the Holocaust must be. What the Eastern Jews had told us about the gas chambers were being confirmed more and more.

Besides the winter's cold, the daily work, and the general disadvantages of life in a small camp, our work on the infrastructure also weighed heavily on us. During our so-called free time there were always victims being selected to work on these internal facilities. The posts upon which the huts stood had to be regularly repaired because the building materials used were so inferior. The muddy paths had to be replaced with a kind of gravel. The water drains and sewer outlets had to be worked on, and we were also given tasks for the brick houses which accommodated the S.A. outside the camp. After a day's work, we were assigned all the jobs for which the S.A. could use us, not just in the evenings but also on Saturday and Sunday. The Kapos then organized a raid under orders from the S.A. To escape from such a raid was impossible. We were surrounded as if in a roundup. The only way of escape, was to hide under the huts. These huts rested on poles some forty centimeters above the ground. But during the winter there was an enormous pool of mud under the huts, a dark, suffocating accumulation of filth. And whoever crept into that pool also took a gigantic risk. A heavy punishment awaited you if you were caught attempting to dive under it. Personally, I never participated in this. Some fifty men were needed for the supplementary work. The only thing that one could do was hope and pray that you were not selected. If you should be picked for this work, you knew that it would be accompanied by the cudgel and much cursing and screaming.

In addition to the internal work there was also the misery of the Stubendiensten or barracks room duties and the cleaning calls. The Stubendienst took place according to a roster. Every two or three weeks you were scheduled to clean with a partner from the same living area. The mattresses had to be straightened out, the floor had to be scrubbed, bedbugs, blood spots, mildew and any filth had to be removed. On its own, it was perhaps not a very heavy task, but we did not look forward to it because of the responsibility and the time pressure attached to it.

The cleanliness inspections were truly the worst. These took place every Sunday. All the prisoners in the camp had to be neat and tidy, washed and shaved. In theory, this practice appeared to be a useful initiative—he who no longer washed himself was on the threshold of decline. But for the S.A. the cleanliness inspections were a marvelous opportunity to partake in their sadism. There were always cudgel blows accompanied by shouting and thumping and immoderate bullying. The standards that they applied to us were far too difficult for our abilities. In each little hut, a wash basin was installed; we had to do make do with that. On a plank above the bed, each one of us kept a jug from which water could be scooped. Shaving oneself was obligatory, even for prisoners who were, like myself, still too young to have a real beard. But how we achieved that shaving we had to work out for ourselves. Often it was the case that we could call upon the services of a prison barber. He was not appointed by the leadership, but he worked in accordance with an agreement among the prisoners themselves. The barber's profession was quite common among the Jews. And like anyone who knew a useful profession or had a talent, the barbers could capitalize on their ability. They snipped and shaved you in exchange for a bit of bread or a few small potatoes or for some other service. Tailors also earned a bit extra when they repaired your rags.

Still, the results of our cleaning sessions left much to be desired. It was impossible to satisfy the demands of the S.A. And thus, on one occasion, there was an act of vengeance on the part of the camp leadership. An unreasonably strict control was announced. We were informed that anybody who was not neat and in order could expect the worst! All the dirt which came from work, all patches of sweat, and all traces of blood had to be removed! All frayed pieces of clothing had to look good again. When we heard all this, panic reigned among us. We feared that the oil stains from our work had penetrated so deeply into our skin, into our hands, and into our necks that they had become indelible. We used sand to rub our hands, arms, legs, necks, and faces until we nearly bled from the friction. To our great surprise, we seemed to be really clean again by the evening before the following Sunday. But when the S.A. saw the results of our efforts, they seemed to be rather more disappointed than satisfied. We were beaten because we had not been so clean sooner!

As it was in all the camps, so it was in Bismarckhütte: the rhythm and the sense of the day was determined by the mealtimes. One lived for them always. A day consisted of two halves: the half before eating and the half after eating. The distribution of food took place in the evenings. We had to hold out for twenty-four hours on the bread that we were given until the meal of the following evening. Most people ate all their food immediately. If you tried to save a bit you were tortured with hunger until you gave in and gobbled the rest up. Sometimes you got a bit of margarine or, very seldom, a bit of jam.

It was only in the bigger camps that the hot food, the soup, was brought to the rooms. In Bismarckhütte, everybody went to the kitchen under the control of his Stubenälteste. If one got there late, there was nothing left in the pot. There was also much shoving and pushing because everyone was so afraid of missing out.

After eating, everyone could go to his sleeping place. Only one advantage existed compared to Laurahütte: instead of a gigantic hall, we were housed in small wooden huts to pass the night. Each hut housed thirty-six prisoners. It was almost like a kind of sitting room. There was a small stove in the middle of the room. After work, we could go and sit next to it and, because of the sudden heat, we began to shudder and shiver. Our skin was painful and our fingers began to burn.

At nine o'clock the lights were dimmed. Then everybody had to be in his bed. Older people or ill, emaciated people who did not have to work the following day and who, in fact, did not do much more than sit and wait for a certain death, sometimes stayed sitting in the glow of the stove until deep into the night. If they still had a little scrap of bread left over from their ration, they tried to toast it. It was especially people with diarrhea who did that: they could hardly digest the ordinary bread. If someone had a little potato, he laid it on the hot ashes under the stove to warm it. There were endless discussions about these roasting and baking techniques, especially among the people who were a bit older. They asked themselves how best to eat it, when, and in which sequence. But I never bothered to toast anything myself.

Sometime in February, the Lagercommandant unexpectedly burst into our room, at two o'clock in the morning to check on how we were doing. It was clear that he had been drinking. He looked stirred up, agitated, and wild, and he stank of alcohol. A couple of prisoners were still sitting at the stove, chatting about this and that. We stiffened when the Commandant flung the door open with much noise. A deadly silence ensued. He paraded along the beds and ran his finger over our wash tubs. If a layer of grime was found in a person's tub, that person received ten lashes with the whip. We were all pigs, he said. We had to learn what discipline and order was. Because the stove had been burning so fiercely, some soot had settled into each tub. The Commandant became furious. We had to come forward one by one in the hut, and each person received ten lashes with the whip on his bare bottom with his trousers down. After that, chatting around the stove became a thing of the past.

During this period, I had little contact with people from my own living quarters because I was a part of a night team. But also everybody was so exhausted by the work that no one had the energy to speak to each other. In my room, I got on very well with Benjamin Brachfeld and Salomon Stern.* They were the only ones here whom I had known in my neighborhood from Antwerp. They had been with me in the camps since the time of Saccrau. Now they slept in the bunk beds next to mine so that we could exchange a few words with each other in the evenings. We were not close friends; our differences in age were too great for that. But they were my companions, my comrades.

Brachfeld had an optimistic, witty character and a lot of willpower. He always had courage. During the last days in Laurahütte he was still very much "in form." I remember that on New Year's Eve he hopped

*Benjamin Brachfeld was the father of Sylvain Brachfeld, the well-known journalist and writer of, among other works, *Uw Joodse Buurman* (Your Jewish neighbor).

onto a table with a cup of Malts coffee in his hand and he sang us a jolly song. He tried to cheer up all the people around him. "Oi Chevre tomid pi," he sang, "Gibt's euch taki mi, und trinkt ein gläsel nach ein gläsele!" [Oh, people, let us have fun. Let us drink glass after glass!"] But in spite of the best willpower in the world, poor Brachfeld fell deeper and deeper into depression. He went downhill rapidly after the move to Bismarckhütte. He became more silent, thinner, and less concerned about his appearance.

Salomon Stern was much more refined in his nature. He was tall and slender, not at all able to take the violence of the camps. He also became more and more depressed and deteriorated physically.

One day in January, both Brachfeld and Stern returned from work with appalling wounds. They had been knocked to pieces by the guards and by the builder. Their hands were thick and blood-red, their arms were bleeding and swollen with lumps and bruises, their heads swollen. When they retired to sleep at night, Stern began to whisper to me. His voice sounded thin and distant, he had absolutely no strength left. "I'm not going to make it," he mumbled. "I'm not going to make it, I cannot make it . . . I'm not making it . . ." I tried to instill courage in him. I asserted that we had to hold out together and that he would get sick-leave from the doctor—that he would get medical treatment and recover. I told him that the end of our via dolorosa was already in view. But my consoling words did not reach him any longer. He hardly reacted to them. I adjusted his blanket and continued to sit by him for another half-hour. It was as if he was dying in my arms. The next day he was no more. His corpse was carried away to the place for the other dead.

Brachfeld passed away a couple of days later. It was not just from the blows he had received at work. It was also from the suffering that he had bottled up during the past months and which had now come to the surface. He had lost his resistance and had submitted to death. As soon as someone lost his fighting spirit, he was condemned to die in the camps.

Their passing severed almost all my ties to any life before the war.

Prisoners who died in Bismarckhütte were more the rule than the exception. After two-and-a-half months, only sixty of the three hundred prisoners had survived. I have never experienced such an extremely high percentage of deaths in any other camp. Most of the prisoners here were completely emaciated from the beginning. The winter was severe, the work was severe, and the leadership was extremely bestial. We eventually were so few that the camp had to be discontinued, and we were taken somewhere else midway through March of 1943. We all looked so ill that we could no longer imagine what plans they still had for us.

Blechhammer

After having traveled for a good hour, we arrived at the Juden-zwangsarbeitslager Blechhammer. Blechhammer lay in the neighborhood of Heydebrecke, not very far from Auschwitz. The prisoners who were sent away from Blechhammer, as a punishment or because of fatal, incurable diseases, were taken straight to the gas chambers of Auschwitz. The fear that one might land there someday was permanently with everybody. An uninterrupted fear of death hung over our heads and prevailed among us.

Yet, on arrival, I immediately grasped that my chances for survival here could be a somewhat greater than in the suffocating Bismarckhütte. To begin with, Blechhammer was a much larger establishment. Between five and six thousand people were kept prisoner here, depending on the deportations and on the number of deaths at any one time. Regularly, new Jewish prisoners from other camps were brought here. Also those who had been left behind in Laurahütte and had later been deported to other camps finally arrived here among us in Blechhammer. And the greater number of prisoners, the more chances you had of escaping the sadism of the guards. You could move along in the mob and hide yourself better among the others. Also, due to its size, this camp had a better developed infrastructure.

As expected, the hierarchical system here was more extensive than in other, smaller camps. On the Jewish side there were active here some four Oberkapos, apart from Vorarbeiters and ordinary Kapos. The ranks were distinguishable by the number of stripes that they wore on a band around the upper arm. A Vorarbeiter only carried one stripe, a Kapo carried two, an Oberkapo carried three. I remember that among the Oberkapos was a man called Emmers, a German Jew who had emigrated to Holland during the 1930s. And further, I still remember a certain Max Bolle.

The Polizisten or policemen of Blechhammer no longer had to accompany us to work. They now belonged solely to the Lager personnel. In a camp of such enormous size like this one, the Polizisten had their hands more than full with the orders from the S.A. Even though I was not clear about what guidelines the Polizisten precisely received, i.e., what really were their tasks and what were not, I could still discover a clear pattern in their daily work. For example, when there was an inspection in the barracks the Polizisten had to accompany the S.A. men. The S.A. men then gave the Polizisten orders, that is, which of the prisoners were to receive whiplashings and how many, or what other measures for punishment were to be carried out. The Polizisten then started the torture while the S.A. men chatted among themselves or sometimes watched the punishment with amusement. Usually they counted the whiplashes.

At the distribution of the rations again, the Polizisten worked outside the direct instructions of the S.A. When the prisoners who were standing in line in front of the kitchen began to push and shove in their panic to get some food, the Polizisten contained them with blows from their truncheons. The S.A. men did not bother to dirty their hands with that sort of work.

In Blechhammer, there were two Polizisten. The chief of these was called the "Schister," the Jewish word for his profession of shoemaker. The other Polizist was called Rauch. Each was dressed like the other prisoners. The only difference was that they wore a cap with a band around it on which was written the word "Polizist."

Rauch was a somewhat older, grey man who had come from Paris. He was a very unpleasant and cruel fellow. He followed the orders from the S.A. more assiduously and obviously enjoyed the work.

The Schister was an Eastern Jew, from the neighborhood of Sosnowice. He was a somewhat primitive, simple fellow, who was much gentler compared to Rauch. When he was given an order by an S.A. man to give someone a flogging, he would whisper to the victim: "Now scream as hard as you can! Scream as if you were breaking up!" When the S.A. was not paying attention, the Schister tried to hit less hard, with less force. He tried to spare us as much as possible. Despite the fact that he was given such brutal task, he did his best to support the prisoners and to fool the Nazis.

In addition to carrying out executions, the Polizisten were also given other tasks. The Schister was also the leader of the burial detail. On his own initiative, he gave comfort to believers. In his barrack, he had a separate little room, and although he himself was not particularly religious, he secretly kept there a pair of tefillins and a prayer robe. He would now and then allow a prayer to be said with a couple of prisoners who, in their normal, previous life, had been rabbis or really god-fearing people, like Leibisch Wahl. For these people it was an exceptional privilege, an encouragement to help them hold their heads high despite everything. By doing this, the Schister took an enormous risk, but he was a man with a heart, the kind of person one seldom meets.

In the hierarchy on the Jewish side, the Judenälteste occupied the highest position. He was the camp head who had the responsibility for the most common events in the camp. He was helped in these duties by a secretary and by the deputized Judenälteste. Within the Nazis the Judenälteste's superior was the camp commander. The Judenälteste had to carry out what the Nazis ordered him to do, but he could choose his own methods for executing these orders. For so long as he could justify this practice to the Nazis, he also had the power to appoint or to suspend Kapos entirely on his own decision. His accommodations also reflected his exceptional status. The Judenälteste did not live with the other prisoners who were packed together in the oppressive barracks. He lived completely apart from them in a single private room not far from the Schreibstuben or typists' offices in the front of the camp. In theory, he received the ordinary camp rations during daily meals. But it was obvious that he could easily obtain much more food from the Kapos and from the cooks. All prisoners, after all, did their best to remain in the good graces of the Judenälteste.

The direct helper or assistant of the Judenälteste was the Stellvertretender Judenälteste or deputy Jewish camp head. He did not play as important a part on his own. He somewhat controlled things and stiffened the supervision. But, should the Judenälteste die, then the Stellenvertretender Judenälteste could immediately step in and take his place.

We experienced an exceptional stroke of luck—the Judenälteste of Blechhammer was an extremely intelligent and kind-hearted man. His name was Demerer.* His most important quality was that he under-

---

*Demerer was born in Vienna in 1902. He lived in Sosnowitze and was interned in the camps in 1940. He was the Judenälteste during the entire existence of Blechhammer. At no time did he ever allow himself to be seduced to the level of taking personal advan-

stood very well how to approach the Germans. He regularly took risks that he absolutely could not avoid, but in general he knew exactly what he needed, where his limits lay, and how far he could go. In other camps it was almost a rule that a Kapo had to behave as sadistically as possible to please the Judenälteste. In the case of Demerer, the situation was precisely the reverse; if a Kapo was too harsh, he ran the risk of being side-tracked by Demerer. He could not always relieve such a Kapo of his function—that would have been going too far for the perverted power-mad Nazis. In theory, the power of the Judenälteste was limited to the interior structures of the camp, and he had no control over anything that happened outside, in the yards or on the march. But despite this, he could arrange for the transfer of a Kapo to a smaller, more difficult and less interesting detail, or conversely, to a better, more advantageous detail. As a result, most of the Kapos tried to be somewhat less cruel in their treatment of us out of fear of the Judenälteste, lest they so misbehave. Actually, they were only allowed to hit us to prevent something worse from happening to us, that is, to fend off the brutality of the S.A. men and other German guards. Through his relations and contacts, Demerer managed to know about everything. That was simply his nature.

We were also grateful to Demerer that the Polizisten were somewhat milder in their treatment of us, that is, when compared with the Polizisten of other camps. In Laurahütte, Kampf had already been a Kapo and a Polizist; in Blechhammer he was, however, a little less cruel in his nature because he had to abide by the rules laid down by Demerer.

For the appointment of the Kapos, Demerer sometimes took into account their own, personal background. Some of the Kapos in Blechhammer had been prominent in their past civilian lives. Some had been intellectuals. Normally, such prisoners were treated by the Germans extra badly precisely for this reason. Demerer did his best to protect them.

---

tage of his position, of acquiring something for himself at the expense of others. All the testimonies which have been submitted about him speak in his favor, something that was not the general rule for many of the ex-Judenältesten. But, although Demerer was so generous and noble by disposition, he would never again thrive and flourish after the liberation. He died in Israel in 1972. In Yad Vashem, the great Israeli museum about the Holocaust, lies a hand-written manuscript of Demerer's memories from the concentration camp.

The previously mentioned Oberkapo Emmers was one of these persons of earlier prominence. Oberkapo Max Bolle had been no less prominent; in pre-war Amsterdam he had been the chairman of the Netherlands Zionist Confederation and was a well-known and influential person. One of the most important figures that you could encounter was a certain Max, a Czech who was appointed to Vorarbeiter or foreman. He was very sturdily built. As a German Czech, he spoke fantastically good German. More than anyone else he was Demerer's confidant. Also the Stellvertretender Judenälteste in Blechhammer, the Austrian Nieuwes, had been a highly esteemed person. Whatever talents these persons had, Demerer got to know about them through rumors in the camp. He looked after all his relationships and kept well informed about everything that was going on. Most of the Kapos were, however, appointed by the Nazis themselves and were, as a consequence, rather hefty lads whose physical prowess far outstripped their intelligence powers.

As a Judenälteste, it was simple enough for Demerer to obtain extra bread now and then. He had, after all, a close connection with Brandes, the chief cook of Blechhammer. It was generally known that he passed on extra bread to acquaintances here and there. He helped out whenever he could.

It is difficult to determine precisely how much we had to thank Demerer for. Most of the activities that took place in the camps were chaotically organized, without a clearly defined order and without a simple purpose requiring insight. But it is certain that, without Demerer, we would have suffered a great deal more. Without him, sadism and insanity would have been even more prominent and widespread.

One of Demerer's protégés was Leibisch Wahl, the man I had seen being dragged away from his family in the train on the way to Saccrau. During the entire time that we stayed in Blechhammer, Demerer saw to it that he would be spared heavy work. Instead of this heavy work Wahl was required to take care of simple chores in one of the barracks of the building yard. He had to do some cleaning up and had to take care of the stove—in the context of the camp, one of the very best tasks that a man could be given.

The presence of women was something new to me in Blechhammer. Blechhammer was organized for men, but about two hundred women performed domestic duties, among other things. They were separated from the male prisoners. Their living quarters were fenced in with wire netting, forming a smaller, closed-off camp within the larger camp.

Most of the women were put to work in the clothing section, in the kitchens, or in the laundry. Also, they were given assignments in the brick houses of the S.A., a little further away, outside the camp. There they had to do cleaning, maintain the garden, and perform kitchen work, including cooking. The Nazis were forbidden by regulation to have the use of a house-slave—but who was around to betray them? They were all in on the game. A house-slave was regarded as a status symbol.

The imprisonment of the women was, naturally, just as horrible as that of the men. Yet, in comparison, life for them was not as bad as it was for us. Their work was certainly not so heavy as ours. Furthermore, it was simpler for them to get a bit of extra food. The women who worked in the kitchen could occasionally keep some little scrap. They could eat this tidbit or pass it on to someone in the clothing department in exchange for a repair job or a little piece of material. The women who worked in the brick houses often received a little something from the wives of the S.A. men, a few potatoes or a piece of bread. The woman of the house found it pleasant to be able to play the part of the gracious lady.

Because of these small advantages here and there, most of the women in the camp were better off physically than us and had a firmer, healthier outlook. That they were able to support each other to a certain extent gave them a greater feeling of solidarity and community. In general, the women were not yet so numbed by work as we were. They did their best, despite everything, to look as attractive as possible.

In the evenings, male and female prisoners stood on either side of the wire fence chatting a little with each other, or simply observing each other. Some of them were couples who had already known each other before the war or who were married or engaged and had been separated by the Nazis. But mostly they represented relationships that only more recently had arisen in the camp. Particularly in the case of the Kapos, it was customary to have a lady friend. They tried to give each other hope, consolation, and courage. It was also a matter of prestige: anyone who announce that he had a girlfriend could feel he was be a bit superior to the others. He felt himself to be special and somehow more popular than the rest, a favorite. And perhaps the most important thing was that one could sometimes get a little extra food from his lady friend! A few little potatoes or some bread. These things were then furtively pushed through the wire netting.

The wife of Demerer, the Judenälteste, also lived in Blechhammer. But she lived with him in his own quarters. He even had his two children with him.

One day, a woman gave birth to a baby in the camp. When the Nazis discovered it, they immediately threw the baby, still alive, into a rubbish bin, and on the same day the mother was taken to Auschwitz.

After the first roll call in Blechhammer, those of us who had come from Bismarckhütte were taken to our rooms. I was lodged in 12.6 together with a couple of others. The first number, 12, indicated the hut or barrack, the second number, 6, the room itself. Room 12.6 was as good as full; we prisoners from Bismarckhütte filled in any "vacancies."

I immediately observed that in my room there was a larger mixture of nationalities than I had previously been used to. Up to now I had been chiefly among Belgians, Hollanders, and Luxemburgers. Now I also saw many Jews from France and Eastern Jews from Poland.

We were shown the sleeping facilities. Mine was to be the bottom wooden plank in a series of three bunk beds. Next, we were introduced to our new Stubenälteste, a Jew of about forty years of age from Groningen in the Netherlands. His name was De Hertog. De Hertog was a German Jew on his mother's side. To me, he looked like a severe, strict fellow, yet not excessively violent. From his eyes, something intelligent spoke, something calculable. Apart from being a Stubenälteste he was also a Kapo. He wore an armband with two stripes.

We had hardly any time to get our breath back before the Kapos rushed in. With cudgels and sticks they drove us outside again. "Los! Los!" they screamed. There was work for us.

We were put to work in a Gelegenheitskommando or casual work detail, which informally was soon given the name Scheisskommando or "shit" detail. At the time we arrived, Saturday morning, March 13, 1943, it appeared as if the entire cesspool system for several blocks around 12.6 was blocked up. The muck flowed over the ground between the barracks. We were forced to clean it up.

At a distance of about twelve meters from our block, an electrically charged fence had been installed. The Germans had switched off the electricity and had cut an opening with shears. From the cesspool up to 150 meters outside the camp, we had to form a human chain through the hole made by the opening to pass on the excrement in buckets from man to man. These buckets had a capacity of about ten liters; yet they all overflowed. The transfer from hand to hand had to be done as quickly as possible and with such heavy force that, after a few minutes, we were all covered from head to toe in excrement. Around each three or four prisoners stood a guard, screaming at us; apart from the usual guards were also several S.A. men who had been brought in to help. They carried machine guns and other very heavy firearms and they all stood around, intimidating us and driving us on. Should any one of us be too slow, even just a little, then this long, infernal chain of prisoners could be interrupted. The guards would hardly approach us because we were so filthy, but if we did something wrong, we ran the risk of being shot down immediately, which, fortunately, did not happen.

It was one nauseating, sickening pool of excrement, from the man who stood completely at the front to scooping in the excrement right up to the end. The work lasted for a day and a half, from midday on Saturday until late Sunday evening, without the slightest break from this detestable work.

But by Sunday evening this hell had past. We were completely broken. We had hoped for something a little better when we were finally driven away. In the camps it was customary that, if one had had to work a whole night on internal work, one received a little more soup or something. But all that we got as a reward for that catastrophic weekend was a kind of hopelessly sour tomato soup that had obviously gone bad. I tried to taste a spoonful of it, but immediately spat it out. No matter how hungry I was, it was so horribly sour that I pushed the plate away. Even the most emaciated, half-starved among us could not swallow that terrible soup.

The weekend of the Scheisskommando would be remembered by us for a long time. After that beastly, revolting work all members of our barrack were so filthy that we sort of became the scapegoats of the camp. There was not much that we could do about it. Our clothes had been soaked to their fibers with the excrement and were permeated throughout with the awful smell. These clothes now lay in a primitive wooden hutch soaking under water in two long zinc troughs. We hopelessly tried to get them clean again, wringing them out and hanging them up, but it did not help very much. We also did not have any detergent. Sand was the only scouring powder against the immense, inexpressible, appalling stench that surrounded us. But it too was hardly a remedy.

The guards who did not know that we had worked in the Scheisskommando held their noses when they stepped into our quarters. These men were out to make our lives more sour than they already were. During the weekend, the S.A. were all for rousting the prisoners of 12.6 out of our room for all sorts of work. Fellow prisoners tried to avoid us. Access to the hospital hut was made difficult for us; our stench was a nuisance there. And as soon as the stench had at last disappeared, slowly and only weeks later, we still were shunned in spite of everything. Overtime, the idea of our rejection was reinforced and became an accepted thing.

The fact that our barrack stank so badly was not only due to the Scheisskommando. Also sleeping in our group was a boy, a bright friendly Frenchman of about my age who wetted his bed. During the day, he comported himself more than respectably. He could also lash back very well in his own defense. If someone should make a mocking remark, he shouted abruptly, "Shut your mouth!" He always knew everything better than the others, and above all he had a charming smile. In spite of all this, all signs indicated that he wrestled with inner problems. In the evenings, he sat in a corner biting his fingernails. He also was none too clean. And at night when he went to sleep he had nightmares. He slept to the left of me on the second bunk, and I could hear him regularly rambling on and scratching deliriously. Because of his bedwetting, the place where he slept was rotting away. We had no sheets, only a cheap, shapeless sack of straw. It sometimes happened that De Hertog, our Stubenälteste, could arrange to get a new straw mattress. But to achieve this he had to struggle through a entire bureaucracy to make contact with the clothing Kapo who was in charge of the textile stores. For us it was not so necessary; we had already become used to the rotting stench. However, the people from outside became nauseated by it and regarded us as lepers.

Most of the prisoners of block 12, and therefore of room 12.6, had been deported from Holland or France. Because there already had existed in Holland a Jewish proletariat for hundreds of years, these Jews came from different strata of the population. Thus, Joop Swaap, who slept behind me, was a carpenter from Amsterdam. His brother had been brought here with him and was a station porter in Rotterdam. Also among my roommates, there was a certain Boekie, a Hollander of about thirty, who spent nearly all his leisure hours on matters of religion. In the camp, he walked about with a little prayer book in his hand, mumbling verses of prayer. Morally, he was no better or worse than anyone else, but he possessed something that was essential in the camps: the urge to survive at any cost.

Of the Frenchmen in my room, I remember a professor of French literature who had taught at the Sorbonne. An older man with thin, grey hair, he was not very sociable and kept to himself as much as possible. He was also personally appointed as a Kapo by Demerer, although he was not so impressive as Emmers or Bolle.

Two boys in my room would become my very best friends. One of them was Bubi Ausubel. He was a boy from Antwerp. We had been in the same school and in the same youth organization, Agoedath Israël. Although he was three years older than I and therefore in another group, we spent our weekends there together. My other friend was called Henri Benzen. Benzen was already in the middle twenties and had been at the University of Brussels. But above all he would be that ray of hope during my via dolorosa. He was intelligent and a very warm-hearted fellow.

On Monday, March 15, 1943, immediately after the Scheisskommando weekend, I was attached to my first permanent detail in Blechhammer: the Kommando Dorfslager.

The Dorfslager was a settlement of wooden barracks outside the camp. Accommodation was given to non-Jewish workers (Belgian, French, Polish, and Czech) who were called up from occupied territories for obligatory labor. They worked here for the Germans. During the day, they went to work on a farm or somewhere in the industrial sector. In the evenings and at night, they stayed in this Dorfslager. Their barracks looked about the same as ours but were much more luxurious, with much better hygiene facilities. The workers of the Dorfslager could go in and out as they chose.

Our work was to develop further this part of the settlement. When new barracks had to be built, Aryan specialists took care of the craftsmanship, but we had to bring in the materials—beams, posts, and all sorts of timber. We also had to help with the laying and maintenance of paths between the huts. We had to fill up holes in the ground, level the bumps, and pave it all. For transporting the sand and the gravel, we could make use of a little horse and a cart.

Considering everything, the work in Kommando Dorfslager was not terribly heavy. There were thirty-five of us. Out of my barrack 12, I was the only one who had the good fortune to belong to this group. All other prisoners were put to work on a gigantic building site further away, the enormous yard of the Obersylesische Hydrierwerke. These Hydrierwerke were a subsidiary of the I.G. factories, the largest coordinating organization for which a range of firms did contractual works. The Hydrierwerke in turn gave orders to, among others, Siemens, Krause, Niederdruck and Betonomenir for electrical supplies, road-making, metal work, and concrete construction, respectively. Compared to the work demanded in the Dorfslager, most of the work for these firms was downright hellish. Rails had to be replaced at an intolerable pace. Stones and cement had to be loaded and unloaded. Gigantic cables had to be pulled free and moved. My friend Benzen, who kept me informed about all this, was put in a detail that worked for Niederdruck. He was part of a transport column for steel construction. Because there was so much pressure for results, Niederdruck quickly became a firm with severely sadistic guards and foremen who were continually standing and watching their workers. It was even unbearable for such an athletic and well-built fellow like Benzen. Accidents at work were the order of the day, and it was a daily occurrence for men to drop dead.

Not only was the work in Blechhammer hellish but so were the morning assemblies of the labor forces. The roll calls of Blechammer were not to be compared to those of the smaller camps, which I had previously experienced. Innumerable guards of all ranks came to make the back yard unsafe. The screaming, yelling, thumping, and cudgeling surpassed everything that I had previously experienced. The whole process of placing us together also took up much more time.

At four o'clock in the morning, we were beaten awake. After we had hastily dressed ourselves and had answered nature's call, we were given ersatz coffee. Then, at around about half-past four, the roll call itself began. These roll calls could last for up to an hour and a half, depending on the incidents which arose.

By detail, we had to present ourselves in rows of three within the inner yard. First, the Kapo came along. In our case it was Martin, or rather, "Redhead" Martin, the Kapo of the Dorfslager. He counted his men and inspected them. He looked at our clothes, our shoes, and our physique. Throughout, he shouted to us how we should stand: "Come forward!! Go backward!! More to one side!! Pull in your bellies!!" Here and there he gave somebody a slap in the face or a shove in the ribs, until we all stood correctly according to his very strict judgment. And then began the waiting, the merciless, destructive waiting. From the very first minutes, one began to pray for it to end. Every day it lasted longer than one could possible have expected. Our feet, calves, knees, everything ached from standing so long.

Unpredictably, much later, a German of a fairly low rank came walking along. The Kapo clicked his heels in front of him and roared: "Ich melde Gehorsam! Kommando Dorfslager mit x Häftlinge zur Arbeit angetreten!" [I report obediently! Kommando Dorfslager with x prisoners falling in for work.] The specific number of prisoners changed from day to day—especially in the detail other than those of the Dorfslager because prisoners fell away almost daily for reasons of illness, injury, or death.

The German counted again to check that the number was correct. He also began to celebrate his sadism. As a rule, he was worse than the Kapo. He walked slowly between the rows of men, with a stiff, arched back and eyes that moved searchingly. Whenever he struck, it was totally without warning. Just when you were thinking, "Oh! He has passed me by today!" he would swing around on his heels, look at you, and box your ears or punch you in the ribs.

Next, the so-called messenger was called in [in German "Läufer," i.e., "runner"] The messenger was a young prisoner of the lager personnel who could run like the wind. The S.A. man gave him a note on which our number was written. Like an arrow from a bow, he ran with it to the S.A. men of the block house at the exit gate. In the meantime, the German looked us over once again. After that, he went calmly to the next detail. The messenger then had to return immediately to his side.

Before we were allowed to march out, we once again had to wait for what seemed like an eternity. These final stretches of the roll call were the worst. Sick or emaciated prisoners could collapse from exhaustion. For the umpteenth time, we were again inspected or punished by any Nazi who felt like it.

The number of details that finally departed the camp was enormous. The Kommando Dorfslager was the Thirty-fifth Detail. Thus could we march out only as the Thirty-fifth. "Kommando, Marsch!!" shouted the Kapo. We made our way to the exit like a dumb, exhausted herd of animals until we stopped right in front of the boom of the blockhouse. The blockhouse was a small brick-built hut in which the S.A. men sat together and calmly began their day. The details stood in a line, shuffling along.

The Kapo turned around to the little gate of the blockhouse, and he clicked his heels together and roared: "Ich melde Gehorsam!! Kommando Dorfslager mit x Häftlinge zur Arbeitsmarsch bereit!!" [Ready to march to work.] Each detail carried its own number. In the current vernacular of the camp, a detail was, however, named after its Kapo. Therefore, Kommando Seidenband, Kommando Kampf, Kommando Goldberg. Our commando was called Dorfslager by accident in place of Kommando Martin.

An S.A. came outside. He had received the report from the messenger. At his leisure, he began to count us yet one more time. He chatted for a while with his colleagues who were standing next to him. He looked around a bit and looked us over as if with horror and disgust. What he intended to do with us depended on his mood. Often he came forward to give a prisoner yet another whack. Finally, he yelled: "Abmarschieren!!" [March off.]

Slowly the boom was raised.

"Kommando Marsch!!" shouted the Kapo.

Detail by detail, we went outside. We formed a shockingly long row. The work that we had to do varied from the relatively manageable to the absolutely murderous. And yet we were relieved when the roll call was, at last, over. At least we had survived that!

The work would go on until about a quarter past or half past four. After this we had to assemble once again. This time, not for a prolonged roll call but just for the purpose of collecting all the prisoners. We were counted again, and at about five o'clock we could return to the camp.

The Dorfslager was nearer to the camp than the Obersylesische Hydrierwerke. After we had covered several kilometers on the way out, we separated ourselves from the others. This separation happened at a place called the Sammelplatz. It was only in the evening, on our way back to Blechhammer, that we would again join the others here at the Sammelplatz. At about a quarter past six we were back in the camp.

Although our work in the Dorfslager was relatively very advantageous, our Meister or foreman was a very dangerous man. He was a Silesian partyman, a member of the S.A. He always went about dressed in his S.A. uniform, a behavior that was quite exceptional for a work foreman. The S.A. cap, the band with the swastika . . . from a military point of view, he was nothing. Nearly every day he arrived at work drunk, with his thick, tangled moustache hairs accompanied by a heavy smell of alcohol. As with the majority of Volksdeutschers [Germans from the annexed territories], he felt obliged at all times to demonstrate his worth. His frustrations were echoed in the way he spoke: a noteworthy mixture of a broken German and a somewhat childish lower-class Polish. In nearly every sentence that he pronounced, he used, like a caricature, the little word "*pierunie*" [Polish for "goddamn," "damnation," "bloody hell," and other horrible things]. With everything that he undertook, he seemed more rough and sadistic than the majority of Germans themselves. He was a really violent person. With his boots always polished and his hands hanging loosely on his body, he kicked your backside until you fell to the ground. With a rasping voice, he came to tell you how you were to work. He explained how you had to hold your hoe, spade, or shovel— or the easiest way to carry your stones. "What you do in one day," he screamed, "I do in one hour!!" Originally, he had been a laborer, but because of the war, he had risen somewhat in the world.

The only way to escape his punishments was to work very hard. Only when you were busy was there any chance of being left in peace. But in the Dorfslager, there was not always a consistent amount of work. Thus, when we had to pave a path, we did it with exaggerated precision until the whole road surface looked truly as flat as a mirror. Only when the foreman had turned around or had disappeared from view could we stop and rest a bit. But if he had the slightest suspicion that we were not busy working, we were in danger of receiving a beating.

Redhead Martin, our Kapo here, got on well with the foreman. Often they stood together chatting at the edge of the yard. Martin was actually far from being a bad fellow. He tried to keep the foreman off our backs as much as possible, and warned us when the foreman was in the vicinity of our work detail.

As a Kapo, Martin also had a lady friend in the women's section of Blechhammer, and she looked after him well.

It was Martin who gave me the nickname of Cucekl. "Cucek" is the Polish word for "infant" or "nursing child"; Cucekl is the affectionate diminutive form. Among the laboring prisoners, I was still one of the youngest; I was seventeen and slightly built. The idea of calling me a suckling babe was meant to be a somewhat mocking reference to my youthful age and my immature, still not fully-grown, juvenile body. After a short time, everybody called me this. Yet, this nickname was also a blessing for me. Many times it occurred to me that I could take advantage of this name. When we were working in a team and a relatively easy task presented itself, one of the prisoners near me might say: "Ach, let the Cucek do that job! He can use it!"

Blechhammer consisted of about 115 details. Most of these details were so heavily guarded that they worked in complete isolation. But four or five of these details could sometimes, with a considerable luck, establish contact with foreigners. The Kommando Dorfslager was one of these units. If everything went well, we might see French, Belgian, or Czech forced laborers. We also saw Poles, but we could not expect much from them. They were, on the whole, not only anti-German but also very anti-Semitic and unreliable.

It happened now and then that a foreign worker, because of illness, got leave and passed the day in his wooden hut. We could then try to approach such a man as carefully as possible. Such a dangerous undertaking was only possible if our guard was absent for a while. A guard of the Dorfslager had extremely monotonous work. Therefore, he sometimes would wander out to visit a colleague a little ways away to chat or smoke a cigarette, even if it was only for a few minutes.

Contacts with foreigners were moments of extreme anxiety. A prisoner would make it look as if he had, coincidentally, to go past the foreigners' hut. As he walked past he addressed him, hardly moving his lips as he spoke. Both looked away or down to the ground. Sometimes the foreigner would appear as if he had to go somewhere, in the hope of meeting us. His solidarity declared itself at least through the one thing we had in common: the same enemy. Our intuition told us that the enemies of our enemies had to be our friends.

The best contacts were between the French workers and the French-Jewish prisoners. Many French Jews were war veterans who had fought on the same side before they had been repatriated as French prisoners of war and then deported as Jews.

Some of the people who were forced laborers of the Dorfslager could surreptitiously listen to the BBC or to other radio stations forbidden by the Nazis. Through these sources, we receive exceptional news on how the war was developing. But some of our sources extended further. Most of the foreigners of the Dorfslager received permission once a year to go home for a while. Several prisoners who had the luck of being in contact with an outside person succeeded in sneaking a communication through to a friend or relative far beyond the camp. My friend Benzen, for example, had been able to send a letter to his fiancée in Wallonia through me and through a Belgian worker in this complex but completely secret manner. He even received a reply from her. In the same way, Kapo Martin sent a letter to a fiancée in Brussels.

Also during our period of starvation the foreign workers sometimes gave us their support. A Frenchman or a Czech who had remained behind in the Dorfslager made a gesture to a prisoner from behind a little window, to signal that he had something to eat. Most of the time it was only a little leftover, but it was fresh and hot. This favored prisoner did his very best to get to him, but he had to take the risks accompanying this gesture. As he arrived there, he very quickly raised his billy-can, and the foreign worker scraped his plate into it.

Yet this method of giving us something to eat was a rarity. It was confined to a very few special individuals. Most of the personnel wanted to have as little to do with us as possible out of fear of the guards. Nevertheless, if they continued to help us, they did so at a distance. The barrels were most important for this. In the Dorfslager there stood outside on the side of each barrack large wooden rubbish bins or barrels, about twelve altogether. The foreign workers shook out the leftovers from their plates into these barrels for us. They did this mostly in the evenings, when we and our guards were away. But compared to the food that we prisoners received directly from a plate, the food that we found in this barrel was usually not good. Often, it lay in contact with the rubbish, so it was sour, rotted, and moldy most of the time. But at least it was food. Everybody who was faint with hunger ate up what he could grab. One threw himself at the food with the instinct of an animal. The weaker one was the less control he had over himself. Some members of my detail were real dust-bin specialists; they lived on it. They always found some way of getting at the food. Speed was needed here above all. You had to be quick to grab what you could when you were standing next to the bin. You also had to be quick to eat it up immediately. But the best, the more or less edible food, always lay on the edges of the bin. Also, if the bin had recently been emptied and cleaned, the rest of its contents proved to be acceptable as well.

For myself, I only dared once to approach such a bin. The food that I found there consisted of preserved mussels. Since childhood I had known that mussels were actually a very dangerous food if not fresh and that they could go bad within one hour. Many members of my detail had diarrhea, and the bin was the chief culprit! I quickly stuffed one of these mussels into my mouth and bit into it, but spat it out immediately. I decided never again to allow myself to be seduced by this temptation.

Only once, to my knowledge, had food laid in the bin that was truly good. On that occasion, a Frenchman had gone to the kitchen especially for us. He himself was too ill to eat. He carefully shook out his whole portion, which was still warm, into the bin. He even took care that not too much of it landed among the rubbish. The prisoner who had been able to get that food was blessed!

At our camp our Stubenälteste issued us a coupon every day. With this, we would go each day to the kitchen where we could shuffle along in rows, one left, one right, for our portion. The policemen had to bludgeon us with their cudgels. Otherwise it would become utter chaos.

We received our portion of soup in exchange for our voucher. The voucher was then punched by a woman appointed for the task to make it impossible to get a second helping.

Anyone could choose the exact moment at which he could get his food. Some ran immediately to the kitchen to try to get there ahead of everybody else. Others followed somewhat later to join the large daily stream of prisoners—resulting in a half-hour to fifty minutes of shuffling along in a crowded, pushing line. And, finally, there were prisoners who only arrived at the very end: the sick, the weakened, and those who no longer had the strength to endure the pressure. I preferred to go to the kitchen a little after the peak hour, but certainly not with this last group. It could happen that, towards the end, the distribution of food would be more stingy, should the amount of available food less than expected. Obviously, it was better to avoid this.

Blechhammer was such a big camp that the prisoners who worked in the kitchen formed a separate group. Because they had to cook for five to six thousand people, they did not have to work outside at all but belonged exclusively to the personnel of the Lager. The chief cook was called Brandes. He was an eastern Jew from the region of Sosnowitz. He had under him a whole range of personnel: cooks, washers, servers. Most of the cooking techniques that they used were very primitive, and most of the foodstuffs available to them, the soup vegetables, cabbage, a few potatoes, for example, were of an appalling quality and unworthy of human consumption.

The prisoners who were busy with the carrying and handling of greens, potatoes, and turnips were a part of what was called the Kartoffelkolonne or potato column. Everything that was needed to keep the kitchen going, breads, potatoes, cabbages, but also plates, soup ladles, and cutlery were stored in separate, very strictly guarded, huts. Yet someone who was put in the Kartoffelkolonne was enormously lucky because, despite everything, he regularly had the chance of putting something aside for himself. Stealing loaves of bread was impossible; the bread that the S.A. gave us would be very precisely counted. But potatoes, for example, came into the camp in sacks by weight and were worked into the soup. The control was strict and the punishments, if one was caught, were severe. Despite this, people of the kitchen staff managed somehow to hold back a certain number of these potatoes.

Anyone who had been able to obtain a few little potatoes from a person of the Kartoffelkolonne could always try to warm them up on a little fire or in the smoking, glowing ashes. He could also try to exchange them for bread. Personally, I have never wanted to exchange my bread for these potatoes. The prisoners who did do this probably cared more for the quantity of the food than for its quality.

One did not have actually to be working in the kitchens to take part occasionally in a very small amount of bartering. If one had the exceptional luck to be in a work place where other, non-Jewish workers were busy, he sometimes had a chance at bartering. But although I myself was able to arrange numerous things, such transactions remained extreme exceptions. On one hand, we were kept under close observation through a severely attentive and unthinkably aggressive surveillance. On the other hand, there was but very little to be found that could truly be exchanged. Also, most of the prisoners were too severely emaciated and emotionally blunted to think about such a thing.

I succeeded, for the first time during my work in the Dorfslager, in buying a loaf of bread. By that time I had been living exclusively on the camp's rations for some nine months. I was already seriously weakened and thin. If I did not take this opportunity now, however dangerous it might be, I would gradually starve. I simply had no other choice.

The breads, which we received in the camps, had the shape of a brick. They weighed about 800 grams. They were cut into four pieces at the time of distribution and that quarter-loaf of bread comprised our daily ration. Only 3 or 4 percent of the prisoners in Blechhammer came into contact with foreign workers. But, if you were lucky enough to have that opportunity, you could sometimes buy an extra loaf, risky though it was. If you bought a loaf in the yard that looked like a loaf of camp bread, it was advisable to have three trustworthy colleagues: one could then cut the loaf into four pieces of equal size and give each colleague a share to smuggle into the camp. Under those circumstances, it was practically impossible to be caught; that quarter piece of bread was the same as our own ration. Compared to the yard, the value of a bread in the camp was somewhat higher, so that one could sell it there with a profit.

Most of the breads that you could buy in the yard, however, looked quite different from the camp bread. If you bought those, you literally risked your life.

Many prisoners of Blechhammer had a mess tin in their possession in which they could hide food leftovers and small goods. It was a long, cylindrical piece of zinc with a lid and a cord for carrying it over a shoulder. Incidentally, we had, not received these mess tins from the Leitung, but because we led such chaotic lives, the tins were simply indispensable to us. Everyone knew how to get one for himself. My own mess tin was a bit conspicuous; it was bigger and clumsier than those of the others and, therefore, not trouble-free.

The mess tins were made by prisoners who worked in an industry where zinc was used. After a short time, it became the custom to ask that the tin be made with a double bottom. The secret was known publically; even the S.A. knew about it. Under the false bottom, you could keep small things, like a cigarette, a piece of paper—that is, if you owned such a thing. My double bottom was bigger than the average, about five centimeters deep.

Such a mess tin had mainly psychological value. It gave you the feeling that you had something of your own, something that was fully private. It also served as a protection against theft. But against German guards it naturally did not offer any resistance. We were carefully frisked when we entered the camp after work. Not everyone was checked, only here and there, at random. On those occasions, the mess tin was also examined and searched. Should you be caught in possession of something not permitted, the punishments then were horrifying. In the best of circumstances, you were given twenty-five lashes with the whip; in the worst, you were sent to Auschwitz. Yet the stronger prisoners who had the opportunity continued to make exchanges. The prisoner who took no single risk would automatically perish from deprivation. There was no time to think this over. If you took a chance to undertake something, you had to start immediately and do it—and you did it intuitively.

To accumulate my starting "capital," I had hardly eaten any bread over a period of eight days. Because of our pitiful rations, this proved to be an enormous sacrifice. Most of us were not even capable of exercising such restraint. But all the little pieces, which I could keep aside with the greatest of efforts, I sold again and again to a fellow prisoner. By the time I could no longer part with my food (wasted away and gaunt with hunger as I was), I had managed to acquire six marks. I was lucky that despite this I could still keep going to the Dorfslager for my work.

The moment of the first exchange was indescribable—for the first time after many horrifying months, I could hold a whole loaf between my fingers. This victory also gave me enormous moral support. That I had alone been able to achieve this, entirely of my own accord, was a symbol of my resistance. It was a confirmation of my individual power to survive.

I sold the bread in the camp for eight marks. I was thus able to make a profit of two marks.

In this manner, I toiled on for months. How I succeeded is nearly incomprehensible. But after a really difficult, nearly impossible period, which demanded the utmost from me, I had enough money for three or four loaves, and I sometimes succeeded in keeping a whole loaf for myself. The feeling of triumph, which I then experienced, was magic. I was cleverer than those monsters who exterminated us, one after another.

Eventually, my transactions began to take on a degree of regularity. The risks that I ran each time I returned to camp started to become too great. I had to conduct myself more carefully. Together with Ingber, the tailor from Luxemburg, who had already been with me in Breendonk, I came up with the idea of having a double lining made in my jacket, a secret cut behind which I could hide away my gains. As I previously mentioned, the double bottom of the mess tin had cease serving as a sufficient method for a some time.

Ingber made an opening over the whole length of my lining from the hem up to the top. He then closed it in such a way that I could just get into it with one hand. This concealed extra pocket helped me smuggle things on different occasions.

One day in June 1943 I had bought a loaf of bread in the Dorfslager that was far too big. Furthermore, it looked completely different from the typical camp bread. I actually should have seen that this specimen, which weighed about two kilos, would be impossible to bring into the camp. But we all had a chronic hunger, and when I saw the bread I could not restrain my desire for food. I could not resist the temptation. My salivary glands ached when I saw it. I held the loaf between my hands and immediately pushed it into my double lining, without giving it a second thought. An insane undertaking! The loaf stuck out quite clearly. My fellow prisoners looked at me incredulously, with gloomy, furtive glances. "The Cucek has gone crazy," I could hear them thinking. Yet I did nothing about it.

At the end of the day, even before our detail had assembled itself, I was taken to one side by the Wachhabende or duty officer, a man in an S.A. uniform. I thought that I would faint from the fright. It flashed through my mind—either I would receive a whipping until I collapsed, or I would be sent away to the gas chambers.

"What have you got there?" asked the duty officer. He pointed to my jacket. "Open up your damned jacket!" he roared.

I did what he asked me to do. Totally disheartened and nearly paralyzed with fear, I showed him the loaf. He looked at it with a serious, expressionless face. Next, he looked at me. With my most innocent, most artless look, I raised my eyes upwards. But then he moved to one side. He walked away from me. "Antreten!! Antreten!!" [Fall in! Fall in!] I heard him scream at the others. I quickly closed up my jacket again, with the loaf still with me. I joined the rest of the detail.

What had now happened? I now stood in line with my fellow prisoners, as my knees turned to jelly with fear. But nothing more was said or done. I had stepped into my grave and had immediately stepped out of it again. It had been a miracle.

I can only speculate about what must have possessed this duty guard at that critical moment. Perhaps he had, on that day himself, experienced something special, something decisive. Had something happened in his private life? He was a man of about forty: did he, perhaps, have a son of about my own age whom he had lost on the battle front at about this time? I do not know, but for one reason or another he must have found himself overcome by doubt. Normally, a detail was kept under the supervision of the same duty guard for a period of at least a month, but this particular duty guard, on the following day, totally and unexpectedly disappeared in the middle of his term of duty. We never saw him again.

Beyond these suppositions, I also had the good fortune that the duty guard and I were the only two present at the moment that I was caught with my loaf. Should there have been other witnesses, he would have been obliged to take measures against me. Otherwise, he would have been in danger himself.

Between the wars Palestine (now Israel) was under British mandate. At the outbreak of the Second World War, some six hundred thousand Jewish people were living there. Many of them served voluntarily in British army units. When such a unit was taken prisoner by the Germans, the Jewish soldiers were not as a rule brought to a concentration camp but sent to a separate camp for prisoners of war. About twelve hundred Jewish Palestinians were taken into captivity in this manner.

One day in the spring, on the way from the Dorfslager or village camp to the Sammelplatz or assembly point, we saw such a group of Jewish prisoners of war. They wore English uniforms and were guarded by two ordinary Wehrmacht soldiers. As they passed, these prisoners were able to inform us quickly that they were Palestinian Jews. Through our misery we were already so severely numbed and stupefied that we could hardly think anymore. The idea that other Jews were not so badly off as us was simply astounding. It was a moment of great happiness, of encouragement. These fleeting encounters occurred twice, one shortly after the other.

Many years after the war I made the acquaintance of a certain S. Wolfstein. In the thirties he had fled from Germany and moved to Palestine. At the end of 1940 he went, together with some four thousand other Jews, to join the British Army as a volunteer. He was attached to the British Army of Palestine in the Eighth Army. Their flag was Jewish (white and blue), and all the officers there were Jewish. Only their commanding officer was an Englishman from the United Kingdom. Their army did not form a fighting unit but was a Pioneer Corps. They served in Egypt, Tobruk, Athens, and Salonika. In February 1941 they were taken prisoners of war by the Nazis in Kalamatha.

The Sammellager or collection camp for these prisoners of war was in Lamsdorf. Regularly, they were sent out of here in groups of two to three hundred to work camps, where they then stayed and worked for a few months. But they returned to Lamsdorf everytime, which was their in-between base.

For several weeks, S. Wolfstein worked in the Obersylesische Hydrierwerke. He could not believe his eyes when he saw all that happened here. As a prisoner of war he was much better off; he received decent rations, was well dressed, and was humanely treated. He had little reason to fear our German guards. On the contrary, "if we ever see you beat up such a poor, emaciated worker again," said Wolfstein's colleagues on one occasion to a Nazi, "then we shall bring you down a peg or two!" They pushed two packets of cigarettes into the hands of the duty officer. During the whole time that they worked there, the Nazi kept as quiet as a mouse.

When I myself arrived at the Hydrierwerke, these Palestinians had already been transferred elsewhere. Wolfstein was part of the group that I met twice in 1943 on the way to the Sammelplatz. Getting to know Wolfstein long after the war and to reconstructing these happenings with him was for each of us an unexpected, wonderful event.

The system of the Holocaust was very simple. The Nazis wanted to destroy all the Jews and had at their disposal all the necessary techniques to accomplish this goal. Beforehand, they decided on a number of Jews based on the gas chamber and incineration capacities of Auschwitz. That number of Jews had to be increased. Which Jews were selected was of no importance to the Nazis. As long as there were enough of them. Smaller and sometimes richer Jewish communities were able, for that reason, to keep out of the claws of the camps by playing on the corrupt nature of the Nazis. At best, deportation could only be postponed, never avoided entirely.

On a Friday in September 1943, three hundred Jews from more prosperous circles arrived in Blechhammer. They were brought to block 15. It was an exceptional day for those of us who were aware of their arrival. These new arrivals had absolutely no idea of what was awaiting them and, for this reason, could not estimate the economic value of their food. On the first day they simply gave their food away.

Because these newcomers were not yet so underfed, they gave up portion of their rations more easily or participated in unlikely exchanges. But eventually the news that they were there spread rapidly through the whole camp. In the first three days, their huts were overcome as if by a plague of flies. The elderly prisoners especially came begging and rummaging. By Monday, there was nothing more to be obtained. They had exchanged their hot food for some bread and a cigarette.

Among these new arrivals was a brother of Mordechai Anielewitz, the chief commandant of the uprising in the ghetto of Warsaw. He was with them by chance; the raids happened so quickly that there were still displacements occurring. Most of these newcomers were, however, known to each other. There were also married couples among them who, immediately after their arrival, were mercilessly wrenched away from each other. The women were transferred to the smaller inner camp behind the fence.

Just as in other camps, so also in Blechhammer, a so-called Stubendienst or barrack room duty had to be performed, the cleaning duty by turns. Every five or six weeks one was appointed for this with a fixed partner. Then, for a whole week, before the roll call, one had to tidy up and clean the barrack room of which one was a part. Everybody had a turn at this with the exception of the foremen and the camp personnel.

The Stubendienst took place immediately before one went outside. The Stubenälteste was the one who, with partners who were indicated for the duty, had to go and fetch the Maltz ersatz coffee from the kitchen. As soon as this beverage had been drunk, the cleaning work could begin. One looked under the beds to see that no dust lay there. Our miserable strawbags contributed a good deal of dirtiness because most of them were torn. One also had to check the beds to see if they were properly covered. And the most important work was to sweep the floor. For this duty, there was a small cardboard dustpan and a homemade hand brush made of twigs which was tied together with other flexible twigs.

If it was not too cold, the other prisoners went to stand at the entrance of the barrack room so that the team, whose turn it was, had enough space to move about. It was really too cold in the winter, and everyone stayed inside. We then all shuffled ourselves from right to left over the beds depending on where the cleaning was being done.

Actually, the Stubendienst was not a very heavy task. We put all the cleaning work behind us after ten minutes. But the responsibility that it carried was enormous. If a wisp of straw by chance still lay somewhere on the floor and a Nazi should pass by and catch you, some punishment was certain. On the weekend, the Stubendienst was more difficult because invariably there would be an inspection by the S.A. leadership. The room then had to receive a scrubbing session with water. You could be given a sound thrashing for the slightest negligence.

One of the reasons my relationship with Benzen had become more solid was because he was my steady partner for this Stubendienst. He was a very clever, very handy fellow. On one occasion he had seen that other prisoners did not just clean the floor but first rubbed oil into it. That oil rubbing itself did not cost much time, but once it had been done, the planks became much smoother and the dirt itself remained more on the surface. Benzen suggested that we should also try this.

An unexpected inspection occurred exactly on that day. When they observed our alternative method, we received severe slaps in the face until we bled. We then had to scrape the oil out with an iron chisel.

Benzen, the future lawyer, still had some good ideas. He had discovered something new when the new arrivals came to us. Now, every morning during coffee time we ran from barrack 12 to barrack 15 as fast as possible to take care of the Stubendienst there. Barrack 15 was not a couple of huts away but somewhere else in the camp—five or six minutes of running time away. The agreement was that we would get food from them in exchange for the work. The new arrivals gave up a spoonful of cold soup for each minute of exchanged work, which could amount to a full plate. It was especially difficult for us to go over there during that first week because we were also responsible for the Stubendienst in our own room. But that extra work, for as long as it lasted, was worth our sweat. After two or three weeks, however, the newcomers too began to need their food as much as we did. From then on, they did their Stubendienst themselves.

During that period when we would run to the newcomers, Benzen and I began to realize what we were worth to each other. This extra Stubendienst was our first team effort based on our own initiative. We knew that we could occasionally arrange things, each in his own way. We agreed that from now on we would share or cooperate like brothers. Together with Ausubel, my other friend, there grew a firm, faithful partnership and friendship.

The beginning of September 1943 marked a new period for me. In the Dorfslager, I had been able, a couple of times, to obtain a loaf, and I anticipated that this loaf would extend my exchange value. For this reason I had bought something different from one of the workers: a dozen onions. I learned, however, that onions were the specialization of my Kapo, Readhead Martin, something I had not known earlier. Because I had paid a higher price than was customary for the onions, I had, without intending it, created some competition for Martin. When he became aware of this, he did not strike me. I still remained his Cucekl, his little one. But because he wanted to preserve his own business, he immediately put me out of his detail, the Kommando Dorfslager.

Although with great difficulty, I was still able to sell these onions to Simcha Schönberg who had arrived with the more fortunate newcomers of the camp. His wife was with him, but immediately after their arrival she was transferred to the women's section. Both of them have survived the camps. They came from the neighborhood of Sosnowitz, but after the war they settled in Antwerp.

All things considered, the Kommando Dorfslager was, compared with the other work details in the camp, one of the most favorable details imaginable, truly exceptional. That I was thrown out of it for a few stupid onions, onions that I could later only manage to exchange with difficulty, was a crying shame. Where was I now going to land? And in what kind of a hell?

I was assigned to the Obersylesische Hydrierwerke, where nearly the whole camp worked. The firm for which I worked was called Niederdruck: the firm of steel construction. I was part of a team of about twenty men. We were responsible for the transportation of heavy metal pipe with a diameter of thirty centimeters to one meter or one meter twenty. Our Kapo, the Parisian Goldberg, was a very brutal, unpredictable fellow. Because his detail was so large, he had three foremen under him. It was they who gave us the instructions and were permanently chasing, harassing, and shouting at us. We hardly ever came into contact with the Kapo Goldberg.

Benzen also worked for Niederdruck. We were together for roll call. However, we never met each other during work.

The yards of the Obersylesische Hydrierwerke were extensive. Where the Jewish prisoners worked, a chain of guards was necessary to keep everything together.

The guards available to the Nazis were not numerous. Furthermore, they were principally Wehrmacht soldiers: somewhat older adults who were no longer considered to be suitable to serve on the front. An S.A. man stood on guard only here and there where there were columns.

The firms that worked us had their own hierarchy. At the top were the engineers. We hardly ever saw them, unless they came to take samples of liquid concrete. They were mostly at work in their little hut and kept aloof as much as possible from what was happening outside their environment. The Poliers or site foremen worked under the engineers. After the engineers, these Poliers were the most schooled of the workers. They also carried the greatest responsibility. They distributed the work, set the goals, and attended to the proper interaction between different work units. The Meisters or master craftsmen were the big bosses who handled the execution of the work, and the foremen finally were the men who worked closest to us.

Wachhabenden or duty guards were guards of the Nazis, mostly common soldiers of the Wehrmacht or armed forces. Normally, the Wachhabenden only had to ensure that none of the prisoners tried to escape. They often could not resist the temptation of meddling with the quantity, the quality, and especially the pace of our work. What kind of Wachhabende had control over you was all a matter of fate. Mostly, he was a maniac and a sadist. If you were lucky, he could be a tiny bit less meddling and a tiny bit more amenable to reason. But in any case, a Wachhabende had to know about handling any situation. Should he be too gentle with his team, he could be reported to the S.A. by the master craftsmen.

Most everyone knew that the Nazis were all envious of each other. Jealousy always reigned. The Nazis always took any opportunity to play a nasty trick on someone. In this mutual game of power, the more prisoners a Nazi had at his disposal the better. Although every Nazi killed off his Jews, he was also convinced that those Jews were his property. One Nazi regularly complained to another: "My Jews work themselves to death while those of yours have it less hard!" And the answer had the impact of a rock: "Bother yourself with your own affairs! These here are my Jews!" The rule said thus: " 'each one to his own Jews!'. If you take the risk of coming here to hit my Jews, I shall then come there and hit your Jews!"

When I worked for Niederdruck, I got up at four o'clock in the morning, and I only got back to the camp by half-past-six in the evening. The march to the yard took up another hour and our assembly in the yard half an hour. Thus, altogether I worked eight or nine hours per day. During the work itself, we were given a twenty-minute break. The only reason for giving us this break was because the other, non-Jewish workers had one: the German workers and the team leaders. We could not begin anything without their supervision. When it was really urgent to get the loading and unloading done, we received absolutely no break at all and had to work through without stopping.

We longed for a bit of rest throughout the entire day. The latrine was the only place where we could catch our breath even a little. But to be allowed to go there we had first to announce our intention. The leadership had to maintain some order and, therefore, they only let everybody go in turn. Our waiting to be allowed to answer a "call of nature" remained part of the daily course of events.

In the toilets we could rest a bit, and we could also try to make contact with other prisoners with the hope of organizing or ordering something. With a bit of luck, I could also do this in the camps themselves, but in the latrines we could meet each other for unexpected or unplanned purposes. Of course, the Wachhabenden kept a close eye on us and on how long we stayed away. And some of the Wachhabenden simply forbade us to go to the lavatory at all, even if we had done it in our pants.

Naturally, you also had to go to relieve your bowels. Prisoners who suffered from diarrhea needed to go with urgency. They were often ill with stomach cramps. The latrines were a nauseating and stinking mess, and it was impossible to walk into the latrines without getting soiled. Furthermore, the latrines were always being visited by a large number prisoners with incipient dysentery or other infectious diseases. With such cases the infectious diseases were present in the feces. Going to the toilet carried the risk of contracting disease. But we were used to taking risks, whether they represented a simple danger or a danger to life.

A more drastic break in the work took place if it rained. The climate of Upper Silesia was such that it could very suddenly begin to thunder and rain heavily. In a very short time everything and everybody became dripping wet. The so-called Aryan work forces took it for granted. In a great hurry, canvas sheets were pulled over the cement wagons as protection against the downpour. We sometimes could find shelter in a building that was being built. This protection gave us the greatest pleasure. Nothing better could have happened to us. With the prisoners in groups of twenty-four or thirty-six, a Wachhabende stood guard over us.

On two occasions because of the heavy rain, we could not even leave the camp for work. But this proved less pleasant. We were dragged out of our barrack during barbarian and sadistic raids of our quarters. We were indeed put to work on the infrastructure of the camp and then had to drag ourselves about through the mud in that beastly weather and in our flimsy clothes while the S.A. regularly kept us in view, with their truncheons ready.

In autumn 1943 the number of epidemics had increased so greatly that the ordinary field hospital could no longer cope with receiving all the victims. Typhus fever had not yet broken out, but soon the Nazis were being warned about what was happening in other camps. With great haste a hospital barrack with a quarantine department was added. The hospital barrack was just an ordinary barrack next to the hospital and surrounded with wire netting. By chance, it was not very far from our room, 12.6. When we emerged outside we could discern its netting in the distance. A sombre, silent sign of our decline.

To get into the hospital barrack, one had to go behind the surrounding fence and then pass through a small wire-net passage where a Kapo or sometimes an S.A. man stood. You had to have a very good reason for wanting to pass through: a fracture, a severe case of diarrhea, dysentery, or serious or extensive inflammation. If you were suspected of malingering, you were beaten to a pulp on the spot.

The consultations began at half-past-six in the evenings. The kitchens also opened around that time, so that it was difficult to be the first person at the hospital. First, you ran to the kitchens for your ration. You had to have a friend who kept your food for you while you ran immediately on to the hospital. If you arrived too late, you ran the risk of remaining in line too long, often without achieving anything. The next day, you then had to start all over again. Five hundred to eight hundred victims daily stood in line at the hospital, slowly shuffling along. The doctors had their hands full. They certainly acquired a great deal of experience. Prisoners who carried an epidemic disease would immediately be taken out. But it still remained a very difficult task for the doctors to set priorities. Everybody screamed for help.

One of the most common illnesses in the camp was diarrhea. About a quarter of all prisoners had it. Because we had no underwear, you could see the diarrhea pouring out of the victims' trouser legs. A remedy against this illness was a kind of coal powder into which saccharin had been mixed. It had to be eaten with a spoon. We called this sweet-tasting powder "soot" because it was so black. It remained on our mouth and hands, and it was as black as pitch. Anybody suffering from diarrhea could thus be recognized at a distance of several meters. Actually, it was a fairly accepted remedy.

I was only a victim of diarrhea three times and each instance only for a short time. I had luck on my side once again.

For the kind of dysentery that was infectious you were allowed to go directly to the hospital. But the doctor and his two assistants could do little to combat it. In most cases dysentery meant a certain inescapable death.

Wounds had virtually no chance of healing. There were no medications and no casts, only an improvised, roll-like bandage. The food that we received was by far not sufficient to enable us to build up our strength. Because we were still obliged to carry on with our work, whatever our medical condition, the wounds could only get worse and rarely healed.

The plague of winter cold knocked us all to pieces. Freezing to death did not mean that the victim expired on the spot. But certain parts of the body froze and failed first; a victim's knees weakened and he fell to the ground. If it happened during the roll call, the victim was usually carried away to the field hospital. That person then ran the risk of being sent to Auschwitz. If he collapsed at work, he fell into the hands of the sadistic guards. He was pulled up straight and received severe slaps. Then, he was forced to go on working as if nothing had happened. That practice continued until he came round. It was impossible for the rest of us to intervene. If the guards suspected that we desired to support a victim, we could be punished. We had to observe silently with sad and suffering eyes. We had to watch our fellow prisoners as they were being tortured to death.

My work in the transport column of Niederdruck fortunately lasted only a month. In the Dorfslager, I had been able to regain some strength but now, during this month in Niederdruck, I had deteriorated both physically and psychologically. I was exhausted, emaciated, and had a very low morale. Now, in the beginning of October 1943, I was transferred to a building firm, Betonomenir, one of the biggest of the yard. This firm delivered bricks, gravel, and cement and laid foundations. My task consisted chiefly of the loading and unloading of wagons. It was work done at a terrible pace, specifically, one wagon had to be emptied and taken to another rail while the following wagon returned for the same treatment. We never had a single chance to catch our breath; we had to heave and drudge away every minute of the time. And on top of that, the S.A. men, the Kapos, and the terribly sadistic Baumeisters or master builders were constantly putting pressure on us. For the slightest thing that displeased them, the Baumeisters summoned the S.A. men.

The most difficult things to move were the pieces of rock. Two men were needed for this purpose, and they had to lay the load on their backs. Within a very short time, our fingers, our hands, and our upper arms were cut open and skinned. The loading and unloading of gravel would have been bearable if the kicks we received weren't so severe. Carrying a sack of cement was a little less difficult; the material was certainly heavy but shapeless and thus less painful to transport. When you became tired, you could reposition the sack against your shoulder. Naturally, we were too emaciated for this sort of work. English prisoners of war who were working some twenty meters further on could comfortably carry two bags of cement in one trip. They were men in good physical condition, received good food, and wore appropriate clothing. We Jewish prisoners were so pitiful in comparison that *one* bag of cement was already too heavy for us. Regularly, one of us would collapse under its weight.

Precisely how hard you had to work at unloading a cement wagon could vary. Various factors played a part. Should you stand in the wagon to unload the bags and pass them on, or did you stand below to take them and turn away? If you stood below, and by chance things progressed more slowly above, it was a stroke of luck! Also, distance within the wagon was a factor. In the beginning, when there was not very much that was unloaded, the cement bags lay somewhat closer to the edge, but when more bags were removed, you had to steel yourself one more time to run deeper and deeper into the wagon. In short, such was the division of labor. One group of the prisoners worked itself practically into a state of collapse while the other group was able, from time to time, to catch its breath cautiously. You learned to enjoy it for as long as it lasted because in the middle of this work the Kapo who supervised could, without warning, make you change places. And there was nothing that you could do about it. If, twice in a row, you were sent to a difficult or oppressive section, you had to clench your teeth to avoid collapsing under the load.

Our work lasted the whole day long with hardly a break. Only at midday were we allowed a short pause, never to exceed a half-hour. It was especially hard when the work had to be done under a time limit, such as when the movement of the wagons began because of their need by other works in the yard—this was when things were especially hellish. Then they all descended upon us: the S.A., and the Wachhabende, and the Meister. "Schnell!! Schnell!!" [Quick!! Quick!!] they screamed, with the cudgel and the whip in their hands. "Los!! Los!!" [Move!! Move!!] The Nazis addressed us in the polite form with "Sie." The expressions then went like this: "Kommen Sie, dass Ich Ihnen einen Arschtritt geben kann!" [Come, please, so that I can give you a kick up the arse"], "Drehen Sie Sich um, Ich erschiesse Sie!" [Please turn yourself around, so that I can shoot you!] They screamed at us day in and day out, as if we were cattle.

Besides our own firm, the Krause firm also worked within the camp. It stood next to the roads on the yards itself. Our own work, for the building firm, was murderous. But that of Krause was still worse, so bad that it defied the imagination. The prisoners that you saw there had to pass the whole day long with a bent back and crouching down on their heels, hacking at stones as heavy as lead to give them shape. With bleeding and torn-open hands, they had to fit self-fabricated cobblestones into the ground under extreme surveillance. Whenever we looked carefully in the direction of Krause, we saw someone being beaten up, tortured, or killed. It was the same there as it had been in Königshütte or Bismarckhütte. The chances of survival were virtually nil.

The English prisoners of war in our building firm received precisely the same tasks to do as we did, only for other wagons. The Germans did not verbally abuse them. They wanted to show that, as far as their prisoners of war were concerned, they honored the Geneva Convention. Either that or they were simply afraid of the English. Often these English prisoners were better off than the Germans themselves; they were psychologically counseled, they practiced sports, and they wore the appropriate clothing. In the winter, they wore a thick, strong, uniform and often struck an imposing appearance. They did their work according to the international agreements: as soon as they fulfilled their work requirements, they would return, whistling or singing, to their camp. Depending on their diligence, they only worked five or six hours per day.

Yet, our own achievements, those of us prisoners, were always being compared with those of the English. "Look, Jewish Schweinhunden!" [pigdogs] the reproach rang out. "The English over there, look! They carry two sacks at the same time! If they can do that, why can't *you* do it? Retarded bunch of idlers!"

One day, a not too careful Kapo of our detail went to a Meister or foreman. He wanted to propose something to him, as humbly as possible: if the Jewish Haftlinge or prisoners were allowed to work according to the same agreement, the Kapo conjectured that, with a rest break, we would be able to work harder in the future and that the final result would produce improvement. The Meister reacted at first as if he were appalled at being addressed by a Jew on such a matter. But, once he had calmed down, he began to consider the idea. He said that he actually did not have anything against it. In any case, it was certainly worth trying. The agreement was that we would be allowed to rest in the yard for a short hour after we had done our work.

Although we did our best to remain skeptical, the prospect of a rest break was truly astonishing to us. At first, we felt really encouraged. With the last dregs of strength that remained in us, we did our work harder than ever. We beavered away and raced about frantically. After a while we did, indeed, rest, although not as soon as the English. We went and sat somewhere on a heap of stones or on a stump. Others would lie down on the spot, completely exhausted. But just at that moment an engineer walked past. The surprise at seeing us there seemed to kill him! What was happening here? The Jewish prisoners who were trying to get their breath back in the middle of the day in the yards? Immediately, he became very upset about such a terrible situation. He went to fetch an S.A. man from somewhere. "What kind of a

Schweinerei [scandal; dirty joke] is this?" he screamed. He became purple with rage, with swollen, stiffened neck muscles. Back and forth he began to beat up prisoners, clouting them and banging their heads together. He even beat up the Kapo, something I had never seen before. "Such a rotten, dirty, nasty trick," he kept on repeating, "Such a rotten, dirty, nasty trick I have never seen before!"

The S.A. man was especially furious because he considered that we had cheated him. The fact that we rested indicated to him that we had not been working as hard as we could.

"Now you see that you really can work!!" he continued to roar. "Lazy, lazy pig dogs!!"

After he had delivered his blows, he gave the Kapo the order to knock hell out of us all.

The presence of the English at the building firm occasionally offered us an exceptional chance to do some bartering. They had their own specific goods. Every month they received from the Red Cross a parcel containing raisins, prunes, chocolates, puddings, oatmeal for making porridge, and cigarettes. The cigarettes, I remember, were of the brand called "Players," in a packet with a picture of a sailor. The English had enough material to put together some trades.

Cigarettes were not exchanged so frequently. A prisoner managed to obtain such a luxury only sporadically. But the prisoners who were addicted to the smoking of tobacco would give everything for it. Those men were a tragic phenomenon of the camps, the most pathetic creatures of the group. In exchange for a little tobacco or a couple of cigarettes they sometimes even gave up as much as the half their ration of bread. Their soup was often mortgaged for weeks ahead, simply for a small cigarette.

During the month that I worked for the building firm, something unusual happened with Ausubel, my good friend in the camp. The food distribution in Blechhammer took place through a system of vouchers. Each person who came for his ration had to hand over a voucher to a woman who had been appointed to the task; she would then punch the voucher in the manner of a train or bus conductor. To come back for a second helping of food was impossible. But on one occasion, Ausubel ran up to me with an amazed expression on his face. "Look!" he said, hoarse with excitement. "Look! They have not punched my voucher! It is not punched! What must I do!" We carefully considered this exceptional situation. I advised him to simply go back for more food but preferably in another line. Perhaps someone would recognize him? After hesitating a while, Ausubel screwed up his courage. And it worked! He could simply get a second helping! He was simply out of his mind with joy, to such an extent that he even gave a bit of the food to Benzen and to me.

He decided always to go back to that same line every day. And yes, for two or three days the miracle was repeated—his voucher was again not punched! Completely confused and incredulous, Ausubel kept asking himself to whom did he owe his thanks for this remarkable phenomenon. How was it possible? The privilege continued for a couple more times; the woman who was responsible for the vouchers had, perhaps, felt so sorry for Ausubel that she put her own life at risk for him. The luck that Ausubel had with this experience was so exceptional! One chance in one hundred thousand!

After a month or so, those attendants who stood in the kitchens were changed. New female prisoners came to replace them. The one who was now responsible for his line did not know Ausubel. The miracle had passed and nothing could be done about it.

At the end of October 1943 my friend Ausubel became infected during an epidemic of typhus, and this condition resulted in the very last stage of his short, but complete deterioration. His physical condition had never been altogether strong. He was on the delicate side, and psychologically he was much too sensitive for the brutalities that surrounded him. For a few weeks he remained in the field hospital. From a distance Benzen and I could see him walking. He looked like a sick, gaunt shadow without any strength. Contacting him was absolutely impossible. We helplessly watched him grow thinner and thinner. And then he died. He had only reached the age of twenty years.

In those days the Jewish corpses were still buried in the ground, in a limestone quarry a half-kilometer outside the camp. The mass grave was not very far from our block 12.6. In the distance behind the wire fence we could even discern the dismal place.

The death of Ausubel was a tremendous blow to me. How many people had I already seen dying in the course of these fifteen months in captivity? Acquaintances who lay in their beds near me, who had been alive the day before, were found the following morning motionless and not breathing any more. Closer friends, such as Brachfeld and Stern, had passed away in my arms. But in the case of Ausubel it was still different. Ausubel was a real, true friend. We had a solid, profound relationship. As soon as I had received the news that he was contaminated with the typhus contagion, I began to prepare myself for the fact that, sooner or later, I would lose my friend. But when, finally, it was over, it still took many months before I had recovered even a little from the shock, from the deep bewilderment. All along I was pursued by thoughts about him.

My friendship with Benzen grew even closer. The two of us were now the only ones remaining. And our bunks were next to each other, so that in the evenings before the light went out we often had very long talks and sometimes very candid discussions.

What we did *not* chat about were our families—who would be deported and who would not. We also did not talk about this terrible reversal in our lives, this impalpable misery into which we had landed, head over heels. These events were all facts. To this there was nothing more to be added. Our most important subjects were simply the things of every day: the subject of survival, our strategy to avoid collapse, the discussion of relationships that we perhaps could make. Practically all our thoughts were based upon these things.

In the camps we had no feelings of sensual desire, not even the Kapos, and certainly not the emaciated prisoners. This condition probably occurred because bromide was mixed in with our food. But in Blechhammer the twenty-four year-old Benzen took on a little of the big brother role for me and told me all about being in love and everything associated with it, should our lives return to normal. When I had been arrested on that fateful day in the train I was just sixteen years old. And, because I had had to play the part of a baby-sitter for such a long time, I hardly had the chance to get to know any girls. The lower school, which I had frequented, carried out a very orthodox policy, and the trade school was also a school for boys. I had had little to do with girls. It was just because of this that I became fascinated by the thought of them. Part of me considered that all infatuations, with all the frills and other things that go with them, meant little—just silly, exaggerated fantasies. But something fascinating, almost compelling was also attracting me to them. The only so-called "affair," which I had as a child, was with Tilly, the daughter of Leibisch Wahl and the little sister of Feiwel Wahl, the boy who was in my class. Tilly was well known as one of the prettiest girls of the neighborhood. Many of my school comrades were in love with her and I not the least. But with whom was Tilly herself in love? Everybody wondered about that and everybody asked that question. On a certain day in the spring of 1938 her brother Feiwel brought me a letter. It was a letter from Tilly. It was a love letter, a passionate love letter! I felt that I was on cloud nine. I could simply not believe that I was the chosen one. Throughout the entire summer we maintained a secret correspondence and regularly saw each other in group settings. Then we made eye contact and small, clandestine personal contacts—small, but full of significance. There, however, my love-life stopped. But by the following school year, it was over between us. I was still so young.

Very moving conversations with Benzen took place when the subject of the girl to whom he was engaged came up for discussion. Benzen had got to know a non-Jewish girl while he was at the University of Brussels and, cost what it may, he wanted to marry her. In his home, Benzen came into contact with very orthodox Jews. His parents were not so severely orthodox but had a hotel in Spa under orthodox supervision. One could eat kosher there according to the most strict standards. The family of his fiancée, however, belonged to the rich bourgeoisie of Liège. Benzen was deeply impressed by this, but from my point of view I did not understand what he could have seen in such a mixed marriage. I was perhaps still only eighteen at that time, but I nevertheless had my opinions. I believed then that a mixed marriage had less chance of success, that it was full of risk, not the least for the children and their education. Benzen's argument only centered on the fact that he was deeply in love. He said that I myself could not understand this because it was something that I had never experienced. Should he survive the concentration camps, Benzen was always saying, he would immediately ask that girl to marry him. And that was final!

Also, for pure survival, Benzen and I became all the more important to each other. We shared our successes but also our setbacks. If, through circumstance, I became isolated at work, it was impossible for me to organize anything. But the same thing could happen to Benzen, and that condition could not be predicted. Benzen always worked for the same firm and performed their transportation. He often arrived at places that indeed resembled the end of civilization. At such times, it was necessary that you know someone who could help you—often it was a matter of life or death.

Benzen came into contact with a French-Jewish dentist rather by chance, but probably also due to his intellectual background. Apart from his daily work, the treatment of prisoners' teeth, the dentist also had to take care of the teeth of the Nazis. He was an extremely accomplished professional. According to the Neurenberger laws, it was strictly forbidden for non-Jewish people to let themselves be treated by a Jewish doctor. But it was a public secret that the Nazis greatly valued some of the captured Jewish doctors. They even allowed their wives to be examined gynecologically by these doctors.

The Nazis gave gold to the dentist, who in turn made crowns and bridges for them. But because gold is a material that is difficult to weigh, the dentist succeeded regularly in keeping a small amount every two weeks for himself. He gave that gold in safekeeping to Benzen, with whom he had a relationship based on mutual trust. In turn, Benzen tried to buy something with it in his yard. I too, via Benzen, was able to make a few exchanges with that gold. From the Czechs, I could get bread and sausages, or sometimes even a bottle of schnapps, and from the English prunes and raisins.

In the meantime, within the building firm I had been given another assignment that was different from loading and unloading trucks. At one side of our place, I had seen a job that involved the changing of switch points in the small rail trolleys. The trolleys were used for the distribution of concrete. By using turntables, they could be uncoupled and then be pushed further in the required direction by several workers. When I observed this work, I became convinced that the work would not be excessively heavy and that it could even offer an occasional break from the loading and unloading. And, once again, because I was the youngest among the working prisoners, I was given permission to work at this task.

However, the assignment turned out badly in all respects. Above all, the pace was unbearable. I could not rest one second during my work. All the time, I had to run backward and forward, riding with the trolleys. The Wachhabende or duty guard who was in charge of me was unusually brutal. He saw perfectly well how enormously difficult it was to get the trolleys together. And yet he hit me nearly every time as he passed me. Furthermore, the coupling of trolleys was dangerous. I had to ensure that my fingers did not get between the iron of the couplings. On one occasion, I had so wrongly calculated the time when such a trolley came at me that I pulled my right hand away just in the nick of time. Had I been a fraction of a second slower, my hand would simply have been flattened—smashed to smithereens. And in those circumstances, that experience could have meant my death.

Toward the end of October 1943, something exceptionally good finally occurred. It happened on a cold morning. If I touched anything metallic, such as the rails or the couplings, my hands nearly stuck fast to them from the freezing cold. Some twenty or so meters further up stood a sturdy Englishman who was busy fixing a truck. At a glance, I had already seen him standing there. Fortuitously, for half a minute, no Wachhabende was to be seen in the vicinity. The Englishman whistled to me. He gave me a furtive sign that I should come to him as fast as I could. I glanced to the left and to the right. I took a chance. What did he want with me? After all, we did not even know each other. I understood nothing of all this.

While I was standing by him, he quickly stuffed a piece of textile into my hands. And then he immediately moved away.

I could see that he had given me some clothing. It was an old, worn-out pullover full of holes and loose threads. The fact that I had simply and suddenly been given a present from an unknown person, just for nothing, was terrific. I put it on under my shirt. Immediately, I got warmer. I was an inexpressibly lucky dog! Something like that just never happened to anyone.

In November 1943 my work with the trolleys was history. I was now assigned to work in the Schwellerei, a part of the power plant that provided all other firms with electricity and other forms of energy. Here the so-called "ovoid coal," a fuel from before the war, was made from pressed coal dust. How I landed in the Schwellerei, I do not know. We did not get the slightest indication of what business decisions were made by the S.A. Perhaps at that moment they had received a better offer from the Schwellerei than from elsewhere.

The so-called Schwellerei could best be compared to a coal mine in the middle of a gigantic yard or wharf. We were taken one hundred and fifty meters underground in large impressive elevators. All day long we plodded away in the oppressive, pitch-black dust. We had to load and unload ovoids in clattering trucks, which we had to push further on to the lifts. The ovoids had to be piled up in cellars. The dust penetrated into your body, into your lungs—you nearly choked.

At ground level outside the Schwellerei, each of us in our details was readily recognizable. We were pitch-black over our entire bodies. We could, of course, wash ourselves, but the washing barrack was far away from our block. And it was winter, to make matters even worse. It was very difficult, almost impossible, to stand there in your bare torso and scrub or wash yourself with water that was nearly frozen. Whatever you tried, the dirt seemed to have penetrated into the skin around your eyes and your mouth. It simply could not be removed.

For me the heavy, beastly work in the Schwellerei was made extra difficult because I still had that old wound in my hand, an inflammation which I had acquired in Laurahütte. Because we received no gloves, the wound could never heal. In the winter the wound became broader than before, and my hand swelled up from the freezing cold. Thanks to Benzen and the dentist, I obtained part of bandage, but that thin, worthless little rag did not help.

The Schwellerei, like the Krause firm, was considered a punishment detail. I was a part of a weak and broken team. We were a ragbag of prisoners whom the work bosses of other details only wanted to be rid of. The foremen of the Schwellerei were excessively cruel; there are no words that can adequately describe them. They stood around like devils, so deep under the ground, so far removed from the outside world, roaring and screaming at us in an altogether hysterical and frenzied manner. It was like a vision of Hades. From morning till night we were knocked about. Sometimes a rebellion broke out. All prisoners had their individual temperaments and not everybody could easily stomach this madness. One prisoner, who had all of a sudden been assaulted in a entirely brutal attack, leaped with flailing arms at his alarmed guard. The guard grabbed his revolver and shot down the Jewish prisoner.

Fatal accidents at work were now the order of the day. We had no helmets, no adapted footwear, nothing. With the smallest collapse of any coal dust, everything fell on the workers who were without any safety equipment. To have to die like this, in the oppressive darkness of the Schwellerei, was the perfect example of utter horror. Nothing worse could exist. And most of the prisoners condemned to the Schwellerei lost their lives. The weaker we became, the harder it was for us to endure it, thus, almost guaranteeing our end.

I was in the Schwellerei for two months. Had this situation lasted for another week or two, I would surely have drawn my last breath in all of this dust. But, on Thursday, December 30, 1943, my luck turned. Once again, following a decision from above, of which I had no idea, I was transferred elsewhere.

I now landed in a Czech building firm. My first task with this firm involved a concrete machine. My detail was called Kommando 38, and my Kapo was a Netherlander called Jopie Brasem who was also in room 12.6 with me. Brasem had two Vorarbeiters, of which one was called Max, a Jewish Czech.

I became the helper for non-Jewish specialist bricklayers. Together we worked for small firms which had to be provided with small buildings of one story and with cellars and small rooms. The bricklayers with whom we, the Jewish prisoners, worked were Czechs. The English workers assisted English bricklayers. But we could make contacts with both the Czechs and the English. About six of us worked on one house; in the meantime, others works continued on other houses, some in the cellar, others higher up, on different walls with different types of bricklaying. It was, of course, impossible for the guards to be everywhere at the same time. The only thing that they could do was to set themselves up in a huge circle around the entire building firm. Thus, for the first time in my camp life, it was possible to sit together with foreigners, Czechs and Englishmen. This situation made the detail unique.

Inherently, the Czechs fostered an intense hatred of the Nazis. For this reason alone, they were willing to sell all sorts of things to us. Contacts were made according to rank. Czech workmen managed deals with Jewish workmen, Czech foremen conducted their bartering with Jewish foremen, and the Polier or site foreman spoke to our Kapos.

Most of the Czechs lived just across the border, some forty to fifty kilometers from Blechhammer. They obtained rations both from home as well as from the Dorfslager where they stayed. The most important products available for exchange were toothpaste, shoe polish, sausages, puddings, and bread. Kapos sometimes had access to a bottle of a home-brewed alcoholic drink—schnapps, which was eagerly sought by the English and anybody else who could afford it.

The bread from their lager ration was more interesting to us than the bread that they had received from home. Their lager bread always looked the same as ours and, therefore, could more easily be smuggled into the camp, cut into four portions, and distributed among us.

Each form of bartering, however, remained difficult and, in some cases, even life-threatening. It was, and remained, a nearly impossible endeavor to approach a trading partner in safety. And it could happen that the person from whom one had ordered something was suddenly transferred on the following day to another place of work. This departure would mean that one was again without business connections. One had also to be careful that he was not being cheated. It sometimes happened that you received a portion which was smaller than originally agreed to. In the whole camp there were only about three hundred prisoners who were in a position to make exchanges.

If you succeeded in obtaining something, it was not so easy to keep it hidden. In the case of the Czechs, if you had bought something from a foreman, then he sometimes kept it for you in one of his boxes for a half-day. But in the case of the Poles, the foreman might deceive you by suddenly reporting you to an S.A. official after the exchange.

Anybody who was caught by the Leitung immediately got whipped, pushed, and punched. According to the prevailing procedures, what followed in the camp was at least twenty-five lashes with a whip, and two more sanctions could follow: transfer to a punishment detail where one would probably die or removal to some unknown place outside the camp. On several occasions, I have been a witness to a prisoner being caught. Whatever punishment followed, it was always something hellish, something that was insanely cruel. Nothing good ever came of the punishment.

Once during my work period in the Czech firm, something gruesome and horrifying happened. From well-informed persons, such as Jopie Brasem or Max who regularly visited our Judenälteste Demerer, we overheard the rumor that our entire camp would be transferred on the following day to Auschwitz, straight to the gas chambers. We did not go to work that day. We were standing in roll call the entire day while the Nazis were busy dividing us up for transport. That was perhaps the most sinister, the most dismal day of my life. No one knew where he stood anymore; there was a dead silence everywhere. You could have heard a mouse squeaking. We were all standing stock still, as if we turned to stone. Everybody was preparing himself for the worst.

Later in the afternoon we were sent back to our barracks. We sat there awaiting our fate, paralyzed by fear. But then, unexpectedly, four prisoners burst into our Stube. Demerer had sent his envoys to all prisoners known to have something in their possession. We understood that if Demerer sent his trusted men, it meant that things were becoming serious, very serious. "Quickly!" said the "trusties." "We are holding a collection! If you have something, give it now! Give it before it is too late!" We had to hand over anything that we might have in our possession, even the most inconsequential thing. Although we had already been sucked dry by the Nazis, there was always someone who any could still extract something more. One mark, two marks, whatever!

What Demerer would be able to accomplish I did not then understand. At most, he might be able to scrape together several thousand marks from this exercise. What result would he achieve from this? Something, at least? The order to transport us away had come from the very highest echelons, from Auschwitz itself. But each of us, myself included, did his best to scratch something together. This contribution was the rope that, psychologically isolated, we could clutch and hold on to, as a drowning man would do in the desperate hope of saving himself from sinking.

In the evening we were once again called together for roll call. Now we had reached the moment of truth. If we still believed that Demerer would be successful in extricating us from this terrifying situation, we did it against our intuition of an impending doom; we did it so as not to go mad with anxiety. Now we positioned ourselves in rows, looking like exhausted and agitated animals. The Nazis and the kapos began to curse us, call us names, and generally abuse us. They also "did us over," thrashing us without mercy. Several prisoners were beaten so severely that they fell down dead. Then, right at the front of the crowd in the yard, the Lagercommandant began to scream. The nickname which we had given him was Moische Hohn [Moses the rooster], not only because he was so proud of himself—just like a little strutting rooster in the farmyard—but also because he crowed so much! He now shouted at us, as if in a terrific rage. He told us that we were "schweinhunden" [pigdogs], that we were lucky bastards! That we could go back to our barracks! That tomorrow we would go back to our work just as before! Dismissed! The order was given suddenly.

Precisely how Demerer had achieved this miracle was beyond our comprehension. Only a very small and silent elite of trusties knew about that. Perhaps Demerer had been able to buy off the Nazis. Later on, we came to know that he had been able to collect a small amount of American dollars. But, he had also been able to play along with the different mutual interests of the Nazis. All Nazis were corrupt. The most important conflict among them was the one between the Nazis of the gas chambers and the Nazis of the Judenzwangsarbeitslager or Jewish forced labor camp. Nazis who worked for the gas chambers had daily quota of Jews whom they had to exterminate. Who these Jews were precisely and where they came from was of no interest to the Nazis. Their ovens were burning and they had to meet their quota of victims for incineration. Whether this practice was economically advantageous or not was of no interest to them. Additional gas chambers and incinerators were being built regularly, and these facilities had to attain a maximum of productivity. The Nazis of the forced labor camps, on the other hand, were not well served by the gassings. These Nazis regarded us as prisoners whom they could hire out for hefty bribes and kickbacks from firms. According to the guidelines of these firms, we supplied constructive, economically significant work. Of the German labor forces, the majority of them were being sent out of the country to the front. Consequently, the war industry was suffering from a shortage of manpower in its native work force. The result of all this was that Jewish slave laborers were more than welcome. For the industrialists it was a golden business opportunity to be able to put us to work. Being underfed and physically deteriorated, we could provide only a limited amount of work, but against this disadvantage was the undeniable fact that we were so ridiculously cheap. The amount per day that firms paid out to the S.A. for a prisoner was so ridiculously small that if, healthy work-experienced Jews were taken away from a firm to be gassed to death, the productivity of the industrialists would fall. Then there was the language problem. To train new Jewish prisoners to do their work, much time was expended before they could be usefully employed and, in the process, this meant less financial gain for the industries. For an industry's productivity, the Endlösung or "final solution" had a retarding effect—it put the brakes on progress!

Jewish children and old and ill Jewish adults were economically nonproductive. One could not make use of them anywhere. They were being deported to the gas chambers first; some of their transports went directly to the chambers. Only when this "source of supply" for the gas chambers had been exhausted were the other, more economically productive Jews sent there.

When Demerer saved us from Auschwitz, he must have used that sort of argument on the Nazis. He probably played up the idea that we, the adult men, were indeed of economic value. Later in the year, this Judenälteste Demerer, succeeded in keeping us away from the gas chambers on two more occasions, even without taking a collection in advance to bribe the authorities! This was something we did not know about at the time. It was only later that we heard about it from people of the Schreibstube or from those who had been Demerer's personal friends. "Last week we would all have been taken away," they might say. Demerer has succeeded in saving us from death, from the "final solution."

However, the facts speak for themselves. While we, the prisoners of Blechhammer, were saved from the gas chambers, many more other Jewish people were taken there in our place. The gassing was never, or hardly ever, interrupted. But we had been so blunted by the Nazis that we could hardly do anything in the face of this outrage. Our life simply went on, from one day to the next.

In February 1944 I was under consideration for a new coat. We were still working in our civilian clothes, or rather what still remained of them. They had been reduced to rags and patches of material from which those infamous "stars" had been cut out. At the beginning of the year I had applied for a new coat. I had nearly frozen to death in my present clothing. But, a distribution of textiles at last took place. We were all called up to come and stand in rows outside the barracks. On one side stood a Kapo and on the other side stood an S.A. man. The clothes, which they had gathered together for us, lay in a mean, miserable, and untidy heap on a table. Everybody who came past received something thrown at him, plus a slap in the face as an expression of "friendship." One really had to beg and plead in order to get something more or less decent. Most of the clothes that I saw did not even resemble clothes, and they were even worse than what we already had. And how big you were or what size you wore or what kind of an article of clothing you needed—these questions were never taken into account. Everything was dished out haphazardly. Our shuffling along was, in itself, so oppressive, so panic-filled, and so hectic that we could do nothing else but count how many people were standing ahead of us in line. Still five people, still four, still three . . . you saw everybody going away with rags. But I obtained, thank God, a pilot jacket. No coat, but a pilot jacket, a blue one, really a magnificent specimen. When I finally held it in my hands, I hardly dared to put it on. I was so deeply impressed by it. Until I was inside, in 12.6, I did not dare to thrust my arms into the sleeves. All my fellow room inmates stared at me; the Cucek had been lucky again!

But I would not be wearing this jacket for long.

Blechhammer–Auschwitz III

During a weekend in the middle of March 1944, a gigantic change took place in our captivity. The rumors, which we had already heard earlier in the year, were now confirmed: Blechhammer became a branch of Auschwitz, the thirty-ninth field detail. The name of our camp from then on became Blechhammer–Auschwitz III.

On the day when this happened, a fatal, terrifying atmosphere pervaded the camp. What was going to happen to us? Were we going to be gassed? Now it seemed that we would not have to go to Auschwitz; Auschwitz was coming to us. More modern techniques and better conceived, more efficient systems allowed Blechhammer to change its shape. Nearly everything underwent a serious alteration.

The most important renovation took place in the Lagerleitung or camp command. S.A., Wehrmacht, and Lagercommandant were dispensed with. The entire external leadership was taken over by S.S. personnel, and their commander was an S.S.-Sturmbannführer, Otto Brossman. The previous guards who were generally older and who were professionally rather ineffective were replaced by these stormtroopers within a day. The essential requirement for this change seemed to be that they wear an S.S. uniform, the uniform with the sinister and macabre skull. Wearing this uniform immediately made one an S.S.-er.

Throughout the vast, extensive yards of the Hydrierwerke a long uninterrupted chain of guards was set up, twice the number of guards as before. And, in addition to the Vorarbeiters, the Kapos, the Meisters, and the S.S. men, the so-called "Flying Brigade" first appeared. The Flying Brigade was an elite body of heavily armed S.S. that had been specially trained for concentration camps. Twenty young fellows who had had their preliminary training in Auschwitz. They spent the whole day wandering around the yards in order to "keep an eye on things." They avidly followed up on each and every confrontation with the prisoners and were dangerous to life—totally heartless, monstrous, and hideously cruel. They always carried a revolver, held ready in hand, and they rode around on bicycles or even on motorcycles. Not to be taken by surprise, the prisoners collectively tried to stay aware of their location. From firm to firm, the information was spread among us by means of subtle signals concerning the whereabouts of the Flying Brigade at any time or place. But they could always pop up somewhere unexpectedly and strike us down in a way that could not be foreseen.

The guards of the Wehrmacht (henceforth called the S.S.-ers) were rotated each month. From one day to the next we could have a completely different guard standing over us, someone utterly unknown to us. It was then a matter of watching out and shuddering with anticipation.

The worst of all the innovations was, without a doubt, the arrival of the Politische Abteilung or the political department. This separate unit of S.S.-ers, including university-trained people like law students, had the power of life and death. If you were caught for some reason by a Kapo or by a Polizist or even by an S.S.-er, you were roughed up with a rifle butt or a whip. But so long as the punishment stopped there, you had no complaint. If, however you were sent to the Politische Abteilung, you were in much deeper trouble. Here and only here would it be decided what the precise nature of your punishment should be, how many lashes of the whip you should receive, to which detail you were to be transferred, or if you were to be sent to Auschwitz or shot immediately. Nothing more horrible, more terrifying than the Politische Abteilung existed. One broke out in a cold sweat at the mere mention of its name.

The innovations of Blechhammer–Auschwitz III were not only limited to the external leadership. The management staff of the prisoners also underwent some alterations. This staff was largely replaced by personnel from Auschwitz. These prisoners sent from Auschwitz were non-Jewish Germans, condemned criminals who had already been in the camps for five years. They had risen to the highest positions of authority among the prisoners. Instead of a red triangle (for political prisoners), these captured criminals wore a green triangle.

The system of the Stubenälteste and of the Kapo remained unchanged. But a so-called Blockälteste was added to this system. The Blockälteste had to be responsible for the everyday affairs of the barracks in his block. The Stubenälteste gave him the authority for these daily things. There were twenty-four blocks of which sixteen were inhabited. The remaining barracks served as kitchen, infirmary, Schreibstuben or orderly rooms, and storerooms. About eight of these Blockältesten were criminals from Auschwitz.

By definition, the Blockälteste assumed a high position. The best position, of course, was that of cook. After cook, the position of Bekleidungskapo or clothing kapo and then the Blockälteste were the most desirable. This Alteste controlled the hygiene in his block and distributed the food. Because three hundred and fifty to four hundred people lived together in a single block, it was possible for the Blockälteste to secretly hold back some food from time to time.

An important difference existed between the position of Stubenälteste and that of Blockälteste; the latter did not have to work together with the prisoners. He belonged exclusively to the lager personnel. He was also much stricter than the Stubenälteste and had much more power. One had to be very wary and careful of him because he regularly distributed slaps and blows.

It was extremely difficult to just go anywhere because the Blockälteste kept watch on the paths between the barracks. Our captivity became more suffocating.

The Kapo who previously came to observe the barrack rooms was now relieved of that authority. However, duties of Kapos and Blockälteste generally went hand in hand, and complemented each other.

The manner in which we prisoners were accommodated in our barracks also changed. Previously we all lived mixed together, not by any specific criterion. However, we were now brought together and housed by work detail. I was sent into the room of Kommando 38, that is, room 16.15, directly opposite the barrack where I had performed room duties with Benzen. Now I was here with prisoners from my work team, including the Kapo Jopie Brasem and the Vorarbeiters Rosenberg and Max.

For food, we did not have to go to the kitchen anymore. The Blockäteste and his little men went to fetch the rations, together with the ersatz coffee, using a little trolley, and then they would distribute them among their roommates. The only advantage of this complete reversal in routine was that our ration was extended somewhat. From now on, once a week, we received a little block of margarine, which weighed about ten grams. And once a week we also got a small spoonful of jam. One could not think of a greater pleasure! Also, we received a little tobacco each month, the so-called Machorka tobacco. It was thick, coarse, Russian tobacco. I did not smoke; thus, for me it was a means of exchange.

Brandes, our cook, was not deprived of his job but, unfortunately, many condemned criminals from Auschwitz were put to work in the store rooms and in the kitchens.

The burial ground in the limestone quarry behind the camp was shut down. The S.S.-ers had a crematorium built, not for gassings, but for the incineration of corpses. The ovens were not used daily; there first had to be an sufficient number of mortalities. But during the course of the months, the crematorium was in use for much longer and more frequent periods of time. After a very short time, the number of deaths in Blechhammer–Auschwitz III was to double, and then to increase again. One could breathe the smell of burnt human flesh as it penetrated everywhere; from chimneys the broad, dark clouds of ash billowed forth. It was so ghastly. There are no words adequate to describe it.

We were all sent to the showers on the fateful day that Blechhammer became part of Auschwitz. Our hearts sank and seemed to shrivel up in our chests. We were already aware of those tales about the alleged showers! But after a brief hour the word spread that we really were only to be washed thoroughly and closely shaved. Shaving was to be free-of-charge from now on and entirely organized by the Lagerleitung.

Our disorderly civilian wardrobe was now a thing of the past. Because of this decision, I was forced to hand in again my recently acquired, smart blue pilot jacket almost immediately after I received it! In the place of my clothing, they gave us a thin, pajama-like shirt and trousers, all striped blue and white. We were also given a bare, very thin vest. For headwear, they gave us a small, striped, almost shapeless little cap.

The Judenälteste wore the same uniform as we did, with the same stripes, but of a better quality. His clothes were also made to fit perfectly. The tailors of the camp who worked in the so-called Schneiderei always did their best to do things as the Judenälteste wished. They wanted to give him the best of the best. He was allowed to keep his own haircut and was not forced to wear a cap.

The clothing for the women was the same as our own, except that they wore skirts instead of trousers. Also, they were not so smoothly shaven as we were; their hair was simply clipped short.

Stars were no longer cut out of our clothes. They simply sewed a little triangle with "J" for "Jew" onto them. And if this were not already sufficient, we were also tattooed on the Saturday of that same weekend. We were called up for this, barrack by barrack. Prisoners were no longer allowed to be individuals with a name. We had now simply become a number. The S.S. wanted to make any escaped prisoners still more recognizable than they already were. Should they be caught, they now could be more readily identified.

At that time, the tattooing was still not being done electrically. An ordinary, everyday, needle with ink was used. The expertise of the tattooer decided whether or not the operation was painful or whether the result was mostly clean and painless; some were experts while others were apprentices. The most significant pain, however, did not come from the actual tattooing but during its aftermath. A considerable number of the prisoners developed infections from it. Antiseptic was not used. The practice was very primitively done, as if borrowed from the Middle Ages.

The prisoners of Auschwitz had been given the first numbers. These numbers were visually very large and could be found near the wrist. With the prisoners of Blechhammer–Auschwitz, the figures were smaller and were placed on the middle of our upper arms. My own number, which I still carry, was 178448.

All things considered, our takeover by Auschwitz meant a much stricter regime than that which we had known in Blechhammer. Because the hierarchy of the supervisors had become more complex, the sadism also became greater. The roll calls lasted longer, and now noise was always the order of the day—an uninterrupted cacophony of screeching, shouting, cursing, ranting and raving. Much more than before, we now had to be vigilant for all types of dangers that could arise literally from nothing. We only had to turn our heads, and we could be in trouble. We lived like the beasts of the forest, according to our lowest, most anxiety-ridden instincts.

I found myself in a completely new environment now that I had been transferred from room 12.6 to 16.15. Under the old regime, I was able to find out from my roommates what was happening in other places of work, under the supervision of other Kapos unknown to me. I knew what was going on, where the work was most horrible, and where perhaps it could be a bit more bearable. All prisoners shared their knowledge of these things. But from now on, the details were cut off from each other, and we lived in a much more isolated state.

Furthermore, I personally became much more lonely. I had suddenly lost overnight the roommates with whom I had lived for a whole year. I especially missed my good friend Benzen. It was only at meetings, which we specially organized, that we still saw each other. Mostly, I went to see him, as my presence in his barrack was less conspicuous than his in mine.

Around June 1944, I met two friends, old acquaintances from Antwerp, during one of my visits to Benzen in the block of Niederdruck where he now lived. They were brothers, Leibel and Menachem Wajsbaum. As I mentioned earlier, the Niederdruck Kommando was so immensely in its activities and so spread out that most everyone saw only a fraction of their comrades now and then. These two brothers were three to five years older than I and had been deported from France. Leibel was the elder, and Menachem the younger, of the two. But our backgrounds ran a parallel course. Menachem was the same age as my brother Samuel, and Leibel was about the age of my late dear friend Bubi Ausubel. We had attended the same school, Jesode Hatorah, and the same youth. organization, Agudath-Israel. The youngest brother, who was in a classroom below me, was named Paul Wajsbaum. He was spared from the camps. At first, when I met Menachem, it was a cheerful reunion; he had always been a staunch friend of my brother Samuel. He also brought his brother Leibel along. At that time we had already been in the camps for two years. The meeting was warm-hearted and genial, but our past had but little reality—we had been blunted by so much in the camps. After a short conversation we had to part. Occasionally, I still saw them here and there.

A figure in my new room was Rosenberg, one of the Vorarbeiters or foremen of Kommando 38. Originally, he was from Bendin, near Sosnowitze. He came along with one of the later transports to Blechhammer, after he had been caught during a police raid on Jewish insurgents. These insurgents were not all of the same political persuasion: some were Zionists, others were leftist socialists, and so on. But all of them were Jewish; thus, by definition, they fought against a common enemy. That was their bond.

That Rosenberg was so rapidly appointed to a leadership position in Blechhammer spoke highly of his powerful and lively character. He was one of the most dynamic prisoners that I ever got to know.

His brother, who at that time was about forty years old, was also with us. He had a much calmer, much more peaceful nature than that of Rosenberg himself. You would hardly have guessed that they were from the same family. This brother had been a bookkeeper by profession. The younger, more vital Rosenberg had indeed always taken good care of him.

Shortly before Rosenberg and his brother were brought into Blechhammer, a nephew of theirs had joined us, an eighteen-year-old boy. He too was now in 16.15. Because we were both about the same age, we soon developed a more personal relationship. The relationship was somewhat undemonstrative, but, for all that, it was a sincere friendship. This nephew slept next to me: I lay in the third level and he on the second next to it. At night we spoke to each other. I learned different things about the workings of the resistance in which he had participated. He told me how, day in, day out, they had lived in underground bunkers. Now and then they could send someone into the woods with an assignment. It was especially when this boy was talking about the arms traffic that I began to understand what a difficult time the Jewish partisans had of it. Both the Germans and the Poles were by nature hostile toward the Jewish people. Despite this, they could sometimes buy weapons if the orders looked worthless or insignificant enough. They were often cheated or betrayed during these sales. An impossible task rested on the Jewish resistance. Everyone who was in the resistance knew in advance that they were doomed to lose. Their only motivation, the mainspring which drove them forward, was the idea that at least they would not voluntarily allow themselves to be led to the slaughtering block. When the insurgents, including the nephew of Rosenberg, were caught, they were taken by surprise in their bunkers by the S.S. Most of the Jewish people were shot down on the spot.

The nephew of Rosenberg had a fiancée. Because he was so much younger, his relationship was less serious than Benzen's. But still his girl was an important subject of conversation for us. We were friends and, therefore, kept no secrets from each other. He told me that she was of the same age as he. Next, he described to me in the smallest details how beautiful and gentle and kind-hearted she was. They had lived together underground in the bunker, and there they also slept together. They did not have actual sexual intercourse; for that, he first wanted to marry her. But at the time of the police raid, he had to see whether she was caught and loaded into the truck. He found out later that she had been taken to Auschwitz.

In this manner, my life began at Blechhammer–Auschwitz III. Under the new regime there were moments during each day when I felt myself close to the brink of death. My physical condition became progressively more intolerable. The only thing that kept me upright was a deep, almost animal-like urge to survive.

Something out of the ordinary occurred in April 1944. I was still a part of Kommando 38, which had been put to work at the Czech building firm. It was the end of a day's work, and we all had assembled, ready to march back to the camp. But the S.S.-ers did not allow us to leave. They made us wait for hours, with us standing still in our exhausted rows. What was going on *this* time? By word of mouth the rumor began to spread that, in another detail, one prisoner was missing, a Jewish prisoner from Paris. During work, he had been able to escape from the yard.

I literally began to tremble with fear when I heard all of this. The S.S. would undoubtedly seek revenge, that much was certain. It was only a question of what horror they would concoct for us. I feared the worst. The unmentionable.

Still, after more than two hours of waiting, nothing happened. Dusk was already descending. We stood there freezing, lifeless and speechless in the night air, not knowing why. It went on and on. As soon as night fell, we began to understand: a chilly, pitch-black darkness was hanging over our heads. Here on the yard, we would have to stand in assembly the entire night in our thin work clothes. The whole camp leadership—everything that was wearing a uniform—had turned out to participate in this event, in these punitive measures. When anyone of these sadists stepped up to us, he began to scream and beat and then to beat some more. Toward midnight, the first prisoners started to collapse from exhaustion. Here and there victims in our row began to fall to the ground. It was impossible to help them. We were obliged to stand staring straight ahead.

What personally made it possible for me to stay on my feet until early morning was the thought that, at least, we had escaped the gas chambers. Because we might just as well have been taken there. It was bad enough that we had not been given anything to eat for the whole day—but this was terrible. We were stiff with the cold and sick with hunger.

We were given a helping of soup only on the following morning. At last something warm! But we had hardly any time to swallow it when we were again knocked about and pulled by the shoulders. Back to work! Time! Time! Back to work! With cudgels we were driven further along the yard. We had been awake for twenty-seven hours, but now we must again tackle a full day's work.

Once again something exceptional happened in that same April—this time, something which affected me personally. I was working with the bricklayers. One day, I was hastily taken aside by an Englishman, a certain Johnny. He asked me if, by chance, I could help him to get hat, a small soldier's beret like those that are fashionable with the Silesians. In exchange for such a beret he would get me prunes and raisins, he said.

I seized my chance immediately. "Naturally, I can help you to get such a beret," I said quickly. "That's child's play for me." And to make it sound even easier, I added the information that I had been a tailor by profession.

The Englishman gave me an old uniform so that I could cut it to pieces and make the beret out of that material.

In the camp, I immediately went to Benzen. We discussed the situation and weighed the risks of taking on this challenge. Together, we had a few portions of bread to barter. Then, with Benzen's approval, I ran to Ingber, the tailor from Luxemburg who was in 12.6. Ingber agreed to make such a beret for me for the price of a loaf and a half of camp bread. He would need a week or two to make it.

The tailor kept his promise. He had done a splendid piece of work on the beret, and it was just the type that had been fashionable at the time. In exchange, I gave him the loaf and a half of bread for which Benzen and I had saved so hard.

I took the risk of taking the beret with me to the yard. This was very risky in itself because it often happened that a prisoner could be searched. I encountered the Englishman again on the yard: he himself had come in search of me. Feeling rather proud of my achievement, I handed him the beret. I stuck my other hand out, eager to receive my part of the bargain. But the day upon which this exchange took place was a Friday, and the answer from the Englishman when I asked him for my part was an abrupt "I'll pay you on Monday!"

These words sounded hard and untrustworthy when I heard them. My heart sank. I did not believe what he was saying to me. Back in the camp, I became nearly sick with doubt. One loaf and a half of bread—the equivalent of six days of rations—I had given to that Englishman on credit! I felt sick to my stomach when I reflected on this precarious position. To make matters worse, fellow prisoners came to tell me that this Johnny was no more than a swindler, that he had quite frequently cheated others. And what I had feared turned out to be true. On Monday, I saw the Englishman again in the yard. He behaved as if he did not know me. I tried to follow him, but the whole day and during the week that followed he kept me on a bit of string. "I'll pay you tomorrow!" he kept on saying, "tomorrow, tomorrow!" In the end, I had to give it up. I had been too gullible. I had wasted my reserve bread on an Englishman. Although this man was also a prisoner of war, he had not shown the slightest spirit of solidarity. He was a heartless crook.

Shortly after I had been deceived by Johnny, I once again took the risk of undertaking something with an Englishman. Unlike the previous Englishman, this Englishman worked right next to me for the Czech firm. We often stood room next to room. Twenty times a day he passed by with bricks. In a hasty chat, he told me that he was interested in shoe polish. I would be able to get that out of the Czechs. We made an agreement, and once again I staked everything to be able to keep my promises. After a short time, once again on a Friday, I was able to deliver his order of shoe polish. But then, to my great dismay, I received precisely the same answer as I had earlier been given by Johnny: "I'll pay you on Monday!"

The fear that I suffered through the whole of the following weekend was even worse than on the previous occasion. I could no longer sleep, I just fretted and fretted. For goodness sake! How could it be possible? How could I now have been so trusting for the second time? I did not give myself the faintest hope of any luck! But see what has happened! See how I have been deceived again! But Rosenberg insisted to me that I really should not be so worried. According to him that last Englishman was a truly trustworthy fellow, the most honest of the lot in fact. As a foreman, Rosenberg sometimes completed much bigger deals with him, and they were always honorable. In spite of this reassurance, I continued to speculate about a potential loss.

On Monday morning, I saw the Englishman again. Instead of addressing him carefully and casually, I went straight up to him and immediately asked him if he had thought about me. In the meantime, I had become very heated up. From the twitching of my face alone, he could have deduced how worried I was.

He went to his little box and took his things out. "Here, you have your goods!" he snapped, entirely offended. "You don't have to be afraid of me! I know what I do! I'm not like the others!"

From his manner I could see that he was insulted. I had offended him with my mistrust. In the future, he would want nothing to do with me. He turned around and went to another room in the building.

I had now successfully completed my exchange, but I had wasted my contact with one of the best, most honest Englishmen that one could meet. In any case, I would now never be able to arrange anything with him.

The earlier setback with my bartering enterprise with Johnny had meant a line drawn through my account. I was one of the very few in the camp who received the chance to trade, and I made use of that chance as best I could. But my small, bitterly earned supply was depleted—and not only for me, but for Benzen too. It was an enormous blow.

The English were also in need of razor blades. Unlike the Czechs, they could not go home now and then to collect extra personal items. The English were permanently stuck in their camp throughout the whole year. Because their morale was still reasonably high, they took care of their hygiene and wanted to shave themselves every day. I understood their need of razor blades and realized that I could do something about this.

Quite by chance—everything in the camps was by chance, even the distribution of rations—I now came into contact with another Englishman, one who worked for a firm further up. Our arrangement was that, in exchange for three packets of raisins and three packets of prunes, I would get him two hundred razor blades. But, from now on, I wanted only "cash" deals, that is, hand-to-hand exchanges, no credit deals! "No problem!" said the Englishman.

Razor blades were very small. One thin packet contained five blades. Yet this arrangement had made an almost impossible demand on me. Razor blades were still much more difficult to obtain than bread; they were a specialty. Only the Czechs had them. But I would do my very best to get this order together. If I had any luck, we would see each other again at the same place where we now stood, in this big drafty market.

During the same week, I hurried to the Czech during my half-hour rest break at work. Since the month of October there was soup for everybody at midday, the so-called bunker soup. The soup was prepared with dried vegetables that had been brought directly to the camps from torpedoed ships. To miss that soup was not such a disaster—most of the time it was very bad, salty but edible.

The exchange with the Czechs was happily arranged. Two weeks after the agreement, I went with the goods to the market. The Englishman was already waiting there. He gave me his prunes and raisins, while I handed over his razor blades. It had been a success! I had had a good day, a wonderful day! But, while I was still enjoying this sudden euphoria, a Wehrmacht guard appeared in the entrance of the passage. He was a guard who supervised the English prisoners. Out of the cold, gloomy passage he bore down on me and looked deeply into my eyes. "What is that?" he screamed at me. "What have you got there in your hands?" I was caught red-handed. The guard raised his gun up high and hit me with the butt. "I'm going to report this to the S.S.!" he roared.

The hour of my doom had sounded. My heart beat so hard that my whole body shook. But then, in a flash, my intuition told me something different. Although I was, naturally, very scared, I began to ask myself if this incident was a kind of scam. It occurred to me that this English-man and this Wehrmacht guard might be conspiring. The Wehrmacht guard had arrived at the precise moment that the exchange was taking place. And had he really wanted to take me in, would he not have done it immediately? In such a case he could have handed me over at once to the duty officer. Instead, he screamed at me and beat me black and blue. He took my things away, but after that, I could go. "Be off with you!" he said.

Fortunately, my suspicions were correct. Later, I heard no more of this incident: It was as if it had not even happened. But what was certain—I had lost my raisins and prunes!

I really must state that most of these Englishmen, each one in his own way, were total ruffians. Even now I feel ashamed to say it, but that is the way it was. The Englishmen could see with their own eyes the hellish and outrageous situation that we found ourselves in. They observed how we did our very best to keep going and to survive, de-spite the appalling conditions. Nevertheless, they cheated us and were totally unscrupulously. I had now lost much more than I had gained from them. Only half a bread now and then could I still expect to barter from now on.

At the end of April 1944, we were suddenly taken away from the Czech building firm. For more than four months, I had worked there under relatively tolerable circumstances. But meanwhile the Germans quite possibly noticed that their success in the war was no longer so as-sured, that their luck was beginning to turn sour. Since autumn of 1942 this reversal of fortune was suggested when, at the beginning of No-vember, American troops entered Morocco and Algeria. This change of luck was especially evident when, on November 19, the Red Army began to attack on the eastern front and overrun the front at Stalin-grad. On July 10, 1943, the Allies landed in Sicily, and the Germans were suffering more and more losses in Italy and on the Eastern Front. And now they wanted to introduce measures to save their own skins. Our whole detail was frantically put to work building bunkers for the Germans, iron-strong, immense air raid shelters. Our own Kommando 38 built the first three or four bunkers for the firm Betonomenir. Quickly thereafter, many other details began working to this end—in all, some thirty thousand in the Obersylesische Hydrierwerke, of which we, the prisoners from Blechhammer, only comprised 20 percent. All the non-Jewish workers, more than twenty-four thousand people, would have to be sheltered somewhere.

This new period which we now entered proved to be a real calamity for us. First, an inhuman work pace was demanded of us. We had never had such a difficult time. If someone worked too slowly according to the prevailing standards, he was immediately exterminated, killed more mercilessly than ever before. Secondly, it now became even more difficult to make contact with someone in the outside world. Although, slightly beyond our site, some Englishmen still worked on air-raid shelters, we were severely isolated in our work. We were about three hundred meters from the headquarters of the Czech firm, and further away even later on. Finally, the S.S. and the Meisters behaved even more sadistically than ever. All their frustrations, rages, and insecurities were now being unleashed on us. The engineers came out almost daily to take samples of liquid concrete, to check if the concrete that we made was firm enough, and to determine if any cement was being embezzled by the contractors. The engineers were made responsible for these things. They suddenly became concerned about them.

And the prisoners noticeably began to deteriorate.

Western prisoners from Belgium, the Netherlands, and France had already spent a good twenty months in the camp. The Poles had been here a year and a half longer. We were all completely haggard and wasting away from the deprivations—from the beatings that we had sustained during torture, from the wounds received from accidents at work, from the abscesses arising from malnutrition, and from the general weakening of our morale. Through Jewish partisans we had heard stories about executions, about the most grisly, barbaric Nazi practices. From prisoners of Auschwitz, we had learned about the gassings and cremation ovens, which were unknown to us before. But although we now knew with certainty that it was happening, we still could not form a image in our minds of these terrible truths. It was and remained something unimaginable. We had to give up thinking about our relatives whom we knew had been deported. If we still cherished hopes for them, we did it against our better judgment, of what we knew to be true. Thirty to forty percent of the prisoners were walking skeletons, totally insensate, half-human carcasses awaiting their certain end almost indifferently. The number of dead that were collected daily for cremation rose inexorably. The death detail of the Schister, which was nearly busy full-time with the collection of corpses now, needed to drive around with two trucks instead of the usual one. The morgue was overflowing. The bodies of the dead had to be taken to the crematorium immediately (or at the very latest on the following day) due to the lack of space and also to prevent epidemics.

How serious the situation had become could also be judged from the number of suicides. Suicide had still been somewhat rare in the previous camps in which I had been. Should a person have wanted to turn his own hand against himself, it still required great determination. Truly accurate mechanisms were not available. The only thing that a person could do was to slash his own wrists or, while at work, jump into some machine. In Blechhammer, the fencing which held us prisoners was electrified for the first time. If someone in a fit of desperation and hopelessness was seeking death, all he had to do was to throw himself against the fence to end his life. Also these dead who hung tangled up from the wires had to be collected by Schister's detail. That the corpses of suicides hung here and there at the gate no longer surprised us. Suicides had become a daily event since the bunker building began.

The natural, mutual solidarity among the prisoners began to diminish, not just at work but also in the barracks. A social isolation, a kind of enforced loneliness set in. Earlier, each prisoner had his roommates around him, companions of the same fate through whom he could find support and friendship. But now one tended to withdraw silently from everything. One stared dumbly ahead with a dull, snuffed-out gaze. Each person tried only to survive; it was every man for himself.

The idea of a liberation never arose among us. There was no future for us at all. But the non-German workers, that is, the Czechs, the English, and the French, perceived it differently. Through them we sometimes received reports which encouraged us to rethink the possibility of liberation. The news which filtered through to us that Allied fighting troops had landed in Italy gave us a flicker of hope. We reckoned that perhaps within nine months they would be able to reach us. Naturally, this guesswork led nowhere. We simply had no idea of what was going on in the war outside the camp.

A full-blown state of euphoria arose on June 6, 1944, during Allied landings in Normandy. When we heard stories about the advances of the Allies and the defeats of the Nazis, we began to have a glimmer of hope for the first time. Yet the hope of release remained an abstract one for us; it was simply unimaginable. Nonetheless, the fact that the power of the Germans was on the decline became clear. We even noticed it from the behavior of the Germans themselves. D-Day, June 6, 1944, was a bleak and unpleasant day for them. And then those Germans became horribly cruel. With blood flowing everywhere, you received slaps and blows for simply breathing.

We now hoped that the Americans would come to us at the speed of a quick march. We hoped that within a couple of months the Nazis would be captured and humbled. But, in the meantime, our living situation certainly became appalling. We were weak and helpless, as if we were lying on the ground and someone wearing heavy boots was standing on our backs. But we went on praying: it will come, it will come, it's coming . . . All that time we remained defenseless victims, suffering only to die miserably on the Nazi conveyor belt. Furthermore, there was a grim rumor going around that, should the Germans have to retreat, they would blow up the entire camp.

In the beginning of June, the first air-raid alarm was sounded. A loud and shrill siren echoed and screamed over the yards. I had recognized that sound even before I had been caught, from the time when the Germans invaded Belgium. But what precisely was happening nobody knew at that moment. We went on working for another half-hour. Even the guards had never been given instructions about this response and were just as surprised as we. But then we saw them, a long way away, entire squadrons. Our hearts rejoiced. This was what we had been waiting for! This! It was proof that our rescuers had already penetrated deep into the interior!

Naturally, panic almost immediately ensued. Nobody knew exactly what a bombardment really involved. It was all so new and happening so suddenly and unexpectedly. We had been given absolutely no instructions. What did we actually have to do? We could think of nothing else but to escape as fast as possible to the bunker. That bunker was still surrounded by its scaffolding, incomplete and unembellished, but the most important work had indeed been completed. The walls were of concrete, two meters wide, and the concrete roof was two-and-a-half meters thick. We crept into it like startled weasels, trembling with fright.

The first bombardment was so strong, so violent, and so massive that the whole bunker danced. It was like an earthquake. Every couple of seconds the walls began to shake again. Our feeling of joy diminished somewhat. We began to fear for our lives. We sat praying for mercy.

After a quarter of an hour everything fell silent again. Our ears buzzed. We heard the squadrons retreating into the distance. It was over. One by one we went outside again with blinking eyes and grouped ourselves.

Our building yard now resembled a glowing, smoking lunar landscape. Around the bunker were spread some fifty, deep funnel-shaped craters. There had also been a couple of direct hits on the roof of the bunker itself. They had not penetrated more than a meter and a half through the concrete. The bunkers had thus survived.

As soon as this chaos had passed, to our great alarm, we saw the S.S. bearing down on us. They were furious. The bunkers in which we had taken shelter were meant for the Nazis and for the non-Jewish workers and certainly not for the prisoners! We, the "Schweinhunden," were not allowed to go there! We were now beaten by the S.S. until their arms grew tired.

The Kraftwerk produced the electricity for the entire Hydrierwerke. It took care of all power needs. The bombardment had so severely battered the Kraftwerk that all electrical services were paralyzed. We assumed that, from now on, the whole firm would be at a standstill for a couple of weeks and that no more work would be done. We were on cloud nine with joy. But it was a mistaken assumption; after two days everything electrical was again going full throttle.

From now on, the bombardments continued three or four times a week. They gave us courage and strength. We felt that the Germans daily were on the defensive. A single bombardment, which usually began about eleven o'clock, meant for us that we had two or even three hours of work breaks. You can easily imagine how happy we were about this, even though now and then there was damage to repair, a much higher work pace was demanded of us, and we now had to stay in the yard for longer working periods. But these burdens seemed to assume much smaller significance with each repeated bombardment, during which our lives were genuinely at risk.

We never took shelter again in the bunkers. The S.S. did not really know what to do about us. Should they stay with us? And how could they then keep an eye on us during the bombardments? The second time that the Allies flew over they simply left us out in the open on a spot within the firm that was surrounded by a wall, as in a stadium. That "shelter" under the open sky was one of the most terrible events that I have ever experienced. All prisoners squatted in rows, with their hands on their heads, waiting until the airplanes passed. We hoped that no bomb would fall straight onto our bodies. And the bombardment was really severe that day. As a result, twenty-one prisoners lost their lives, flattened out, torn to pieces. None of our guards was hit; their orders had been to remain outside during the bombardment. Yet as soon as the bombings began, they went somewhere else for shelter.

With the next bombardment, however, the S.S. had found a solution to the problem: we were accommodated in the Schwellerei. The Schwellerei was located in the heart of the Kraftwerk; for the Allies this was an outstanding target, but the whole structure was so deep and solid that we did not even feel the slightest shudder. All the prisoners, some six thousand in number, could be kept there together, plus three to four hundred guards. That was how gigantic the operation was. The only real danger was that we might lose our lives under thousands and thousands of tons of coal dust. But this never happened.

To be able to attack without warning was not possible for the Allies. Their airplanes came straight from England and thus could be spotted and tracked well ahead of their arrival time. Using the routes that the airplanes took, the Germans could predict which places would come under fire. We, the prisoners, could compute the precise time simply through the techniques that the S.S. used to prepare themselves for the bombardments. Just before an attack, the workers of the Hydrierwerke spread little barrels containing a sulphur-like material on orders of the firm and in collaboration with the S.S. This material was then set fire so that, within ten minutes, the entire yard was hidden by a kind of mist. You could not see your own hand in front of you—it was a real pea-soup fog. Not that this system was of much use. The Allies soon caught on to this technique and first made a couple of mock attacks until the fog had lifted. After this, the real bombardment began.

The work on the bunkers in the neighborhood of the Czech building firm lasted another two months. During that time Kommando 38 had become a much weaker team, nearly a punishment detail. A few prisoners who had connections were transferred. In their place, still weaker and sicker prisoners were brought in. And then at the beginning of September 1944, we all had to go 300 meters further out to build more bunkers, but this time we were much more isolated and worse off than before. We were now subjected to extreme, unremitting pressure, and we were watched so mercilessly that it simply became impossible to contact anybody. Even bartering (or anything like that) was out of the question—and then there was the chaos of the bombardments two or three times a week.

With this move Kommando 38 got two new Kapos. The Vorarbeiters Max, that smooth, slippery eel, and Rosenberg, his handy colleague, had left suddenly for another detail, like rats leaving a sinking ship. Also, our Kapo Jopie Brasem ran off. Brasem was one of those with whom the Germans got on relatively well. He had been a boxer and had enormous physical strength. Even the S.S. were stunned by him. The Kapo who took his place was rather second rate, a certain Godel Mel from Liege. A Kapo from Luxemburg was also sent to us. His name was Levy. Neither of the two Kapos tried to bother us. They certainly could not be called sadistic. The only trouble was that the work was so difficult due to the unbearable pace that workers frequently fell over dead.

Jopie Brasem, Max, and Rosenberg still remained with us in the Stube, in 16.15, even after their transfer. The principle of Auschwitz to keep prisoners together by detail was soon neglected by the Nazis. Too many deaths, too much change took place at work. Nobody could keep up with it.

For fourteen days, my work at the bunker became lighter. I was now put onto a railway where small wagons were loaded with liquid concrete. All that I had to do was to take care of the wagon change and send each wagon in the right direction. Once again, it was fast-paced work, but compared with the building of bunkers, it was child's play.

Later in September 1944, the real catastrophe began. The work at the bunkers reached its miserable peak. We were so far removed from the rest of the yard that it looked as if we were now in no-man's land. Although we worked ourselves to death, nothing more happened: no speeches, no discussions, no bartering, no messages for us to receive. Nothing.

After a while, I became aware of a kind of homesickness; I wanted to go back to the Czech building firm where, after all, I had worked for more than four months. I had had one foot in the grave before I had arrived there. With the Czechs I had recovered some of my strength and had become accustomed to receiving a little more food. For this reason, my memories of this time with the building firm were, therefore, very good. I had suffered so much building the bunkers during the past two weeks that I became neither more hungry nor more distressed. But I felt that I was permanently on the edge of succumbing. One day, I could no longer resist my urge. In the middle of my work, I simply left the bunker. At the only unguarded second that occurred, I decided to buy a loaf of bread at the Czechs. With this initiative, I began a totally reckless and crazy undertaking. A terrifying punishment would await me—perhaps even death—if someone should see me running away, this far from my own detail.

On the way, I asked myself the same questions again and again. Why was I actually doing it? What did I hope to achieve? Was I crazy? But I had just enough money for a single loaf. I was starving to death. I walked across the open yards as if I had been sent for by somebody higher up. The chances that I might achieve something were practically zero. And even if the trip should be successful, its benefit certainly could not outweigh the enormous risk to which I was exposing myself, over and back, during this trip.

It was purely by accident that the first person I encountered at the firm was the chief of the Czech workers. His firm had already been out of work for some time. He found himself in a lifeless, disconsolate condition where he saw nothing or no one. When he observed me approaching, he looked at me with amazement. He was happy to make contact again with someone, no matter who it was. He spoke to me about his own initiative and invited me to go with him to his small barrack.

This was not the first time that we had dealings with each other. We were not of the same rank; his normal clientele were Kapos. But through Rosenberg I had been able to buy something from him on two occasions—first a sausage and then a bottle of brandy.

The only things that he now could offer me were again a sausage and a bottle of brandy. I certainly did not have enough money to pay for such luxuries at that moment. The only thing that I was hunting for was a bit of bread. Did he not have that? No, he repeated. Only sausage and brandy. In spite of this, he continued to treat me in a kindly manner. We chatted a bit. He asked me where my detail was now working and how things were going. It only then occurred to me what I had actually been doing on my way back from this unproductive trip. I suddenly felt a wave of panic going through my body. I felt as if everybody was watching me, as if the shadow of death was hanging over these monotonous spaces. For an entire hour I could have easily been caught by numerous parties. This was not normal. When I returned to the bunker building site, I fell to my knees with exhaustion. It had been a senseless, life-threatening, and totally surreal adventure. I simply did not understand it myself.

I so much wanted to be transferred out of this bunker building to some other detail. But I had not a single connection worth mentioning. I did not know anybody who could help me. During September, I felt myself slipping backward to such an extent that I would have taken the greatest risks to leave. If I had to remain here, I would eventually perish in a very short time.

With luck, I turned to a good friend of Benzen's, a certain Zeppi. Zeppi was a German Jew who had fled to Brussels in 1937. Like all the German Jews, he underwent a double tragedy because of the war: to the Belgians he was an enemy of their state because he was a German and to the Germans he was also an enemy of the state because he was Jewish. In the concentration camps, he still succeeded in using the small advantage of his Germanic background: in the Schreibstuben or orderly rooms German Jews were most often used. There were about ten of these prisoners. They enjoyed a privileged position compared to the other prisoners.

Although Zeppi was an acquaintance of my very best friend, Benzen, I had had nothing to do with him. I didn't know exactly why, but the relationship between him and Benzen was only lukewarm at that moment. Zeppi and I only knew each other superficially. When I had been dismissed from the Dorfslager, Zeppi had made the file, and that was the only time that we had contact with each other. And now to enter his Schreibstube to see this "privileged" person was far from a simple thing to do. The Schreibstube was permanently surrounded by Vorarbeiters and all sorts of important prisoners who had to be passed through, one by one. Yet I made a great effort to approach him. Even if he was going to snap and curse at me, I had to take the chance.

With much bluffing and boldness, I was finally able to approach Zeppi. As humbly as possible, I posed the question: could he do something to help me? But Zeppi was far from being sympathetic. He made no attempt to calm me down or to console me. He did not even bother to use his ingenuity to find a way of helping me out of my misery. He simply told me categorically that a transfer could not be arranged, that such a thing was impossible.

Disappointed, I went outside again. I was convinced that I would be dragged down further into personal decline, which inexorably accompanied any work on the bunkers.

On a Friday toward the end of September, I heard the wonderful rumor that I would, nevertheless, be transferred! I heard it from my Luxemburger Kapo who, in turn, had heard it from somebody in the Schreibstuben. But to where would I be transferred? To Niederdruck, the Kapo was able to tell me!

Niederdruck was one of the most horrible firms that existed. Certainly not better than the bunker-building—even worse, if possible! I almost collapsed in despair.

The following Saturday afternoon a prisoner from another block came to our Stube. He had news for me: Kapo Martin, Rosse Martin, had sent him to come and fetch me. Martin lived in another block, but he wanted to receive me immediately. I went there full of curiosity, but also with anxiety, because the unknown was always dangerous.

The Dorfslager was dissolved in the autumn of 1943. Rosse Martin was then transferred to the firm to be the Kapo of the electricians. When I met him in his room he was sitting peacefully on his bed. With a sigh, he said: "Cucek! Ach, I'll never be able to get rid of you! On Monday you are coming to me!"

What he meant by this was that on Monday, instead of going to Niederdruck, I would be transferred to the electricians. Once again, Martin would become my Kapo.

It is impossible to express in words how glad I was to hear this news. The work with the electricians was generally known to be one of the very best duties imaginable. Compared to the other firms it was nearly ideal. And it had happened to me *after* I had the firm in Niederdruck looming over me! I had been removed from Hell to Paradise! Benzen congratulated me heartily. Back in my quarters I was the envy of everyone. I was still being spoiled only because I was considered the baby.

How I had arrived at the electricians I was never able to determine. That Zeppi had something to do with it was unlikely. If he had been responsible, he would surely have said something to me about it, even if it were only to remind me of my debt to him. Perhaps the Kapo from Luxemburg had put in a good word for me with Demerer. In any case, this transfer was a pure miracle for me, truly unbelievable.

The two electrical firms that belonged to Siemens were Siemens & Schuckert and Siemens & Halske. The firm to which I was sent was Siemens & Halske. Very few prisoners did technical work; real electricians took care of that. What we had to do was the preparatory work. There was no talk of real exhaustion. We certainly had to be quick, but the work of the electricians demanded so much precision that the S.S. could not really come and hurry us up. They had to leave us to do our work in peace.

The most important thing that kept us busy was the preparation of the tube grooves. We had to use chisels to make grooves in the concrete constructions. Later, metal tubes could be placed in the grooves for the electric wires. After the tubes had been installed, we smoothed the walls with mortar using a trowel. In this way the tubes were completely covered. Whole buildings were provided with electricity in this manner. It was certainly not heavy work.

An additional advantage within Siemens & Halske was that we again worked in rooms on structural duties and that we, therefore, were not guarded very much. It was again possible to come into contact with non-Jewish workers, master craftsmen, and assistant electricians.

My room in the camp remained unchanged. I was still in 16.15, where I was surrounded by prisoners of Kommando 38 who visibly were deteriorating daily. Also present was Max Rosenberg, whose nephew and the others were still with me in the room.

The bombardments, in the meantime, continued undiminished. There were attacks three or four days a week.

The tragedy affecting a young Dutch Kapo took place in Blechhammer–Auschwitz III during this period. He was about twenty-four years old and was appointed to be a Kapo because he was a very capable carpenter, an artisan. This Kapo had seen a bomb lying on the ground, which had not exploded. It was split open, but the mechanism had not detonated. The Kapo saw a yellow powder lying in the middle of the split bomb. He obviously did not realize that it was dynamite. Because we had no washing powder in the camp, he got the idea of smuggling some of that yellow powder into the camp in a parcel to see if it could be used as a washing powder.

While he was still busy taking the powder in, he was caught by an S.S. man. He was whipped until he fell down. Next, when he came into the camp he was sent to the Politische Abteilung. The S.S. of the political department drew up a protocol in which it was stated that Raphaelson (that was the name of this young Kapo) had "plundered" the dynamite and that he had done it with the intention of committing "sabotage." His deed was stamped as a "terror against the Third Reich." Raphaelson was then forced to sign the statement. But it is worth noting that after this incident he was left in peace. He was not relieved of his function. He was not taken away to a punishment detail or to anywhere else. Four weeks went past without anything happening. But when most of us had forgotten the incident, we realized that the S.S. had something different in store for him.

It happened on a Saturday afternoon. We came back from work. All S.S. who had not been at the building seemed to have dressed themselves up in their very best, most impressive uniforms. We were extremely suspicious. They paraded over the yard in their best ceremonial clothes as if an important holiday were being celebrated. But why? Naturally, none of us dared to ask that question. Normally we were allowed to go straight to our barracks after the routine checks. But today we were assembled in the center of the camp. And there we saw what was really going on. To our great surprise a gallows had been assembled.

All the details were now placed in a surrounding square. An indescribably sinister feeling gripped us all. We stood stiff and speechless, staring ahead. As soon as everything was brought into order and everybody was in his place, which took nearly two hours, Raphaelson was led to the platform where the gallows stood. The youngster seemed no longer to be able to understand what was going on. He let himself be led forward, cowed and stupefied by fear. He was then tied up. The S.S. made him stand on a little stool and, with obvious pleasure, placed the noose around his neck.

Only after a long period of absolute silence, the commanding officer of the S.S. stepped forward. "Sieg Heil! Sieg Heil!" shouted the Nazis.

Only later we learned through the Schreibstuben what precisely the Nazis had arranged. The protocol, which the young man had signed, had been sent through to the leadership of Auschwitz. Only now was an answer received from there. As if he were presiding at a court-marshall, the commanding officer read out the sentence that he had received from Auschwitz. And that which the Nazis had hoped for was read aloud: "Prisoner number so and so is, on the basis of his crime, the plundering of explosives with the intention of sabotage, committed on that date, condemned to death by hanging." The whole thing had the appearance of a lawful trial and a truly democratic tribunal.

By accident, I was standing right in front. Even if I had not wanted to, I was forced to observe from very close range what was happening to Raphaelson. After a very long wait, the stool was pushed away from under his feet with a firm kick. A panicked chill passed through us as if time were falling away. But then it seemed that the rope was not holding. Suddenly, it broke in two. Raphaelson fell unhurt to the ground. Everybody present stood amazed.

We all hoped now that Raphaelson would be given mercy because of that unusual event. But such a thing was, of course, unthinkable for the S.S. The rope was repaired and once again the boy was placed on the stool. Again it was kicked away. But the unbelievable happened again! The rope broke in two a second time!

A sort of providence seemed to have insinuated itself. Everything that we saw was so unusual, so unreal! But the Nazis did not give up. For the third time, the Kapo was placed upon the stool, and the noose was put around his neck. Because of what had happened, Raphaelson came more and more to his senses. He seemed to be clearly aware of what was going on. All of a sudden he yelled, half-choked but with a final ounce of strength: "Friends! Do not lose courage! Those who today want to murder us will themselves soon be kaput!" The two S.S. who stood next to him could not believe what they were hearing. "Hold your beak, you!" they shouted. Quickly they again kicked the stool away. And then Raphaelson sank down. For a couple of long minutes we had to look him in the eyes. After that, he was no longer among the living.

We still had to remain standing for another quarter of an hour. The horror of what had happened spread through us. And as a grand finale, they required us, all six thousand prisoners, lager personnel included, to march around the hanged person. Everyone had to be there and observe everything. Only after this were we allowed to crawl quietly and dejectedly back to our barracks.

We had already seen much deprivation, pain, and torture, but this calamity was truly different. Raphaelson had been a young and still relatively healthy, kind-hearted person. Everyone was desperate. We crept silently to our beds and shut our eyes tightly.

Soon after this, two French boys were also caught at a similar "plundering." Throughout the bombardments, some poles with thin electric cables had fallen over. The prisoners had loosened a few of these cables to use them for replacing the worn-out rope of their mess-tin. An S.S. man had noticed this. He hit them with the butt of his rifle. "Traitors!" he screamed, "Traitors! You are going to have to pay dearly for that!" The Kapo of the two French prisoners, a certain Roger Okshorn, also French, immediately went to talk to the S.S. man. He hoped to obtain mercy for them by trying to convince the S.S. man that it could not really be called "plundering." He begged him to be reasonable and not to make a case of this situation. But if Okshorn wanted to rescue the two boys, he would have done better to scream at them and to beat them black and blue; by so doing he might have been able to satisfy the sadism of the S.S. man. But now, instead of obtaining a pardon for them, the Kapo himself was put in the record for Auschwitz. The S.S. man claimed that the Kapo who had wanted to protect the boys was himself trying to sabotage the camp leadership. On the day of Yom Kippur 1944, September 27, the two Frenchmen were hanged together with the Kapo in the same ceremony that had been performed for Raphaelson. On this occasion three gallows were built with stronger ropes. The hanging of these three prisoners was indescribably hellish.

Afterward we received our food. But some Jews did not want to eat. Despite their hunger, they wanted to obey the highest Jewish commandment: to fast on Yom Kippur, the Jewish day of atonement. When the Nazis noticed this they became furious. Harder and harder they beat us until we vomited. Today we were forced to eat.

From now on, the gallows became a regular feature in Blechhammer–Auschwitz III. To my knowledge, there were forty or fifty prisoners involved in Auschwitz protocols because of "plundering." These cases invariably resulted in death by hanging.

The bombardments began to cause new problems. The English now dropped bombs with timers instead of with ordinary fuses. These bombs only exploded after eighteen to twenty-four hours, depending on how their timers had been set. It was very difficult for the Germans to locate these bombs, and they could explode suddenly anywhere in the work yards.

In order to render the discovered bombs harmless, the engineer troops had to participate. There were fifty defusing specialists in total, and they worked in threes: one leader and two helpers. For each small group, six Jewish volunteers were asked for. Under the supervision of German defusing experts, the volunteers carefully had to dig out the bombs, which lay under rubble, by using their hands—an extremely tricky job! And if the specialists still could not reach the bombs, the prisoners had to lift them and tip them over. Every move that they made was charged with extreme danger and could easily be the last one they ever made. But, in exchange for the risk that we were taking, we were given an extra bit of bread to supplement our meager rations. For this reason there was no shortage of volunteers among us—we were so hungry! Although only hundred prisoners were needed, there were hundreds of volunteers!

Within my detail of electricians I knew such a lad who had been appointed for this work with the bombs. When I asked him why he had volunteered for such work (which was as good as committing suicide), his answer was sobering. Some time ago he had picked up an electric cable with rubber to repair his mess-tin. He was caught at this so-called plundering. Consequently, he was in deep trouble according to the Auschwitz regulations. In the expectation of this death penalty, he still took his extra portion of bread. He had nothing to lose by it.

Quite regularly, such a time bomb exploded, even when nobody was handling it. Some few hundred meters from where I was working, six members of a detail of volunteers died as the result of an exploding bomb. We heard the blast echoing over the whole area and felt hot and cold with fear. A total of thirty volunteers lost their lives in this way.

At the beginning of October 1944, Benzen was reported sick. He was my only true friend for whom I would have walked through fire. Although nobody could exactly determine what was wrong with him, he was promptly taken to the quarantine department. This did not augur well. Two days later, I heard from the dentist that he had typhus. Typhus! The "Tyfusepidemie" which, a year ago had affected Ausubel, had been raging for a good year in Blechhammer; it was doubtful whether many of us could have escaped it. But Benzen definitely did not have a chance. Prisoners suffering from this disease either died after a couple of days or after a couple of weeks.

It was impossible to make contact with Benzen. A couple of times I received greetings from him via the dentist. This response was for me the only sign that he still lived and that he had not been sent to Auschwitz. But I lost my courage. My friendship with him, during all that time, had been the only thing to hold onto. He was my only hope, love, and support. For a long time, however, we had no longer been living in the same barrack but had still kept in close contact. So far, nobody had yet emerged alive from the typhus barracks.

More than ever, I also feared for my own life. First, Ausubel, next, Benzen—would I then be the next victim? The tide had started to turn. Along my path lay only misfortune.

After fourteen days, Benzen died. I was immediately informed about his death. If possible, I wanted to be present when he was to be cremated.

In Blechhammer–Auschwitz III, the dead were always taken to the crematorium in the evening on the day following death. When I saw the death detail passing with its two hearses, it was impossible to recognize Benzen's corpse amongst the others. The mortality rate had risen enormously: the hearses had to be enclosed on both sides to keep the lifeless, emaciated bodies packed together.

The crematorium was not located in any special zone outside the camp. It was located in the camp itself and not very far from our block. From behind a chicken-wire fence, I speechlessly watched the flames at a distance of seven or eight meters. They leaped up three or four meters high and were like devilish, hellish red tongues telling me that my only friend, Benzen, was certainly dead. It was the greatest blow that I had suffered in all my camp life. It felt as if I was being dismembered. Motionless and nearly vegetative, I lost all motivation to continue and was depressed for many days. With a piece of charcoal, I wrote down the name of Benzen and the date of his death. If, at least, I should survive all this, I would remember Benzen by reciting the kaddish in accordance with the Jewish custom on the date of his passing.

Soon after he had died, the business aspects of this calamity emerged. Earlier, we had together accumulated a sum of money that was considerable for life inside the camps. The most important part of it involved the dentist who, at that moment, had credit with Benzen. To everyone in our barracks, it was clear that the dentist must now pay me to clear his debts. Half of what remained of Benzen's possessions now automatically belonged to me and the other half belonged to me morally—that was the opinion of my roommates. If it had been I who had died, then Benzen would have received my possessions. Seen from an ethical perspective, I was the only one who had a right to that money. And yet I had difficulties in getting payment out of the dentist. Perhaps he was not completely aware of my business relationship with Benzen. This thorny problem demanded much of me. I lay awake worrying about it and constantly went around looking for witnesses. I could only approach the dentist with difficulty, but I was persistent. Finally, I became grateful to Zeppi, the Belgian-German Jew from the Schreibstuben, for still being able to shake loose the greater part of this amount—something that I shall never forget Zeppi for. He told the dentist of my relationship with Benzen and convinced him that he had to pass the pot over to me. When I finally got it in my hands, I stiffened with excitement. At last I had something to hold onto!

The fact that I had lost Benzen for good was a certainty, a loss which in no way could be restored. From now on, after twenty-eight months, I stood completely alone, without a confidant, without a friend, without a brother.

With the sum which I now had in my possession. I wanted again to revive my earlier image and restore my old bartering relationships. The English usually had prunes, raisins, and cigarettes to offer us but also something else, something more exclusive: the so-called "iron rations." This food was a survival ration that every soldier had received as a precaution in case circumstances carried him to a location lacking food. The iron ration consisted of vitamin-rich material, a sort of chocolate. It was in a small copper-colored tin of ten by twenty centimeters. One day, when I could find nothing else, I bought the small tin from an Englishman. I could not permit myself to eat it, but I bought it for the purpose of bartering. It was terrific for my morale to have that heavy object in my pocket. I now had access to more food than anyone else and, naturally, that advantage gave me courage. I ran around with the tin for weeks on end. But I could not sell it to anyone. It was too expensive. It seemed as if I had made a bad purchase. And furthermore, I now ran into danger. It was an art to keep that tin hidden from everybody. The guards would do away with me, and certain prisoners would not have hesitated to steal it from me. Too many prisoners were far too hungry to have any moral scruples about this.

In November 1944 a kind of cabaret took place under the supervision of the S.S. Anyone who had some talent or who had performed professionally in the past could produce something if he wanted.

The biggest boss who contributed that evening was the garment Kapo Walter. He could play the guitar like a true blues-playing cowboy from Texas. People laughed a lot, and here and there even an S.S. seemed to be amused. But, in general, this cabaret was an unspeakably misplaced, outrageous, and atrociously cynical joke. We were being forced to "feel good," to create a small and miserable celebration. But only now did we realize the sort of condition that had affected all of us. The wretched grind of all those days, which were now behind us, mercilessly permeated our senses. Myself, I could not even laugh. In general, one was not against humor in the camp; any effort to cheer someone up was always welcome. Jokes were being told daily and all guards secretly received a nickname from us: the Lame One, the Fat One, the Ginger One. But many of those who had come to the cabaret that evening were much worse off than I. They were critically ill. They stood shivering on their crutches, and yet they still had to watch this spectacle. None of us had relatives left. We had no future; we had no life. We had no illusions at all and were living at the edge of our final, our complete annihilation.

I worked for about six weeks on the installation of electrical service. After this, at the beginning of November 1944, I was transferred to the transport detail of the electricians. Other transport details, which had to relay heavy things every day over distances of two to three hundred meters, were hardship assignments. But by contrast, the work was light with the electricians. We transported spare parts, plugs, tubes, wires, screws, etc. We moved permanently back and forth with a hand-car taking these lighter items between the store and the firm. At that time, Siemens & Halske supplied some twenty buildings with electrical service. Thus, we had nothing more to do than run from one building to another.

There were six prisoners in our group. The majority of my colleagues were old and sick prisoners who were nearly incapable of completing any of the work. At best, they were only in a state fit to move forward with the handcart, a shabby little four-wheeled affair. For me, this task was laughably simple. It allowed me once again to recover my strength.

Fortunately, it was also difficult for the S.S. to watch over this transport detail that extended over a distance of several kilometers. Because of this range, we had a good view of the entire yard. We knew the smallest details about different details. And we got to know if the Flying Brigade was stopping somewhere; this information was gathered and relayed by means of undetected signals and secret warnings. On the whole, work with the transport had many more advantages than my previous job where I had to prepare screwturns. I had drawn a extremely favorable lot.

The work went on until the beginning of December. Initially, we had been very busy, but gradually the Siemens & Halske operation began to decline, mostly from the bombardments. Certainly, the transport detail no longer needed six prisoners. With two of the older prisoners, among others, and with a certain Tennebaum from Paris, I was transferred to work with the chief engineer of Siemens. There, I became his jack-of-all-trades. I had to make sure that his stove burned well and that I swept out his work place. On one occasion, I had to clean his bicycle with a leather chamois and a bit of water. These duties were completely outside the scope of the average work in the camps. Actually, most of the tasks to which I was assigned here were fairly light. And the two prisoners who had come here with me had it easier still. In fact, their presence was even more superfluous to the engineers than to the transport detail. The only thing about which they had to be careful was keeping themselves well hidden from the supervisors. Should they be seen by them, they had to ensure that they looked as if they were terribly busy!

On one occasion, a bomb fell into the engineer's inner courtyard. It was a bomb that had not exploded. Together with a couple of other prisoners, I was forced to remove it. First, we had to loosen and remove the coarse sand and some stones with a hoe. Next, we had to pull away any additional sand with our hands and then raise the horrible thing with the strength of our hands and arms. At each stage, we followed the instructions of a specialist. Throughout the operation, I saw my death flitting in front of my eyes. The slightest wrong movement made by me or by anyone else, and we could have been blown to bits. The sweat poured from our faces.

Luckily, nothing went wrong. After our work, the bomb was inactivated by a German specialist and then removed. It was then that I discovered that the bomb, which the English dropped, weighed two hundred and fifty kilos because this was clearly painted on its side.

In the meantime, something new and extremely odd happened in our Stube 16.15. Max, the extremely clever or, more precisely, cunning Czech foreman, had arranged nearly every night around twelve or one o'clock for two S.S. to come into our quarters, not to check on us or to punish us, but simply to play a game of cards. One of these S.S. was someone from the Flying Brigade, a Romanian and a real monster. We named him Tom Mix after the cowboy hero of the Hollywood westerns. This S.S. looked very like him. In addition, he was as quick as a rat.

In a corner of our barrack was placed a pocket torch and an oil lamp. The two S.S. men sat at a little table opposite two kapos. Mostly, they played cards with Max who, as a Jewish Czech from the German zone, spoke very fluent German. Rosenberg also often participated and sometimes also Jopie Brasem.

To us, these card-playing evenings were extremely ambiguous, mysterious. They simply could not be explained. These S.S.-ers were the worst bloodthirsty tyrants imaginable. They tyrannized us day and night. For that same card money, they would easily have sent us to the gas chambers in the morning. Yet they sat here with us, playing a bit, chatting a bit, as if they were the very best chums. We, the ordinary working prisoners, naturally lay low and kept quiet: the less you had to do with the S.S. the better! There was no doubt, though, that Max and Rosenberg intentionally let the S.S.-ers win. They went on playing until four o'clock in the morning, happily drinking together as if they were a small, private circle of friends.

This absurd, schizophrenic situation was indeed partly explained by history. It was now December 1944. Although the S.S. went on murdering us without interruption, most of the prisoners began to understand that their luck was beginning to turn. Possibly they wanted to remain in the good graces of these Jewish kapos, Max and Rosenberg, anticipating a future day of reckoning. Should it happen that one day Blechhammer would be captured by the allies, the S.S. would be able to state that here in the camp they had performed no more than their basic duties: that even among the prisoners they had "friends."

Whatever the reason, these card-playing meetings went on nearly every evening for several weeks. It was the pinnacle of madness. We could not talk about it.

The Czech firm for which I had worked a half-year ago was situated not far from the chief engineer's business. The Czechs worked about two hundred meters from there, and they were always arranging something. Each in his own way, from large to small, the Czechs bartered—for gain, but also because they were so against the Germans. One day, I took the risk of walking over to them in the hope of arranging something. That walk was to be the beginning of one of the most terrifying days of my life in the camps.

I had a small iron wheelbarrow because I took care of the engineer's stove. I filled it up with coal and went with it to the yard of the building firm, pretending that I had an assignment.

The firm was evidently breaking up. But, here and there, I saw a few people still at work. Earlier there had been some two hundred active workers. I was lucky. I still could find a Czech from whom I could buy bread, not the standard bread of the camps but a Czech bread. When I saw it, my mouth watered! I felt I had little choice and entered into the dangerous deal.

Within the engineer's outfit was a safe but small hiding place for my acquisitions. Mostly, I hid them in a corner behind a cupboard. Today, however, it appeared that, during my absence, the engineer had been looking for me. As I was in a hurry to present myself to him, the only thing that I could do was to store the bread artlessly under a nearby bucket.

Then I hurried to the engineer and helped him with his work. We had to draw up an inventory for spare parts. But, all of a sudden, Tennebaum came with a chalk-pale and trembling face: "Cucekl! There has been a great accident! A disaster! Tom Mix of the Flying Brigade! He has been upstairs and has found your bread! He has found your bread, Cucekl!"

I was terribly frightened. I could see the consequences coming at me. I became dizzy and saw stars! I did not know what was happening to me! And then Tom Mix himself came in, the merciless Tom Mix!

"What is that!!" he screamed. He pointed, to the bread and gave my behind a hard kick. I tumbled over the floor. How could I explain to him? What I had done was all so clear! Yet I tried to give an answer. "A stranger had offered me the bread in exchange for my smoking ration, my Machorka packet." Seeing that I did not smoke, I always had a packet available.

"What??" screamed Tom Mix. "What?? Do you think I am a fool??" Once again he started to beat me with his fists, like a street fighter.

After that, his first, most violent rage began to subside a little. With a heavy, slow voice he ordered us to go: go this evening with the bread that I had bought to the Political Department.

To the Political Department!

That was the moment when I experienced the fear. I was no longer a witness of the horror; I was the direct, immediate subject of it. I began to shiver uncontrollably. I felt glowingly hot and then ice-cold and then again glowingly hot. My panic was so fierce, so overwhelming, that a sort of tranquillity came over me. I felt a kind of passiveness settling on me which paralyzed me completely. All the frustrations, all the stress, all the misery which I had bottled up during these years now rose up all at once. With utter clarity, I now could see what I was up against. Where I stood. Who I was. What was in store for me. In a flash I saw the gallows before my eyes; I saw Raphaëlson, the two boys, the Kapo Okshorn. Immediately I had to make a decision. But where should I begin? Okshorn had wanted to defend the two boys: the S.S. had condemned him to death for that. Did I now have to accept what was happening, or should I try to offer resistance? I did not have much time: in a fraction of a second I tried to extract myself. Of my own accord I started to flatter the S.S.-er.

"But I have done nothing wrong," I begged. "I have done nothing wrong. I have always had the impression that you are so humane. Everybody says that."

The S.S.-er did not react immediately. That pause gave me a spark of hope. And then I said truthfully (but very dangerously): "Perhaps there is something that could be done. So that I no longer have to go to the Political."

Thus, I insinuated that I could organize something for Tom Mix— that, in exchange for his mercy, I could get something for him. The fact that I had the nerve to continue begging like that was altogether unbelievable. It did not even make sense to me.

"What??" screamed Tom Mix, outraged. His voice, heated up, echoed through the hall. But I would not let go. I fought for my life. "Bitte! Bitte! [Please! Please!] I went on stammering. "Bitte! Bitte!"

Tom Mix distorted his face. What was he going to say now? Or would he take his revolver? "Tell your kapo, Martin, what has happened!" he spoke. "Tell him that I have been here and that I have found the bread with you!"

He turned round, and just as majestically as he had come, he disappeared with jingling boots through the door. It was a miracle! In fact, I only half-realized what had happened.

Thoughts now began to run feverishly through my head. Tom Mix knew as well as I that Rosse Martin worked one kilometer further from here, that it was quite impossible for me to reach him. And it was already past twelve. I did not have a second to lose. I grabbed my wheelbarrow and once again hurried to the yard of the Czechs.

Quite a long time ago I had succeeded here in buying a bottle of brandy. Benzen had, at that time, sold it for me to the dentist. I now hoped, once again, to get such a bottle in my possession. With such a bottle Redhead Martin would perhaps be able to calm Tom Mix down and get him into a more favorable mood. But brandy was still much more difficult to find than, for example, bread. It was a luxury article. I approached the Polier but he could not help me. At that time he had absolutely nothing in store. For the rest of the day, I rushed around like one possessed, buttonholing everyone I met with a feverish sweating, trembling, and stuttering. The fact that I could be noticed by an S.S.-er or by the Flying Brigade hardly occurred to me, so agitated by panic was I. All my thoughts were directed obsessively toward that bottle!

Purely by chance, I finally came across someone who could help me. It was a Czech who, according to what he said, indeed had some brandy. Once again a miracle! This day had been a succession of miracles! But all these abrupt twists and turns, including the earlier disappointments and how this success, put my emotions very much to the test. I staggered from exhaustion; the physical strain was overwhelming.

After running again for three-quarters of an hour, I arrived weeping at Redhead Martin's. I showed him the bottle. Gasping, I explained to him what had happened, that Tom Mix was sending me to the Political Department, that I had to go to the Politics, to the Politics! I begged him to help me if he could. I was condemned to death; I was to be hanged. I could become crazy with anxiety.

Martin was not the worst of fellows by far. My earlier competition with his onions did not upset him anymore. But he told me honestly that he could not promise anything. He would see what he could do, but the chances were small and, naturally, against Tom Mix, an S.S.-er, he was powerless.

At the end of the day I dragged myself, exhausted and weary, back to work. My colleagues at the engineer's office had already given up on me. During my absence they all had been at my bread. Nearly everything had been consumed except for a few small fragments.

The details were assembled a little after four o'clock. "Kommando 1", "Kommando 2", "Kommando 3" . . . Then they all had to stand in a row. At that point Redhead Martin came up to me. "Know this, Cucekl," he whispered clearly into my ear. I trembled. Here comes the moment of truth, I thought. Then he said: "You have more luck than sense. I have seen Tom Mix, and you do not have to report to the Politicals."

At first, I did not comprehend what he was saying. It felt as if I had been strung up on the gallows with the noose tight around my neck and then lowered down again. It seemed as if I had escaped into another body, so drastic was this flip-flop in my spirits. I could not grasp it. My brain was reeling like mad. What a risk I had run! What mortal danger! And what an unusual amount of luck I had had! What a series of coincidences, one after another—like a combination of wonders, truly incomprehensible. Caught by the S.S.-er, by Tom Mix of the Flying Brigade! Having dared to make him a proposal, him! And then getting *this* chance—it was not normal. And then running around the yards with my little wheelbarrow without being caught! They could have grabbed me by the collar ten or twenty times. And then having the money in my pocket through the coincidence of Benzen's death. Hard cash. Exactly enough for that bottle! That was pure chance—I might just as well have been broke! And I was also lucky to obtain the brandy, which was so scarce. And I had been lucky to find Martin who was not always so easy to find, and lucky too that Martin had been so kindly disposed. My luck simply never seemed to run out. Another Kapo could have made the situation worse for me. He might have kept the brandy for himself or even have drunk it in front of my nose! And that Tom Mix had stuck to our agreement was also purely coincidental. He could have done anything that occurred to him.

Now, all at once, these miraculous happenings penetrated my mind, and I could have fainted from all the emotion. It must have been the hand of God. "You do not have to present yourself to the Political Department," I now heard being whispered in my ear.

What did fate have in store for me? I saw everyone collapsing and dying around me. And time after time I managed to survive.

My financial position had deteriorated somewhat. Several times I had experienced a setback. I had been cheated in the beret affair, and suffered a setback with the razor blades. My iron rations continued to be impossible to sell. And now, with that brandy which I bought only to give it away again, I had come to the end of my reserves. I still had one or two things stored up but not enough by far to enable me to maintain regular bartering. I now also felt myself indebted to the late Benzen. I believed that it was only because of his death that I was now experiencing this good fortune. It was as if he had sacrificed himself for me.

Among the prisoners, there were key figures, that is, persons in charge who enjoyed many privileges: the Judenälteste, the chef cook, and the garment kapo. As I began my next exchange, I was very grateful to the garment kapo, a certain Walter, a German criminal. He had arrived at Blechhammer–Auschwitz III from Auschwitz.

The garment kapo had all the textiles of the camp, and it was nearly impossible to contact him. He was perhaps even more difficult to reach than the Judenälteste. It took simple luck to get into his compartment under escort. But first you had to brave six or seven other posts which, in particular, were occupied by other criminals. In spite of all this, I had the good fortune to get in through the agency of Zeppi, the German Jew from the Schreibstuben. Earlier, the guards around the garment kapo had seen me standing and talking with Zeppi, and because of this, they exhibited a certain regard for me. They were afraid of doing something wrong by not letting me through, so they let me pass.

The Bekleidungskapo was a true businessman. Except for the standard striped suit of clothes that was designed for all prisoners, he tried to sell anything over which he had control. He also did business with Zeppi; the latter was always adequately dressed, for example, with a good jacket and with real boots.

When I approached Walter, I asked him if he had perhaps a pair of shoes for me. He gave them to me, just like that, for nothing. It was an enormous gesture; my old ones, worn out and threadbare, were completely useless. After that experience, I asked him carefully if, perhaps, he might have some other wares. I explained that on the building sites I could now and then do some bartering. But, except for the shoes, Walter had sold nearly all his goods to various prisoners. If, in the future, something should come in, he was certainly prepared to do business with me. That much he promised.

I returned to him some days later. The guards who surrounded him recognized me and let me pass through without any delay. I now hoped to get a shirt or two, anything that I could use for bartering.

Had new goods already arrived? "Nothing," said Walter. Not even a small, valueless reel of thread. Knapsacks, yes! These he had! But, to me knapsacks seemed to be an article of little interest.

Still during the same week, an Englishman came to me at the electrician's. In haste, he asked me if I had anything to offer. Disappointedly, I shrugged my shoulders. "To be honest", I said, "I have nothing . . . except a few knapsacks."

"You have??" shouted the Englishman. I still remember the strength and the amazement with which he shouted this out, not once, but twice. Immediately, I felt certain that I had a good deal in the offing. Naturally, the English knew better than we that the war was slowly coming to an end. For them, the prospect of regaining their freedom seemed more certain than it did to us. They were already thinking about returning home and were preparing themselves for this day. How could they better pack up their things than in knapsacks? Knapsacks had suddenly become the rage; all of the English were anxious to get some.

In the meantime, I had established a solid and trustworthy footing with Walter and proposed a price for his knapsacks. Because the English had already cheated me a couple of times, I only wanted to deal for hard cash with them. And over a period of six weeks, as we left the camp, I put a knapsack on four or five fellow prisoners and then later sold them to the English.

After a while, my smuggling in of any money became too dangerous. The lad who worked in the volunteer detail on diffusing bombs lived on such a short notice that he suggested to me that he should carry the mess-tin with the proceeds in my place. He was condemned to death and had but little time to lose. After a couple of weeks I was so well off that I could pay him for his risky work with a loaf of bread.

By Friday, January 19, I finally succeeded in selling my iron rations. The sale took place in the evening after supper. For weeks I had been struggling to sell it. Now I got rid of it for thirty marks through a fellow prisoner. My financial situation had now more than recuperated. I had the purchasing power of some seventy bread loaves. Compared to the rest of the camp, I was now a privileged person. Every day I could gain access to extra food.

The advance of the Allies in the west, meanwhile, did not seem to be going so well as we had naively been hoping. We had heard that the Russians indeed had started a great offensive in January, but we were still waiting to see the result. In addition, we still feared that all Blechhammer-Auschwitz III would be blown to smithereens . . . and with it, all the prisoners.

Death March

On Saturday, January 20, 1945, an enormously chaotic atmosphere pervaded Blechhammer. We had been standing around for roll call in the freezing cold from five o'clock in the morning, and we had not been directed to go to work. Without being given any explanation for it, we had to stand and wait, fighting against that terrible sensation of stiffening with the cold. From outside the camp came the sound of artillery; salvos of gunfire echoed through the air. We could not understand what was going on. We were stupefied, numbed, and disoriented.

At about four o'clock in the morning, without our knowledge, about two thousand five hundred other prisoners entered the camp. They had come, after marching for three days, from the concentration camp of Gleiwitz.

At about eleven o'clock in the morning, we were finally informed about what they intended to do with us. The whole of Blechhammer had to be evacuated! All the prisoners, all the Kapos, all the people of the larger personnel, everyone was to turn his back on Blechhammer!

While the meaning of this event was only just sinking in, we were already receiving further instructions. Everybody could go to the food store for an extra ration of food! After that, there was still time to quickly get ready! The march would begin within one hour! Finally, they announced that anybody who felt too ill to come along could simply stay behind in the camp!

This last piece of information was very dubious and ominous. We were given to understand that we did not have to go along with the S.S.-ers and the other prisoners. But anyone who stayed behind would probably disappear forever! The fear of such a final ending was too great. Nearly everyone decided to go along with the rest and not to stay behind in the camp—even the prisoners who were really too ill or too severely wounded to be able to stand up. They dragged themselves out of their beds, determined to join the main body in its flight.

But from the prisoners coming from Gleiwitz we heard other views. During the past three days these prisoners had gone through so much misery that it was impossible for them to go further. Many of them who still had a fairly good constitution, nevertheless, reported sick.

"I'm not going to go on anymore!" I heard someone say (a deathly pale yet fairly healthy prisoner). "They can shoot me, they can blow the whole camp up, but I'm not going to go on any further! I can't take it anymore! I would rather die right here than join this evacuation for a single day more!"

His words sounded ominous and terrifying. But I personally did not want to take this significant risk. I decided to join the column.

The ration that was given to us was enormous, two loaves of bread and a 500 gram packet of margarine! But our amazement was so great that we failed to consider for how long this ration would have to last. During all those years most of us had dreamed of only one thing: not of liberation or of freedom but simply of having a whole loaf of bread in our hands! There was pulling and pushing, cursing and screaming. The single row of thousands of prisoners was in movement. It became like a raid, a plundering. The distribution of the rations was so chaotic that some of the luckier prisoners could even get double portions placed in their hands.

At around one o'clock in the afternoon everybody was ready and prepared. The exodus could begin. From the six thousand prisoners from Blechhammer, some one thousand five hundred stayed behind, either because they were too ill or because they wanted to take the risk of waiting here for liberation. Of the two thousand five hundred prisoners from Gleiwitz, more than a thousand stayed behind. Thus, our column consisted of a total of about six thousand prisoners. We made up a column of about one-and-a-half kilometers, a column which struggled forward through meters of thick snow. Even at the exit gate, it became a journey, with prisoners lingering and dragging behind. By the end of January 1945, the Upper Silesian winter had become the worst and most appalling season of the year.

On the way we could still hear the sound of gunfire. An oppressive, apocalyptic atmosphere ruled over the entire landscape. This was the war's front line. The more we became separated from the camp, the more severe the booming and banging of the heavy artillery appeared. Pieces of shrapnel and shell fragments flew around our ears. For the entire time we came to understand that, either on the left or the right, we would be drawn into the middle of a battle or perhaps be caught up in a general assault by the Russians. Sometimes we saw on the horizon a couple of French prisoners of war approaching us. These were little groups of about ten men who had been freed in the next village. Their guards had already been sent to the front. They called to us, full of euphoria, "It's over! It's over!" "Vive la France! Vive la France!" English prisoners of war also passed, similarly crazy with joy. Would we also be released? Within the camps such a thing would be unimaginable, but here it suddenly seemed to be real and close-by. Even the S.S. was clearly confused. They did not know what to do or where to go. Indeed, should they meet with a Russian patrol, the S.S. would not be in an acceptable state to fight back. They were sadists, not fighting men. But, as our hopes began to rise, we penetrated deeper and deeper into the hinterland, in the direction of Frankfurt on the Oder. What was awaiting us there? At thirty-meters intervals the S.A.-ers stood around us with loaded rifles and with their revolvers within easy reach. Every now and then one heard them giving someone the coup de grâce, a flat, echoing crack that passed through one's bones and marrow. Other younger S.S.-ers rode about on motorbikes with sidecars. They roared past us with submachine guns trained on us. Never before had they been so careless with their weapons. Shooting had become a carnival game. They could not touch their revolvers enough; they always had them within reach. Although I had received new shoes from Walter the clothing kapo, I was not adequately dressed for this journey. It was so cold and we were so inadequately clothed that it felt as if we were walking naked. Our physical condition did not prepare us for this trip. On the first day we covered some fifteen kilometers at a snail's pace. Night fell after five hours and we looked for somewhere to sleep. We were led to a number of great factory halls, there to pass the night on the hard stone floors.

The halls were still being built. It was draughty and freezing. With our clothes on, we pressed against each other for warmth.

The rations which we had been given in the camp did not last for very long. After a half-day of walking we had become very hungry, and the rations were nearly depleted. The majority of those who lay around me had eaten everything, including all the bread and the margarine. We well understood that this was a mistake, that we should have saved something for later on. But the temptation to eat yet a little more was always too great, even hypnotic. The majority had, during the journey, torn off little bits from the loaf and gobbled them up until, despite their conscientiousness, everything was gone! Even I suffered from this "greed" although I had been well-trained in the camp always to leave something for emergencies.

The night was hell. Nearby, shots rang out all night long. The air was thick with war and fighting.

On the following day it took everybody a long time to get up. For the first time in my two-and-a-half years of captivity there was no four o'clock roll call, and we were allowed to go on sleeping.

It looked as if the S.S.-ers were waiting for further orders. Because of all the chaos, none among them would take any initiative. Perhaps they had indeed received instructions but instructions which contradicted each other. The entire system of evacuation was uncertain and unreliable. The S.S.-ers did not even know how to begin. Only when we were finally under way, in the middle of the morning, did still more become apparent.

I had placed myself somewhere in the front among the prisoners. The atmosphere of war became so heavy that I believed I would be freed at any moment within the hour. Yet, it never seemed to happen. We were still dragging ourselves forward when the German military columns arrived. They crossed us precisely in the opposite direction. We saw that the S.S.-ers were beginning to doubt their undertaking. What was happening where we were going? And what were these military columns on their way to do? At a certain moment, the S.S. sent the head cook and his team back to the camp. No explanation was given for this. We hoped that perhaps they were going to fetch fresh supplies, new and vitally indispensable food. But later, at about two o'clock in the afternoon, it became clear to us that the S.S.-ers on motorbikes were placing themselves at the head of the row. They allowed us to come to a standstill. "About-face," they suddenly screamed. "Los!! Los!!"

Our hearts sprang up! We were thus going back in the direction of Blechhammer–Auschwitz III! If we reached the camp, we would probably get organized and receive proper food. With renewed courage, the entire column began to return.

It was only later, when we began to think more deeply, that we started to worry again. Were they perhaps going to blow up all six thousand of us prisoners as soon as we returned? Or would we wait there until we were freed by the Russians? Both death and the release from captivity became a reality. No one knew exactly how he should feel. The situation simply became too ambiguous.

After walking for a long time, we again reached familiar terrain. In the distance, we saw the tops of the buildings of the Obersylesische Hydrierwerke. The return journey was a little less tiring than the initial journey because the majority felt themselves relieved and nourished with hope. But then, one or two kilometers before arrival, a motorcycle with a sidecar came along with much noise. It was accompanied by fifteen similar vehicles, with noisy exhaust pipes. In front sat a furious, bustling, army colonel. He shouted to the most important S.S.-ers that this entire road had to be cleared! We were all in the way here! Make room for the army! The entire column had to be halted, stopped, and ordered to do an about-face! What were we thinking of? He cursed and snarled.

Our fate had again been altered through the sudden appearance of this colonel. Once again we would go back precisely in the same direction whence we had come—back to the interior, away from the front line.

From now on everything got worse. Everyone was exhausted and confusion reigned supreme. Whoever could no longer keep up, even for a little while, was simply shot. It was impossible to help the man next to you; by so doing, you ran the risk of falling down with him. And nowhere was there any mercy. You were killed for the slightest delay that you might cause.

We now passed farms, empty or nearly empty barns, and abandoned farmhouses. The atmosphere of war reached a highpitch here. Everywhere we heard the blasts of gunfire, the echoing, terrifying blasts! Earlier that day a grenade had even fallen in the midst of our column. Several prisoners lost their lives this way.

The prospect of being liberated was now so intense, and my own physical condition had become so miserable, that I risked attempting an escape. I simply behaved automatically, without reason. I saw that, for the moment, there was no guard near me and I fled like lightning into one of the empty, nearby buildings. I reasoned that, if I could hide myself for a day or even for a couple of hours, the Russians would come and liberate me. Or at least, the S.S.-ers would be out of my way.

Only then did I begin to think more realistically. Here I was in enemy country. There was a war on. Disorder and aggression reigned. I had no documents, no clothes, no place of refuge. To remain here actually meant suicide. If my guess should not turn out to be the correct one and the Russians should not invade so soon, then everyone of this region would know me as a prisoner. In the meantime, I began to fear that the inhabitants might return to the premises. They would probably be just as dangerous as the S.S. They would immediately betray me and report me without giving it a second thought.

After a minute or two, I decided to rejoin them as quickly as possible after looking anxiously over the little gate at the passing column. The distance between the farm and the column amounted to about eight meters. As soon as an S.S.-er had passed, I could see the following one approaching at a distance of about twenty meters. I hurried out like the deuce and, crouching, jumped again into line to refill the space which I had vacated along the ghostly road. My undertaking was for naught, a fantasy.

How difficult it was to escape from the camps, even during an evacuation, became clear from the story of Moshe Zimmer. Zimmer was a thirty-year-old prisoner from Upper Silesia, whom I had known when I worked with the electricians. I met him again many years later after the war. He told me how, during this evacuation, the so-called "death march", he had been able to escape from the claws of the Nazis.

Zimmer came into contact with a Polish electrician through the work to which he had been assigned. This electrician found out that an acquaintance of his, a Jewish woman, had been able to hide herself in a convent about thirty or forty kilometers from Blechhammer–Auschwitz III. With her address in the back of his mind, Zimmer would have given anything to obtain some civilian clothing. Thanks to his work with the electricians, he succeeded in obtaining such clothes. Now, at long last, during this evacuation, these clothes came in handy. Just as I had done Zimmer slipped out of the line late one afternoon during the march and hid himself in a farmhouse. At that time, he was a distance of ten or fifteen kilometers from the convent. When the march had passed, he continued to wait in great fear for several hours. Only then did he make his move to slip away from that house.

After a while, he lost his way. Zimmer found himself in a desolate place, destroyed by the war. The only thing that he could do was to make for another town where he might ask the way from someone in the village center. That was an extremely life-threatening undertaking, but what else could he do? In the village, he was received with skepticism. The people whom he approached only wanted to know who he was and where he came from. He explained that he was a Pole who had been recruited for forced labor, that he had fled because of a bombardment. But they did not accept his explanation. He was taken to a police station for interrogation. Here even less credence was given to his explanations. Finally, he was put into a truck to be delivered to an S.S. service that specialized in the investigation of unidentified foreigners.

Together with two others, he was placed in the truck, which was parked in a parking space. Then, precisely at that moment, a bombardment took place. The truck was abandoned and all occupants were able to escape.

He wandered around for three more days. During daylight hours, he had to hide, while at night he continued on. When he finally arrived at a convent, half dead with exhaustion and hunger, it turned out to be a convent different from the one he was seeking! But then, luck was on his side. There was a Jewish woman working in that convent who sensed that Zimmer was also Jewish. She demonstrated her support by hiding him in an attic for twenty-eight long days, right up to the moment of the liberation. She gave him food and drink from the very little that she had for herself.

Zimmer told me this story much later after the war had been over, in the 1990s. Most of the ex-concentration camp prisoners rarely, if ever, spoke of their past in the camps. But when I heard that Zimmer was bedridden and expected to die, I went to visit him. Despite his weakened state, he told me about his escape with an unerring memory. He was really happy to be able to relate his experiences at last. He had mentioned them previously but never before in such great emotional detail. He died fourteen days after my visit.

But clearly, for a prisoner like me, such an escape would have been still more difficult. I had no clothes, and no safe-house address. I would not have had a chance, had I stayed in that farmhouse. My intuition had rightly advised me to give up the escape.

On Sunday evening, the second day of our exodus, we stopped after about ten or twelve kilometers. It was already getting dark, and we could no longer got any further. We were to pass the night in enormous wooden barns, a relatively very good place to sleep. There were thick, warm bales of straw in which everybody could find a spot to rest. We dug into them like moles. And, before going to sleep, at about two-o'clock, we actually received a plate of soup. The cooks had improvised a kitchen.

To be able to distribute the soup, the S.S. formed an unbroken circle around us. They left an opening at one place in the row and formed a passage by standing, one opposite the other. That was where the ladders stood, and through there we went out again with our ration in our hands.

In practice, this forced march left much to be desired. Everything occurred in a disorganized manner, and everyone was in a state of panic. In the camps the only question had been whether one would get enough food—or whether one would get thin or thick soup. Here, however, there was so little organization that one could experience the misfortune of getting absolutely nothing at all. Despite our exhaustion, we were all pushing and pulling and looking ahead like vultures. The further back you stood, the more anxious you became. And with good reason. Some succeeded in slipping past the S.S. a second time to get a second helping, but others, especially the weaker ones, received nothing at all. They fainted with hunger.

Like most prisoners, I had received one portion. The hot food steamed through my blood. In the straw of the barn, I became so warm and comfortable that I fell asleep after a couple of seconds.

I had already eaten up my bread at midday. The temptation had been all too great for me and others alike. The power of food's attraction was like a drug. I would have been able to resist it one day longer than most of the others, but I had that same day already eaten my packet of margarine toward evening.

We woke up in the middle of the night and we did not know what was happening. It seemed as if we were suffocating, as if hundreds of heavy bales of stacked straw had fallen on top of us. Taken completely by surprise, we did not know what to do. We crept over each other, coughing and shrieking and gasping for air. A nightmare! I still was lucky that I lay fairly high up in the straw. The prisoners further down could suffocate very quickly.

"My ration! My ration!" somebody began to scream. "My ration!" A prisoner had lost his food in the panic. He was one of the few among thousands who had even been able to save a part of his bread. It was a real disaster to lose it this way! In all probability, a starving prisoner had stolen it from him. We tried to discover where it could be or who might have it but without success. Everything was upside down.

The prisoner who experienced this disaster was Gustav Altman. He survived the camps. After the war, he came to live in Antwerp. We sometimes meet each other and then we talk about this incident.

When we awakened in the morning, the temptation was great to hide ourselves among these bales by creeping to the bottom and keeping quiet, until the Nazis and the column and all misery departed from the barn. But these thoughts only lasted a few seconds; they were just too dangerous to entertain. When I began to straighten up to join the others, I heard a woman screaming not far from me. "Herr S.-mann," she called out stupidly—Silesians did not say S.S., but rather S.-mann—"Herr S.-mann, there is still another Jew hidden in the straw!" I jumped up and got away. A bit later, the S.S. came in armed with pitchforks. They stabbed into every bale and turned each bale over. Had any prisoner been hiding under a bale, he would have been impaled.

After we had assembled and were standing in column, the journey on foot once again could begin.

We could still hear the sounds of the invading Russians around us, the banging and the crazy shots. We were still a bit hopeful. With the front and liberators nearby, there was the expectation that perhaps something good would happen. But the march itself became more and more difficult.

We were now seldom shouted at or beaten. Should a confrontation arise with the S.S., the chances were now greater—even more than at the march's beginning—of being killed on the spot by a bullet through the head. They murdered us routinely, without the slightest hesitation. The intervention of a Kapo was nonexistent. During the march, the hierarchy among prisoners had broken down. There were S.S.-ers and there were prisoners, and that was the end of it. In the meantime, nearly everyone had eaten all of his ration. It had simply been impossible to hold something back for later. I still had my money hidden within the false bottom of my mess-tin, including that money which I had received for the knapsacks and for the iron rations. I had just sold that ration to someone the day before this hellish journey, after having been embarrassed by it for such a long time. But now, one day after, it could have been my salvation! I kept the mess-tin with the money as if it were a lifeline thrown to a drowning man! Should I lose that, I would be irretrievably lost!

Because we were by now so hungry, we began to scrape up and eat the snow from the ground. It did not feed us, but it drove out the pernicious, rotting taste from our mouth. And it refreshed. The snow was brown and muddy and dirty. Off to the side of our column, but still within the chain of guards, I could see snow that was white and still undisturbed. I could not control myself and secretly crept closer to it. While I was quickly scooping some of this white snow with my mess-tin, an S.S.-er came towards me. He had spotted me from that distance. He aimed his gun at me. I was paralyzed with fear. This was the end. Just as hundreds of other people, I would be left behind here as a corpse in the snow. But, instead of shooting, the S.S.-er hit me in the ribs with the butt of his rifle. Already after the second blow, I fell down. He wrenched the mess-tin out of my hands. He threw it away for a distance of several meters, and it landed high on the bank of snow.

All that I had ever owned was now taken from me. I felt so naked! I was completely at my wits end! The column marched on, but I could no longer accompany it. I had to try to get my mess-tin back; I had no other choice. I dragged myself forward between the others as slowly as possible. The S.S.-er who had attacked me had, in the meantime, disappeared. I looked around me and flew up the snowy bank like lightning. If a prisoner strayed but one meter outside the line, he took his life in his hands. But, I thought, even if they shoot me dead I must get it back! Without my mess-tin, I have no chance!

The undertaking demanded some magic. However, luck was on my side. I picked the mess-tin up and immediately rushed down again. I had rejoined the row and nobody had noticed me. All my money was back in my possession.

After trudging on for a long time, we finally reached a bridge by the evening. It was a bridge over the Oder, and in retrospect, the bridge to Hell! The end of all hope! We would again land behind the German front line, far away from all the fighting.

By chance, just as I took the first steps over that bridge, I heard an exchange between the S.S.-ers who guarded us and some soldiers from a group of engineers who were guarding that bridge. As soon as we crossed this bridge, said these soldiers, they would immediately blow it up. Thus, they hoped to create a barrier against the advancing Russians. When I heard this, I felt faint with despair. Escape was impossible from now on. Every step on this bridge was a step in the direction of the Germans.

We wandered around for two or three hours after dark. The S.S. were unable to find any place in which to pass the night. We had come to a halt in the midst of a desolate landscape. We would have to spend the entire night outside in the bitter cold. And no food was available. We crowded together on the ground. He who was lucky enough might find an empty cement bag to creep into. The rest lay on the ice in their flimsy clothes. The only reason why we fell asleep was that we were so exhausted. We were at the limits of the last vestiges of our strength. But we were not allowed to sleep through the night. We had to take care not to stiffen or we would have frozen to death. Every few minutes we had to change our position and try to rub ourselves warm.

By morning we were numb with cold. A great many prisoners could no longer get up; they were either dead or near death and were simply left behind.

The fourth day of our march, Tuesday, January 23, 1945, was one of the worst days of all. We were so hungry and weak that we could hardly move on. The distances which we now covered each day were greatly reduced. The pace of the earlier days simply could no longer be maintained. I had just seen Menachem Wajsbaum and his brother staggering along. We were all so exhausted that only one gave a nod as a sign of life.

We already knew what a typical day's journey would be like. We staggered, dulled and expressionless, over the dreary stretches of landscape, through the most hellish snowstorms, and still we heard the rifle cracks and revolver shots of the S.S. who were acting like lunatics. The safest thing to do was to begin the day somewhere in the line and then try to avoid falling behind during the course of the march. Anybody who became weaker and who could no longer keep up was exposed to danger. He would disappear into the tail of the column, and the man who reached the end of that tail—the utter end of the column—was slaughtered.

There were never any pauses for rest. A prisoner would sometimes stop to sit on a kilometer post for a few seconds of rest in order to, at least, catch his breath and get a little relief. Of course, it would only be possible for him to do this if he was walking in the front. But if he should be caught doing it, the chances of being shot in the neck were very great. Some of the prisoners were so tired, so exhausted, that they had become totally incapable of thinking about this possibility. They just lived from one moment to the next. This condition was especially true of the prisoners who had been discharged from the hospital specifically to accompany us. They had no other choice, and now their bodies simply could not go on any more.

For those prisoners who had diarrhea—and there were many—the absence of any break presented even more torture. There were no lavatories or other sanitary provisions throughout the entire journey. These unfortunate victims simply died, their faces stiffened by the cold.

Even the guards became fed up with the march. There were two kinds of guards: the genuine S.S. who were solidly trained headmen and members of the Wehrmacht who had simply changed into another uniform while in Blechhammer. It was especially these ordinary soldiers who gradually began to falter. Their equipment and their guns began to weigh too much. They were also quite elderly and also longed for a way to rest. This weakening effect on the ordinary soldiers was an advantage for us; their aggression had been somewhat diminished.

The real, younger S.S.-ers, who had been specially trained for the concentration camps, still stayed in formation. They were in much better physical condition and, in addition, were motorized. With undiminished sadism, they rode back and forth. Shooting prisoners down was a sport for them. They amused them greatly with this "recreation."

I was worn out to the extreme. My body was beginning to breakdown from the lack of food. We never again saw bread during the whole march. On Tuesday evening, we were given a little soup, and that was all.

The journey still went on for another three days, up to and including Friday. The days passed by as before. The pace slowed down even more. The population diminished noticeably. Corpses were lying everywhere along the road from Blechhammer to our present location. The column became longer, with gaps in the line. On Wednesday, we slept in an empty factory after being given bunker soup. Many prisoners were too weak even to line up for their food. And Thursday night, the last night of the death march, was again spent under the open sky. On Friday, January 26, 1945, we continued to drag ourselves along throughout the entire day until midnight. A new destiny was awaiting us. Survival.

Grossrosen

We had arrived very late in the evening at the end of the seventh day of our evacuation on Friday, January 26, 1945, at the concentration camp of Grossrosen. We could not see what it was like; all the lights were off because of the bombardments. Everything was pitch-dark. We were led in by the light of hurricane lanterns. "Los!! Los!!" In the open, snow-covered fields whence we had come the nights had actually been fairly light. But here, suddenly, we were unable to see our hands in front of our eyes, rather like entering a darkened cinema. Our fear of the unknown was at least eclipsed by our relief that the nightmare of this death march was temporarily past.

We were taken to a type of yard in the camp, a gigantic, draughty hall. Sleeping accommodations were not arranged well; there was not enough space. With the approximately four thousand people who had survived the evacuation, we now stood pressed against each other. In the best of circumstances, we could squat down on our heels or sit down on the work material or the piles of hollow building blocks. It was also absolutely dark here. Water or hygienic facilities were not provided; for that we had to make our own arrangements. We did not even have a roof over our heads.

Only in the morning after daybreak, when it had become a little lighter, was I able to look around me. I immediately saw that, of all camps which I had seen and lived in, this one was the most horrifying. We were in a murderers' den, inside a den of cut-throats. In the distance, in the inner courtyard, I saw the prisoners of Grossrosen standing for roll call. They looked ghastly. The condition of these people was more appalling and shocking than anything that I had ever seen. Such a condition was not limited to a certain section; each person I encountered was an emaciated, walking skeleton. How could all this be real?

And they were not even shaved normally, like us. In their extremely short hair, broad bare stripes had been made through which other dark stripes arose. The entire aspect of these people was so hallucinatory that it seemed as if I was literally living in a nightmare from which no awakening was possible.

At about eleven o'clock in the morning I was able to make contact with one of these prisoners. He had to work on the infrastructure of the camp; therefore, he was prisoner of the camp personnel. He stood with his back turned towards me, as scared as a weasel. You could not call it a conversation. This prisoner was simply too terrified of being caught talking. He murmured something without any intonation and looked straight ahead as if he was busy with something.

Furthermore, he made it clear to me how bitter life in Grossrosen was. The inhabitants of this camp formed a mixture of Jewish prisoners, political prisoners, and prisoners of the common law. The Kapos here were terribly cruel, the prisoner said. But they had no choice. The S.S. always chased after them, every second of the day. The entire camp was in such a state; sadism occurred in its extreme forms.

Most of the prisoners were sent to work in quarries or stone pits. Of the various kinds of slave labor, this type was the worst imaginable. In each camp it was always the quarry workers who most rapidly worked themselves to death. The work was just too heavy. Also in no appropriate equipment was available in Grossrosen. Only one prisoner in the quarry had an electric drill. All the rest had to work with pickaxes from sunrise to sunset without the slightest rest-break. Furthermore, the stones were as heavy as lead. Often there were great chunks of rock. These had to be carried by three prisoners at the same time and brought over in a trolley. At breakneck speed, the blocks had to be loaded and unloaded. The management of Grossrosen was so gruesome and morbid that it simply defied belief. The Kapos were criminals, which says it all. All guards of all ranks were entirely barbarians, sadists, or opportunists. Twenty-four hours a day, they were out to provoke the prisoners. A prisoner could be tormented, beaten, or killed for the slightest reason. A series of ruses was invented to torture the prisoners.

The prisoner hastily told me that there was no source of warmth anywhere in the camp. Recuperation from the hard work in the stone quarries was even harder to come by. Food was so scarce here that everybody ate snow, just as we did during the death march. The snow lay at the border of the zone where the prisoners moved. Like a released herd of cattle, they were always searching for it.

Grossrosen was even bigger than Blechhammer. Blechhammer was much too small for subdivisions and was actually a section of Auschwitz. Grossrosen was a "mother" concentration camp. Many prisoners had already been transferred elsewhere, to one of the many "daughter camps" of Grossrosen (or Ausserkommandolager).

For us, Grossrosen also meant the temporary end of the evacuation, which had lasted a whole week. We had again been brought together. The enormous chaos of the move more or less disappeared. Also we received a piece of bread for the first time in since the evacuation. For many of us, this food was just a little too late.

The situation suggested that we were only here temporarily. We could not guess what precisely the S.S. had in mind for us, but in Grossrosen there were no barracks for us. The whole time we spent waiting passively in that cold, roofless yard.

We only had contact with prisoners who did work in the camp itself, and we could only see the others when they left in the morning for their work. We also had very little to do with the S.S. of Grossrosen.

Only now that we were isolated here from the rest of the camp and waiting to learn what would happen to us were we in a position to review the outcome of the death march. My estimate was that about 35 percent of the people who had left Blechhammer–Auschwitz III had died, been murdered, or collapsed. In all probability, Leibisch Wahl was among these victims. After Blechhammer I never saw him again. Furthermore, 20 percent of the evacuated prisoners had reached such a disastrous state of exhaustion that they must have been classified as hopeless. About 15 percent had frozen limbs, hands, or feet (particularly the feet—we were still able to move our hands a little). In half of these cases the freezing had advanced so far that an amputation would be necessary, a procedure that was not possible in the camps. For them, only death remained. In my case, the little toe of my right foot was just at the initial stage of a freezing. If the march had gone on for any longer, that toe would have rotted away. The remaining 30 percent of the prisoners were, without exception, so severely broken in health that not one of us was in fit condition for work.

When each of us reflects about the death march and about Grossrosen, we get a specific image of how gruesome the Holocaust was at its worst period. Each of us worthless wrecks now ran the risk of being taken away in a death transport to the gas chambers. Not time but at some point in the very near future. Even today, perhaps. In any case, We could not be of any use to the Nazis. We had been all used up.

We passed through Saturday, Sunday, and Monday without any activity. Although we were so weak that we could hardly move about, victims still collapsed from exhaustion. Like corpses, they were removed from our midst and carried to the crematorium. Thus, the toll of the march had not fully registered among us; in fact, we were only now just beginning to feel its full weight. Many prisoners were too weak to offer resistance and had finally to surrender to their vulnerable condition.

By Monday, January 29, 1945, groups of prisoners were consistently called away for an evacuation. Here, the column of the death march was split up. We were grouped by train. Nobody knew where these prisoners of Monday were going to be taken. To an outside detail of Grossrosen? The stone quarries? We would have collapsed in misery if the thought had come to us in the previous week that we had been so close to liberation. This experience was once again camp life at its worst, at its truly hellish.

I left with more or less 700 people on Tuesday, January 30, 1945. We departed at about twelve o'clock in the morning. In a long, miserable line, we moved on foot through the snow. Our destination was a mystery. The prospect of a new and murderous foot journey made us crazy with worry. It was all coming back: the hunger, the cold, the revolver shots. It was already late in the afternoon when we arrived at a row of freight wagons, in the midst of a snow-covered, desolate plain. In the meantime, some tens of prisoners had collapsed by the wayside or had been shot down.

"Einsteigen [step in]!! Einsteigen, Schweinhunde!!"

We clambered into the wagons, which were open supply wagons. On the floor of these vehicles were the remains of hard, razor-sharp pebbles, which cut into the soles of our feet. There was no roof. Neither were there any benches. We would travel standing, sixty to seventy men per wagon. We were pressed so closely against each other that we could have suffocated. It was actually impossible to move even a hand. We could not see further than the prisoner in front of us, and we had to keep each other warm with our breath and our feverish, sickly bodies.

The wagons started to roll slowly. We hobbled, stopped, and hobbled further. How long was this going to last? Our food supply was as good as nothing. Neither were there any lavatories: each person had to urinate and defecate into his trousers while standing. The stench was unimaginable, like a sewer on wheels.

We traveled for the entire night and throughout the following day.

And then through the next night and day. There seemed to be no end to our journey. After three days we were still standing pressed together like sardines in a tin, sleeping standing up straight, speechless, and paralyzed with exhaustion.

Every few kilometers the train stopped. Then it would go off in another direction. Once we were hindered by a track that was covered with snow. Every now and then, when we stopped, an S.S.-er would come and look at us. He then gave somebody a blow with his gun or pulled him out to shoot him down. The corpse was then left behind along the track.

Prisoners also died everyday in the wagons. A prisoner who died like this remained standing because of a shortage of space. Often the man who stood behind you was still half alive while the man who stood in front of you had died about an hour ago. Whether or not *you* were still alive was problematic.

The most deadly circumstance was the shortage of something to drink, but also dangerous was the icy cold that followed the wagon stops. During the death march, we were still moving at least. Here in the wagons, we hoped that we would not freeze to death. My lungs squeaked and started to ache like a razor under my ribs. I feared the onset of pleurisy.

We could hear the thundering of bombardments everywhere along the horizon. These went on for the entire time that we were in transit. On Friday night, the heaviest bombardment occurred after we finally arrived at a new location. We could not be unloaded, and consequently, we had to spend the entire night in the wagons until the squadrons went away.

The transport of the day preceding our arrival had suffered a direct hit. We saw the ripped-apart wagons laying on the ground. There was blood everywhere. Here and there, we even saw human limbs strewn about in the snow. We prayed that such a bomb would not land on our own wagons. We were deeply shocked. Furthermore, the prisoners in our wagon continued to succumb with monotonous regularity. Everything that happened brought with it only pain and death. It was an unearthly experience defying one's imagination.

Finally, on the last day we were pulled out of the wagons to the accompaniment of physical blows and pushing—a new and unknown destination awaited us. We began to abandon all hope.

Buchenwald

We were pulled out of the wagons at about four o'clock in the morning on Saturday, February 3, 1945, emerging like wrecks into the cold, dark, outside air. There were some forty S.S.-ers awaiting our arrival, and they appeared to be a little less noisy and meddlesome than had earlier been their custom. They hit us with the butts of their rifles, but only if we caused delays or other difficulties. They still had their terrifying, blood-thirsty German shepherds, specially trained for the camps and exactly like those I had encountered two years earlier in Kosel. They growled and barked as if possessed, and they bit at everybody who passed, while the froth poured from their mouths. These dogs left a deep, traumatic impression on all the prisoners. For the S.S. it was a show, a parade with much exhibitionism.

From a signpost we had been able to read that we were in Weimar. We knew that this meant Buchenwald for us. We went stiff with fright when, a bit later, we saw the gigantic fences of the camp and the gloomy, dismal, black entry gate. We had already vaguely heard about this camp. It had been established in 1936 on a hill called the Etterberg. According to what we had been told, there were more than sixty-thousand prisoners there: communists, Jehovah's Witnesses, labor leaders, homosexuals, condemned criminals, and Jews. But more than that was unknown to us.

"Jeden das Seine" [Each his own] was written above the gate. This gate is where we were brought into the camp.

We arrived at the vast, muddy, inner yard. It was a bigger yard than anything I had earlier seen. Several Kapos came to stand around us. "During the march, you all became infested with lice!" they shouted. "You must take all your clothes off and stand in a row to be de-loused! Only after the disinfection will you be divided into groups!"

184

A disinfection? This frightened us as much as if we had been standing face-to-face with Death himself. We feared that we would be killed on the spot.

The Kapos understood our suspicion and did their best to calm our fears. They pointed to a barrel in the middle of the yard. The barrel contained creoline, a sharp, louse-killing substance. We believed from their style of speech that, in all probability, these Kapos spoke the truth. They behaved fairly; they were far from friendly, yet they also were not sadistic.

The coordination of the disinfection was abominable. Instead of arranging for us to undress in small groups just before treatment, they had all of us undress at the same time to be certain that no delays were created. But perhaps the Kapos had thought that the whole operation would be over much faster. What actually happened was that, for two or three hours, we had to stand waiting stark naked in the cold before it became our turn. The group in which we found ourselves was far too large. In addition to us, there were newcomers from other camps. The raw winter raged on and we had shelter from the bitter cold. Starved and shivering, we stood in the freezing cold, huddled together. Here and there, victims were collapsing.

During this ordeal, I had seen myself naked for the first time since Blechhammer. When I observed the state of my body, I could not believe my eyes. I was horrified. All my ribs had become visible, sticking out under a skin that had become nearly transparent. I had become a walking skeleton.

It took about three long hours before I reached the tub. Behind me were hundreds of others standing and waiting. Even more victims were collapsing from exhaustion, as if it were for a waste-disposal competition.

The disinfection was accomplished through the use of a large, wooden wine barrel. The smell of the creoline, which arose from it, reminded me of my childhood and of the de-lousings recommended by the schools. In the barrel, one felt the penetrating, biting petroleum. On each side of the barrel stood Kapos who grabbed my arms and dunked me. It was gruesome and unbearable. But I had to go through with it. Looking back, it literally seemed like a kind of baptismal ceremony: first to be dunked into this gigantic tub and thereafter to be accepted into Buchenwald. I was pulled out of the barrel and led away by helpers of the Kapos.

As we entered the camp before disinfection, we were informed that we were not allowed to bring anything in with us. Everything that we had needed to be de-loused. We had to give up the clothes that we wore, and our whole body would be checked over. It was impossible to smuggle anything in.

In Blechhammer, via Benzen, I had gained possession of a plaster from the dentist. It was a small, elongated sticking plaster. I bundled together the German marks, which I had kept in my mess-tin, and stuck them onto the soles of my feet using the plaster. This is how I passed through the baptism. I took an enormous risk, but that money was my only possibility of surviving. I simply could not give it up. However, during the evacuation I had lost the paper on which I had written the date of Benzen's death, to be able to commemorate him later in better times.

The checking took place immediately after one came out of the barrel. And the soles of the feet of the prisoners who had emerged from the barrel immediately before me were checked over. My heart stood still. Along with the Kapos, some S.S.-ers were also present. I was, therefore, about to meet my death. After all my suffering, I would now be lost. But the Kapos became somewhat negligent when they came to me. They glanced at me and then let me continue. Thus, with the money under my foot, I went on. It was a terrific triumph. I trembled with emotion but could not let anyone notice it. I was immediately led to the following initiation ritual.

We were taken to a shower to rinse off the biting creoline. The rinsing took place in the open air with ice-cold water. Then we were once again inspected and weighed in front of the camp administration. I could see that I weighed only forty-five kilos. In Blechhammer, I had still weighed sixty-two kilos. Thus, I had lost seventeen kilos during the march.

Only now did I get my clothes. They were just tossed to me. They were again the typical concentration camp clothes: a thin, striped, pair of pants, an equally thin, striped little shirt, a little striped jacket, a small bonnet, and a pair of shoes. The clothes were distributed in parcels without taking your size into consideration. They were just routinely chucked into your arms. Up to now, I had mostly good luck with such distributions, but now I received shoes that did not fit me at all. He who had shoes that were too small could, if he were lucky, get them replaced. But he who had shoes that were too big just had to put up with them. Mine were much too big and in hideously worthless condition. This was very bad for my morale. I could not even walk properly in them; I could only hobble along. But, naturally, I was happy that at last I could hide away my money inside such a shoe. Only then did my tension subside completely.

Only after this initiation ritual did we get something to eat. We had not eaten for days, since Grossrosen.

Buchenwald was an enormous camp, one of the largest in history. Earlier, it had been split into two separate parts. One part had been erected in 1936 and was made of stone houses and covered more than sixty hectares. All the prisoners who were held there went to work daily. This was the so-called Old Camp, the typical concentration camp as had originally been conceived for various kinds of prisoners: political prisoners, Jehovah's Witnesses, etc. The New Camp, or "Sonderlager," was much smaller. It was a sort of quarantine camp, separated off by a double layer of barbed wire. A part of this area was set aside for the roll call. Furthermore, there were barracks, a washing barrack with zinc basins, and a shabby, repulsive latrine. After we had eaten, we were taken to this Sonderlager. We would hardly ever come into contact with the Old Camp. There was a barbed wire fence and a guard of Kapos between the two parts. A small, vague exchange existed secretly between the two parts, but, personally, I was never very interested to know what was happening in the Old Camp. By that time, I no longer had the energy left to look around with too much curiosity.

In the Sonderlager, I was assigned to Barrack 53. Our Blockälteste seemed to be a Russian. Most of the management staff prisoners of the Sonderlager were, for that matter, Russians. The atmosphere of the barracks was hectic and oppressive. The sleeping arrangement were a great disappointment. In the previous camps, we slept on strawbags in our three-tiered bunk beds. Here, we had to lie down on the wooden planks without any softness. Also, because of space shortages, we were all pressed against each other. We lay together in groups of six or seven prisoners, often head-to-foot. But during the most chaotic days, particularly when newly evacuated prisoners arrived, we had to sleep in bunk beds with as many as ten or eleven people. In theory, such a bunk bed was meant to be for three or, at the most, four people.

Everyone tried to find a spot and settle himself. Soon after, the discussions began, feverish as always. The political prisoners who had already been in Buchenwald directly informed us that we did not have to be excessively afraid of torture. They said that beatings and torture did not occur very often and that the guards were not always out for a confrontation. The German Kapos of Buchenwald had already been here for five or six years. They were truly toughened, but they did not "play games" any more. And their behavior was predictable. He who kept himself quiet and laid low was fairly safe from them. The same held for the Russian Kapos; these men made much noise and looked rough and raw, but they seldom administered unnecessary blows. The secret here was to behave as correctly as possible. Then you would not have a problem with them. Stand perfectly in the row, immediately let people through who bring the coffee, stand aside when necessary, look away, and keep quiet.

The weakest among us were, however, so blunted that even this behavior was too much to ask. Without realizing it, they always got in the way, like zombies. Each day, they received a couple of clouts until they died.

The food that we experienced in the Sonderlager was minimal, even less than minimal. In the morning, we were given Maltz coffee, and in the evening there was a little soup and bread but never any margarine or jam. I had to give up the trick of holding even a small piece of bread over into the evenings and keeping the rest until the following day (or even midday). I no longer had the patience to achieve this any more. All food that I now was offered was immediately consumed, as was done by nearly all the prisoners here. I was driven by a blind, bestial hunger, a hunger brought on by fasting for an entire day, while awaiting in pain and uncertainty for the next food distribution.

There was also the tragedy concerning the money that I had earned with so much trouble and carried with me during the death march despite all the risks—money which I had been able to smuggle into the camp with much luck. That money now seemed to have absolutely no value. Any deals completed here in the Sonderlager always were done through bartering. Paper money no longer had any value. This was a blow to my morale. How many times in the past had I risked my life for that money! Now I was just as helpless as the other prisoners. To survive now was simply a matter of luck. I could no longer take personal initiatives.

The roll call demanded here meant little. During its twenty, or at most, thirty minutes, we had to obediently and meekly stand in a row. The Russian Blockälteste then shouted "Bistro! Bistro! Rebiata!" which means "Hurry! Hurry! Guys!" If an S.S.-er passed by at that moment, he hardly looked at us. He usually had something better to do or so it seemed—perhaps because he also felt the end of the war was approaching.

In general, a catastrophic, oppressive atmosphere hung over the Sonderlager, not so much from terror itself but because of a general, all-embracing malaise. Over the past years we had endured much too much misery. And now we were here, passively waiting and hoping that yet another day should pass with nothing too horrible occurring. In the past, the murderous slave labor had made it impossible for us to even think. At that time we lived almost like machines. But only now, when we were obliged just to sit still, did we began to daydream for the first time. Despair overwhelmed us. For me it was particularly bad because in the past, over time, I had been good at adapting myself to the difficulties that arose. Despite all the hard work, I still had enough energy left over for making contacts and setting up transactions, whatever the risks may have been. But now, after the death march and throughout my stay in Grossrosen, I was so severely broken in spirit and depleted of physical energy that I had become apathetic. Whatever took place in my vicinity just left me cold. I had neither "guts" nor energy. I certainly still wanted to survive, but I lacked the stamina to struggle for that survival. All the good and strength that I had earlier known had disappeared. I did not have a single thing to hang on to anymore. Earlier, I had had several friends around me, fellow-prisoners whose fate I shared. The only one that I rediscovered here in Buchenwald was Rosenberg's little nephew, the boy of room 16.15 in Blechhammer. After our transport, we all had been divided up so that no one was still accompanied by someone he knew. We were like a deck of cards that had been shuffled, and the result was that one felt like a random two of spades in this full deck. And no one still had the strength to pull himself together and once again seek confidants. Everything here was monotonous, spiritless, lonely, hopeless.

I remember how the emaciated "skin and bones" prisoners speechlessly walked back and forth between the barracks of the Sonderlager. They held a blanket wrapped around themselves and over their shoulders and were hopelessly ill.

Fichel Horowitz was also with them. He was as thin as a skeleton and almost gone. When I saw him, I was convinced that he would never reach the finish line in our race for survival. He did survive the camps and returned to Belgium, but psychologically he was never the same.

My own state of emaciation was by no means the worst among the prisoners. I had caught a murderous cold and a dry cough during the journey from Grossrosen to Buchenwald while standing in those hellish, drafty wagons and also from standing in that slow line while we awaited immersion in the tub of disinfectant. It was not so bad during the day, but at night when I lay down in the barrack I became aware of twinges of pain in my chest and in my loins. I coughed for hours without stopping. I thought that I was going to die. Also, my coughing affected my sleeping companions; they feared that I might be infectious, and I, therefore, kept them from their night's rest. During the slightest fit of coughing, I received a clout in my side. "Shut up, you! We are trying to sleep!" I sought a comfortable sleeping position, turning and returning in search of a solution. But I went on coughing. Going outside to get my breath back was impossible because I might bump into the night guard. I also could not go to the doctor; he was only available for broken bones, wounds, infectious diseases, etc. In fact, I only achieved relief of any kind when the morning arrived. This condition went on for the whole winter.

Next to me in the sleeping quarters lay a prisoner who had come to Blechhammer from Gleiwitz on January 20. Just before the evacuation from Blechhammer he had reported sick, so he simply could not leave to accompany the rest of us. I later learned from him what had happened to all those people staying behind in Blechhammer. They were not guarded at all, not by a single soldier. Thus, they could make use of all kinds of food: roasts, potatoes, anything and everything that they could find. But a week later, unexpectedly, arrived the personnel of the Volkswehr. This was a unit of the Germans who were too old for the ordinary Wehrmacht or for army service. The Volkswehr surrounded the camp and herded all the prisoners into trucks. Twenty kilometers further along they were unloaded at a place where they again fell into the hands of the S.S. They were then taken to Buchenwald.

I can only guess what was going on in the mind of that man when he told me all this. But one could read in his face that it was the most horrible thing one could possibly imagine: to be released from the Nazi terror at first only to be once again held captive in a concentration camp—that was simply evil.

Others who had stayed behind in Blechhammer immediately had made a break for the woods and had hidden themselves in the surrounding area of Blechhammer-Heydebrecke. They waited there for some eight days until the Russians came to pick them up. Once set free, they were able to repatriate via Poland and Odessa.

After two or three weeks, the S.S. again began to call people up out of Sonderlager with the purpose of transferring them to other details of Buchenwald, and among other camps, to Dora. The daily slave labor once again awaited us in these outside work details, but it was even worse than in the previous camps—stone quarry work. The transportation to these other camps took place by train, in locked cattle trucks.

For me, any kind of slave labor would mean my death. The business of sitting passively was suffocating but endurable. However, I was altogether in no condition to work. In the Sonderlager I could, at least, still rest. The idea of opposing this further deportation against all the odds became my only goal.

Rosenberg's little nephew, my only acquaintance, was soon taken away from us. When I heard that he was called up, I immediately went to him. On my own initiative, I gave him half of my money. It was an enormous amount. Here in Buchenwald the money had no value any more; perhaps things would be different where *he* landed. That I gave him so much was crazy indeed. God alone knew what was still awaiting me and how much those German marks could help me. But morally I was so fragile that the whole question hardly interested me. My first impulse was even to hand all my money over to him. "Here," I meant to say, "Here is my money." But, after pondering it, I changed my mind. Rosenberg hardly reacted when he accepted the money from me. He was just as blunted as I was. He could no longer express true gratitude. Without saying much more, we said good-bye, and our ways parted. So low were our spirits that we were practically devoid of all feelings.

In March 1945, the weather began to improve a little. We had come through a very hard winter—a miracle! We began, little by little, to go outside more and gradually to seek some contact with each other. The sun shined a little for an hour or two each day. This experience again gave us renewed courage.

During one of these walks, I met an old school friend of my brother Samuel, one Berel Melman. He and Samuel had been very good friends. I had also been at his home to eat and play there in the old days. I ran into him during a gathering for a roll call. The fact that we bumped into each other so unexpectedly after three years of camp life was something really valuable, really exceptional. We chatted a little and looked at each other. In fact, it was a miracle that we still recognized each other. Like everyone else, Melman looked exhausted and ill, with sunken cheeks and deep, dark eye sockets. He was not yet a skeleton, but, like me, he was on the edge of the abyss. I told him that the Wajsbaum brothers, Menachem and Leibel, had been in Blechhammer-Auschwitz for the entire time. They had also been his good friends. I had still seen them during the death march, but no longer in Grossrosen and Buchenwald. I feared the worst. After the war, it was assumed that they had died during the death march. Our contact with each other lasted a few hours, at most. After we told each other what we had been through, that is, where we came from and what had become of us, that was enough; it was the way things were with us. We came and went; we could no longer offer each other true support.

I only saw Melman once. Later I heard from other prisoners that he had been put on a transport. He was promoted to work in an outside detail, like Rosenberg, and he was to die in that outside detail.

Because so many political prisoners were in Buchenwald, the camp had an organized underground containing a network of contacts, complete with a radio and, apparently, even a secret newspaper! From right and left, news trickled in about what was going on in the outside world. One day we were informed that a United Nations had been established in San Francisco. For us, this was a completely abstract concept. We were still prisoners here, and every day people perished. We did not understand that was necessary for the world to look forward to those times that would follow the war. "After the war" did not exist for us. We lived from one day to the next, just for the day.

The idea of a liberation was still far too remote from our own living experiences. Slowly, the skeleton prisoners among us became so numerous that they started to exceed the other, somewhat healthier prisoners. They could not be taken away to a work detail. Therefore, they all remained in the rubbish heap of the Sonderlager to hang around until they died. Every morning dead ones were found on the wooden sleeping bunks. They were loaded up in droves to be cremated. Dysentery and diarrhea also persisted on a large scale here. The worst victims who were already completely emaciated were taken to barrack 57, a sort of home of the deceased which was named the "Scheissbaracke" by us. He who had to enter there was considered to be lost. Nobody ever returned alive.

All my days looked the same now that spring had arrived. Most of the time I lay on my bunk, looking dumbly in front of me. If it was not raining, I would sometimes go for a stroll to observe what was going on in the general surroundings.

On two occasions I saw something that was incomprehensible. A couple of Russian prisoners walked past with a little dish of fresh red meat in their hands. They wanted to exchange this meat for one thing or another. It looked really presentable and attractive, but how did they come by it? After all, we never received any meat! Until, one day, I was enlightened by a prisoner who stood near me. They had human meat. It did not come from a skeleton prisoner or a sick person but from a fellow prisoner whom they had just killed. Had they killed him following a quarrel or an argument between them? Or had they killed him solely to this food? I was horrified; it was just as if I had been dealt a blow with a hammer! I had already experienced a lot with food; prisoners who ate offal, snow, grass . . . but I had never heard about cannibalism in the camps. I was totally bewildered. I lay awake for days as if in a nightmare.

That it was Russians who ran backwards and forwards with that meat was no coincidence. I do not say that with an accusing finger. But many of these prisoners came out of the depths of Russia. They had to survive their captivity of merciless and inhuman treatment in the most impossible ways, and they had become barbarians throughout their via dolorosa. In spite of all the torture, they remained gigantic and sturdy as bears. Within the camp they formed an uncrushable unit, a kind of mafia.

The calls to go and work in an external detail continued ceaselessly. The Russian Blockalteste came into the barracks and read who had to go. In a broken German he then said, "Los!! Los!! Schnell!! Schnell!! Tempo!! Tempo!!" On a certain day, my number was also present on the list that he called from. The blood rushed to my face. I would not be able to do any work at all. I had now already reached the final limits of my strength. I dived rapidly behind the other prisoners in our barrack and hid myself under the bed space, with my face against the cement floor. My number was repeated. "Number 178448!!, Number 178448!! Mitkommen!!" Where was I? Someone from the prisoners at the entrance of the barrack answered for me. "He has gone to the doctor," he replied. "Because of his dry cough and his temperature."

The explanation was accepted. I escaped. But the practice remained the same. Another prisoner was taken in my place, which again made the totals correct. He was transferred in my stead to an external detail. This is not to say that the transfer was absolutely negative for that prisoner. The days in the Sonderlager of Buchenwald were also miserable and led one into a life-threatening existence. It is true that one received a bit more food in an outside detail and that you ran less of a risk of catching an infection. The fact that I myself did not want to go depended particularly on my own appalling physical state of health, not from an objective rational consideration of the advantages and disadvantages.

This single call seemed to be a forerunner of a whole series of new ones. From every source we heard that the Russian army was rapidly advancing. We did not expect as much from the Americans; they seemed to us to be somewhat more cautious. And what I had feared for so long seemed now to have become reality: Buchenwald, the whole of Buchenwald, was to be evacuated.

My intelligence and my intuition suggested to me that this event would be the last experience of my life. I had just begun to gain a little more strength once again. My cold had diminished somewhat. I had once again gathered together a little hope. But now I imagined the whole evacuation from Blechhammer unfolding before me again, step by step, day by day. The suffering from hunger. The unspeakable cold. The collapsing of the prisoners who could go no further. The sadism of the Nazis, the incessant murders. I would not be able to stand the pace anymore. I no longer had the guts to face it. I decided to evade this evacuation at all cost. To participate in it was impossible. However, what could I do about it? If I was to be put on a transport, I would be put on a transport. There was nothing that I could do about it.

Yet, there was one essential difference from the evacuation of Blechhammer; Blechhammer had only six thousand five hundred prisoners. This number of prisoners could be taken entirely on one march. Buchenwald, on the other hand, was immense. There were infinitely more prisoners—sixty thousand, nearly ten times as many. The evacuation would have to take place in separate contingents with units of no more than five thousand prisoners each.

A disadvantage was that the first prisoners would have to be assembled, not out of the old lager of Buchenwald, but out of the Sonderlager, which was of little importance to the work or labor effort. The Nazi leadership would, in fact, rather lose us than gain us.

The first raid before the evacuation took place at about four or five o'clock in the afternoon on Friday, April 6, 1945. The S.S.-ers again became active, exhibiting pleasure while causing suffering as they had before. A zone was established in the camp with ten to fifteen thousand people. The camp would certainly have no problem assembling groups of five thousand. We were chased like animals, cudgeled and kicked. A tornado howled through the barrack. Stumbling, cursing, screaming, clouting. Following an instinctive impulse I quickly decided to hide myself. I crept away under our barrack, behind the supports. This was the classical method: I was packed together there with many other prisoners. Shivering like frightened rats, two long hours, we stayed immobile there, lying in the stinking, suffocating mud. We were scared stiff, and we remained scared until long after the tumult had diminished. Nobody dared to be the first to emerge, until we heard and recognized a few of the prisoners who had been rounded up. They told us that the S.S. had managed to assemble their five thousand victims. The rest they allowed to come back.

I was exhausted and went in to rest on my trestle bed. How long would I enjoy this small relief? What I had experienced today was surely just a stay of execution, certainly no cancellation, no release.

The next raid took place immediately on the following day, in precisely the same way. Already in the distance, we could hear the S.S.-ers coming. What now? I thought again about creeping under the barrack. But I believed that this time I could not do it. In the first place, I no longer had any strength to, once again, lie crushed for two hours in that slime, gasping for air. Secondly, I had been so exceptionally lucky yesterday that I certainly could not duplicate that luck again! I could not keep on trying. Also, I suspected that the S.S. had probably long ago spotted that little trick! In fact, several prisoners had previously been pulled out of their hiding place and shot dead for their trouble! So, I remained standing at the entrance of the barrack, paralyzed with fear. The S.S.-ers came closer and closer. I let myself be surrounded by them. They led me together with the others along a straight road that was guarded on both sides by heavily armed helpers. There was no longer any hope of evasion. I staggered along with the crowd to the macabre outer gate. All of that, the entire raid, took place in a couple of minutes, like a vortex dragging us down to our doom.

Next, we went to the exit through the Sonderlager, through the old camp. They had to be flogged as a group because nearly everyone tried to resist.

I could now see the gates some five hundred meters further on with the iron arch over which were written the words "Jedem das Seine" [each his own]. I was being led like a lamb to the slaughter. I thought that I was headed for a bullet; for me, this evacuation meant an even more certain death.

On one side, in the colorless grass which grew around us, I saw prisoners lying there who were being kept apart by the S.S. They were mostly emaciated skeleton prisoners, cripples, and invalids. They could not go with the transport, that much was clear. They lay there, listlessly staring into nowhere. And for myself, I began to limp as if I was lame, as if I had become wounded in my left leg. The closer we got to the gate, the more I pretended to limp. I could already hear the S.S.-ers in front. "I still need a hundred and sixty-seven," said one of them. "Still a hundred and sixty-seven, and my five-thousand is complete." And then it was my turn. They observed me as if I was an insect, as if I was a bit of rubbish in their way. They discussed among themselves whether I should accompany them with that leg of mine. And then I began to plead, very humbly, with my eyes downcast to the ground. I mumbled quietly that I was severely ill, that I was crippled, that all my strength was gone. Normally, I would have been shot on the spot for this, and certainly, in an evacuation like this, I was overstepping the bounds. But the S.S.-ers could care less. They were in a hurry; the train was waiting. Behind me were many more prisoners, more than enough. One of the S.S.-ers grabbed me by the shoulders and through me aside with a powerful movement. I staggered and let myself fall down on the grass. I now lay among the others, among the prisoners who were truly ill.

Full of anxiety, I now waited to see what was now in store for us. Nothing was certain. The S.S.-ers were in such a state that they were capable of anything. They could easily shoot us down and carry us away to the crematorium. When they finally had their required quota of prisoners ready, somebody marched up to us. He made it clear what we had to do. "Los!! Los!!" he screamed. "Weaklings!! Pigdogs!! Los!! Los!!" He chased us back to the Sonderlager. And although most of us were truly crippled, we hurried like lightning. The deeper we penetrated into the camp, the faster we ran, just in case the authorities should change their minds!

Back in Barrack 53, I felt as if my head was going to burst! I had now had extraordinary luck on two occasions. The first time was when I hid myself under the barrack, the second when I pretended to be crippled. Every day we could expect them to come on new raids. But on a third occasion I could not expect to have fate on my side. That would be impossible. I had to invent something to keep myself safe. Anything. The whole night, I lay thinking, sweating with anxiety, with my heart beating loudly. In the end, I got the idea of going to the Sanitäter or medical orderly. The next day, at the first glimmer of light, I went to see him immediately.

The Sanitäter was the loud nurse. He did not work in the area but outside the barracks—whereever accidents occurred, accidents producing hemorrhages, severe wounds, or other acute conditions. He was not a Nazi, but a prisoner like the rest of us.

When he saw me coming he was very surprised. My physical condition was certainly not extreme enough for me to come knocking on his door. But I told him, without evasion, that for the last ten days or so I had been suffering from severe dysentery, that I did not dare say anything to anybody because I was afraid of being sent to Barrack 57, the Scheissbaracke, the home of the deceased.

The Sanitäter did not trust me. He looked at me and ordered me to drop my pants. Victims of dysentery had a messy bottom, full of inflammations, bright red swellings, and traces of water loss. With me there was not the slightest sign of this. The Sanitäter sighed. "You are bluffing," he said. "No," I replied. "I am as sick as a dog. I can't go on any more. I am dying of dysentery . . ." And the Sanitäter got angry. "Please don't talk rubbish to me!" he said. "I can recognize dysentery at once! For years I have been doing nothing else than seeing cases of dysentery! You have no dysentery! Enough!" "I must run the whole time," I insisted. "I cannot hold it for a minute, really. Don't you believe me?" And then he became furious. "If you have really got dysentery, then you must go to the Scheissbaracke! That is the only spot where I can send you in that case! To Barrack 57, the end of your life!"

He gave me a sort of sickness certificate upon which he had written that I had dysentery and therefore should be admitted to Barrack 57. In other words: I had achieved my purpose! I knew well that it was life-threatening to have to go into the Scheissbaracke, if only because one could so easily become infected there. But I chose to go. It was the only way of protecting myself from the raids and from death during an evacuation.

I went there with the first light of day. When I entered the barrack and handed over the sickness certificate, everybody looked at me with suspicion. Only emaciated victims came here who died of dysentery, who lay down in the stench, ready to be taken away after two, or at the most, three days in the mortuary cart. So what was someone like me coming here for? I was not like them. I should have been outside! I was assigned a bed half-relieved, but rather shocked by what I now saw, I lay down.

Here in the hospital block no wooden bunks existed, only beds. But they were beds of only two levels. To climb three levels was impossible for the patients here. They were too weak to make the effort. I was given a top bunk.

The days which I passed here in the Scheissbaracke were the most unreal that I have ever experienced. Everyone lay like a lifeless skeleton, waiting for death. If there was someone there who still moved, he did it like in a slow-motion film, with slow, exaggeratedly lethargic movements. Each person turned slowly around like a tortoise, unbelievably slowly, and stuck out a hand. Very seldom did you talk to anybody. It was oppressively quiet there, like some subterranean morgue. And everybody was listless. These people still lived, still tried to live, but they absentmindedly languished in their own excrement. The little piece of bread that they were given—every day one tiny little piece— was the only thing at which they still clutched. Except for me, nobody here was still able to eat. Any kind of food was dangerous for them. Their stomachs could not stand anything any more; everything that entered their bodies was immediately rejected.

Next to me lay a non-Jewish Belgian, a political prisoner called Vos. When I came in, he was already fully in the throes of death. Altogether, he weighed perhaps thirty kilos. At times, he slowly turned toward me and looked at me. He tried to say something. Despite his desperate plight, it was apparent that he was a very civilized man. He was still mentally alert. He still could understand where he was and what was awaiting him, and that made me feel that he appreciated my presence there. But after speaking for only ten minutes, he was so desperately exhausted that he had to turn away again with the little piece of bread in his hands. Gradually he would lose consciousness.

The Blockälteste of the Scheissbaracke regularly tried to organize something to obtain extra rations. He used a separate technique to achieve this end. If someone died, he did not immediately hand over this corpse to the corpse service, but he kept the body hidden for a few days. The Blockälteste kept for himself those rations that would have gone to the prisoner. This appropriation did not last for very long. After a few days, the corpse had to be passed on because it began to stink from decomposition; some corpses decomposed more rapidly than others.

This form of manipulation also took place in other barracks. The only difference was that here, in the Scheissbarak, the number of corpses was much greater. There were several deaths here daily.

The swapping of corpses was a regular feature in all the camps, and certainly in such a gigantic camp like Buchenwald, which had an extensive network. Someone who was awaiting a punishment—for example, a death by hanging—was reported to have died. There then needed to be a corpse available to be substituted for the condemned prisoner. A deception like this was only possible if neither the prisoner in question nor the corpse bore a tattoo. Thus it took place in all the camps, except in the case of Auschwitz-Birkenau and those places where all prisoners were routinely tattooed.

While I lay in the Scheissbaracke, I had little else to do other than simply await my death. I became visibly weaker and weaker and eventually became as listless as all the others who found themselves in this plight. The air was so stifling there, as oppressive as above a swamp, totally unbearable. We lay together like dying reptiles.

It looked as if my hour had come, or so it seemed.

Liberation

On the third day of my residence in the Scheissbaracke, April 11, 1945, at around three o'clock in the afternoon, we suddenly were alarmed by the incessant sound of distant machine-gun fire. We did not understand what was going on. Perhaps prisoners were being shot. We were as scared as rabbits being chased by a weasel. A bit later, things quieted down again outside, and a strange, oppressive silence fell over us. We felt each second intensely and believed that something abnormal was happening, something which we had never experienced before. But what was it? We could not guess. Vos, who was still lying next to me, ceased to move. All the time, from hour to hour, I had been observing his agony, his via dolorosa, but during this agitation caused by the sound of gunfire, he escaped my attention for a while. Half an hour later, his life had slipped away. He had perished from exhaustion.

After more than an hour, some prisoners who worked as nurses came in. They shivered like mad. Their eyes were popping out with excitement, and the sweat poured off their foreheads. Stammering with emotion, they came to tell us what was going on: the liberation . . . the liberation . . . we were liberated. American armies had taken Weimar; they had surrounded the concentration camp below the Etterberg. From there, they had already given a sign to the underground troops in the camp. There had been a real battle between the S.S.-ers and the prisoners of the underground network. Hardly any of the S.S. had wanted to surrender just like that. But the rebels seemed to have been extremely well equipped. For years, they had been preparing themselves for this with the courage of despair. There were 150 S.S. in Buchenwald; they all had to be overpowered. By surprise, the troops had been able take them all prisoner. When the male nurses told us this, I was overcome with relief. For my entire time in the camps, I had been longing for this moment of liberation, keeping the illusion of a future freedom in the forefront of my mind. Now it had become a reality! But it came so unexpectedly! Soon after, we saw prisoners marching past with captured S.S.-ers. The S.S.-ers had their hands up and were as tame as little lambs. Guns were directed at their backs. This image defied the imagination; the world was now upside down! The prisoners who formed the resistance behaved themselves in a very disciplined and correct manner. But, how was that possible? How could that be true? I was dreaming; it could not be otherwise!

In our barrack, an indescribable exhilaration arose. With their remaining strength, these sick, emaciated skeletons emitted their shouts of joy. Those who were still physically able heaved themselves up to go and look. Other remained lying down and laughed hysterically, completely immobile. And one of the walking skeletons, an Italian, shrouded in a blanket, tottered across the floor. He began to sing: "O sole mio," "Mama son tanto felice," and "Santa Lucia." With these songs that rang out over our beds, he gave expression to what we were all feeling: a heavenly, unreachable happiness on the one hand, and a completely desolate, broken, and desperate loneliness on the other. Although a dream had now been realized, a dream that we had been dreaming for many long years and for every second of the day, a dream that, in reality, we no longer had dared to dream—we suddenly also became brutally aware of the enormous cost of this tragedy through which we had lived. Thirty percent of the prisoners had been past help, irretrievably lost in a hopeless struggle against death. Everybody whooped with joy, but everyone saw these walking cadavers, corpse-like men, half-skeletons who today or tomorrow were inevitably going to be dead. There were people with frozen or broken limbs, people on crutches. Ninety percent of them were going around with a blanket around their shoulders, as the first signal of their inevitable doom. How many of these exuberant people in Barrack 57 would, anyway, reach the finish line in their race for survival? And how many were there among those like Vos who, even at the moment of liberation, had died? For them this nightmare had never come to an end—the countless unhappy wretches in the camps, already in a vegetative state of mental decline, who stood expressionlessly looking around and who did not even realize what was going on.

Personally, I was too weak to be able to participate in this happiness. I knew that I had been freed, but, at the same time, all the misery and unhappiness that I had had to bury in order to survive came flooding back. The death of my mother, my father, my brothers, my whole family . . . I now saw before my eyes how, in Auschwitz, they must have been gassed and incinerated. I felt that I was totally alone in the world, with nowhere to go and nobody to turn to. Where had I to go now? I had nothing to long for, nobody to support me. I was only a teenager and I was sitting in a lonely black pit. Totally hopeless.

One hour after the liberation, the Americans were already approaching us in the camps. When they saw us they could not believe their eyes. They were deeply shocked by the indescribable beastliness in which we had had to live and the physical condition into which we had declined. But now they were going to put everything right. They were going to take care of us.

Because there was not enough water in Buchenwald to make it possible to prepare enormous amounts of food, the Americans had to bring water to us in tanks. We, the prisoners of Barrack 57, had always received food from the S.S. at about one o'clock in the afternoon. The physical condition of most of the walking cadavers in this barrack was completely dependent on this routine, just like a biological clock. Because of the delay with the water, however, we got food at four in the afternoon, that is, three hours later from when we were accustomed. Our hunger was so great that this difference (or delay) was nearly unbearable. I heard a prisoner close to me complaining: "Why is it really necessary to be liberated?" he said. "Before, at least, we already got food at one o'clock! And here we are now sitting in agony waiting!"

The irony of this man's remark is, naturally, incredible. Most of these prisoners were so severely blunted that they could not even think logically any more. They acted on impulse. Their perspective was simply too narrow for them to realize the full significance of this liberation.

Eventually the most unbelievably rich foods were served up to us: goulash, potatoes, beans, all with sauces; it was too much to describe. We could not believe what we saw. We could have fainted from the aromas alone. But this distribution of food was too reckless. This sudden change had a deadly effect on quite a number of the ex-prisoners. They died before the far-too-rich food had even been half-digested in their bodies. Later on, we were given somewhat lighter food, milk porridge, macaroni, etc.

Many ex-prisoners, and certainly the Germans who came from within the immediate region, wanted to get away as soon as possible, to leave Buchenwald behind forever, even though the war was not yet at an end. The head of the Scheissbaracke was such a German ex-prisoner. Immediately after the liberation, on the night that immediately followed it, he moved on and disappeared. He had nothing more to do here. But the majority of the ex-prisoners had nowhere to go. We still had to stay on here for days on end. And the male nurses, the guards, and other camp personnel now placed themselves at the service of the allies. Except for their rate of pay, they remained unchanged in function.

Prisoners who had slightly better health and who were still somewhat physically able gradually began to head for Weimar. They were going to satisfy themselves with food and drink. The people who saw them coming were too afraid to refuse them anything. The prisoners also tried to get clothes. For days on end, we still had to be satisfied with our camp garb, the striped, very flimsy, little suit of clothes.

The excursions to Weimar and back for these ex-prisoners began to cause much chaos in the camp. Everybody now used his own initiative. After a few days, the Americans had to set some limits about this. If one wanted to go away, one had to first ask for "leave" twenty-four hours in advance. This leave was always granted.

All this was not possible for me. Physically, I could not manage it any more. I lay down without strength in the dark Scheissbaracke without any special interest in the outside world. For me, every minute was still a question of surviving. Had the liberation occurred a little bit later, I would probably not have survived to see it. I was drained so much, almost a vegetable. Enjoying my liberty was really quite impossible for me at the time.

My only activity amounted to listening to the radio. The wireless sets were brought in to us, even as far as the Scheissbaracke. We could receive announcements about the advances of the allied troops, about the other camps which had been freed, about the transports of prisoners that had been intercepted, about the terrible condition in which they were found or even how they had died. On the day after the liberation, April 12, 1945, we also heard the news of the death of President Roosevelt, a noteworthy and significant announcement. The entire war effort was now on the decline. A new world was beginning to take shape. The new American president was Truman.

After a day or two, a medical corps came to Buchenwald. We were deloused with D.D.T., a kind of powder. After the fumigation, it looked as if a bag of flour had been emptied over us. In the meantime also, American war correspondents came to see us. With pen and paper in hand, they turned the whole camp upside down, examining every-thing and questioning everybody. One of these reporters also came to me, in the gloomy Scheissbaracke. He wanted to have an interview with me. He introduced himself to me and told me that all news about Buchenwald was front-page news. He asked me a few questions. But while he busied himself with questions, I only looked at him speech-lessly, hardly interested. Throughout all that I had experienced, I had become so lonely and isolated that I could no longer accept that some-one could be interested in me or in my own personal circumstance. I thought that this interviewer was pulling my leg, taking me for a ride. It felt as if I was posing in front of a camera without any film. He went out without receiving anything from me. Go and make another joke, I thought.

On the second day after the liberation, the Americans made all the inhabitants of Weimar, after they had surrounded them, come to the camp. They were obliged to come and look at what had happened here, at what shame, disgrace, mischief, and calamity had occurred. In rows, the frightened citizens walked past us, as if it were a passage through a museum. The alarm and fright could be read from their faces. The Americans asked them for their opinion. We heard for the first time their infamous and disreputable comment again and again: "We knew nothing of this." That was it. That settled everything! "We knew nothing of this."

Little by little, they began to reconstruct our identities. We had to supply our names, our date of birth, and other information; in return each of us received a temporary or provisional identity card. Photos could not be taken; we supplied our thumbprint instead. I attached a good deal of importance to that little slip of paper because it was like an annulment of the number on my arm. It was a first step in the direc-tion of becoming a human being again. For hours I held that little pass-port between my fingers and stared at it.

In the meantime, we naturally and urgently wanted to go back home. What were we doing lying here? How much longer did we still have to wait? They told us that they were busy preparing the brick houses of the S.S. for us, the places where the S.S. had lived together with their families, wives and children. While awaiting the evacuation, we would be taken there. And indeed, around April 18, we were taken to these brick houses from the barracks of the concentration camp. In the meantime, the Sonderlager was substantially evacuated.

The move to the brick-built barracks was quite a relief. In fact, I had been exposed to the danger of becoming infected for one long week. And now, for the first time since 1942, I lay in a clean, soft bed under a spotless, sumptuous sheet. The sensation that this gave us beggars has no description. Only now did we feel truly free. We were exalted.

Although, I had partly recuperated physically, I still found myself among the invalids and among the most washed-out, emaciated physical wrecks. Here, I was in a sort of convalescence. There were still ex-prisoners who died daily. The causes of their deaths included fully advanced tuberculosis, dysentery, and exhaustion. Victims with infectious diseases were taken somewhere else.

There were also children with us. It was only now that I came to know that within Buchenwald, in the Sonderlager, there had also been a children's barrack, a special barrack for prisoners between the ages of six and fifteen. A shocking piece of information that defies the imagination. Two of these children, still younger than I, were Elie Wiesel, who was later to be awarded the Nobel Peace Prize (in 1986), and Rav Lau, later the Chief Rabbi of Israel.

In this room, I made the acquaintance of two Jewish boys from Czechoslovakia. One of them was named Max Neugroschel. He was a very pleasant and also religious lad. From the first moment following the liberation, he decided not to eat any meat that was not kosher, and observing in the camp that there was no kosher meat available, he ate only milky foods. The other boy was the grandson of a rabbi. He was always discussing deeply the dark Talmud questions. During the first two or three nights in the brick-built houses he began to ask himself so many questions about the Talmud and about his destiny that at night he immediately began to hallucinate. In his sleep he recited entire Talmudic passages. It got worse and worse. He had to be shaken awake and calmed, but a little while later, as soon as the light was put out, he began again. He experienced a phenomenon that affected many other ex-prisoners—a pure mental derangement, a total disorientation that obliterates all other thought processes. He had to be admitted to a psychiatric clinic. Thirty years later, in a discussion with Max Neugroschel, I learnt that the boy later recovered and was getting along well.

One day a barber came to us. We were all given the opportunity to have a haircut as we ourselves would wish it, within the bounds of possibility. In fact, our hair was still too short for anything to be done with it. But if all the hairs around our ears and at the sides of our head

Ausweis — Certification.

Herr Rosengarten Jaques
Mister

geb. am 27-2-26 in Rzeszow (Pol.)
born *at*

zuletzt wohnhaft Rue de la Couronne 200
last domicile

Anvers

wurde vom 23-7-42 bis

in nationalsozialistischen Konzentrationslagern gefangen
gehalten und vom Konzentrationslager Buchenwald
bei Weimar in Freiheit gesetzt.

was kept in captivity from 23-7-42 to
in Nazi-German concentrationcamps and was liberated from the
concentrationcamp of Buchenwald.

Unterschriften und Stempel:
signatures and stamps:

Lagerkomitee   Lagerkommandant

Weimar-Buchenwald, am

The first identity card given to me at Weimar-Buchenwald after my liberation,
May 9, 1945 (in two parts).

Provisional identification card
for civilian internee of Buchenwald.

Vorläufige Identitätskarte für Buchenwälder Zivilinternierte.

Current number ....   Internee number 130462
Laufende Nr.   *Häftlings-Nr.*

Family name .... Rosengarten,
Familienname

Christian name .... Jaques
Vorname

Born ..27-2-26 ....   at   Rzeszow (Pol
geboren   *in*

Nationality .... Polish
Nationalität

Adress ..2oo Rue de la Couronne 2oo
Adresse   Anvers

Fingerprint:
Fingerabdruck

Signature:
Unterschrift

Weimar-Buchenwald, am 9-5-45

were made any shorter, the remainder looked, simply by contrast, a bit longer. I remember that Max Neugroschel had all his hair shaved off with a razor, in accordance with the tradition of most orthodox Jews.

A week later, still in Buchenwald, regular political declarations began on the roll call grounds of the Sonderlager. These declarations were made mainly by ex-prisoners from the communist side who had particularly been attacked by the Nazis. Amongst others, ex-senator Glineur came to say his bit. At that time, I met during roll call a certain Jack Graubart who would later become a well-known Antwerp diamond merchant. I also met a person called Krygier who after the war occupied himself extensively with helping ex-prisoners from concentration camps.

And then, gradually, the great evacuation began to take place. We Belgians were told that, within a few days, we would be flown back to our own country. We were put on lists; I was the only Belgian in the brick-built barracks of the S.S.

Indeed, sometime later a military airplane landed in the neighborhood of Buchenwald. We were informed that the prominent Minister Paul Van Zeland would be coming here, to take with him all the ex-prisoners with Belgian nationality. Because I was still wearing that much-too-thin clothing of the concentration camp, I was given a new outfit, washed and ironed, and a blanket was wrapped around me, and I was taken in a kind of ambulance to the aircraft. I was all excited, ready to leave and to say good-bye to this place of doom. But right in front of the steps up to the aircraft, the Belgian ex-prisoner chiefs came to the conclusion that I could not go with them. The reason was that I was not a demonstrated true Belgian. I was registered as originating from Belgium, but because my father came from Poland, the chiefs began to have doubts about my nationality. I explained to them that I was most certainly Belgian because I was naturalized—which was not completely the truth, but would anyone have done the same to get out of this hell. But the chiefs again began to confer amongst themselves, and they concluded that in no way could I be considered for repatriation with them in their aircraft.

When I heard this, I felt as if I had been slapped in the face. I was sent away in disgrace and left to my fate. The ex-prisoners who came after me and who had the same status as I—a certain Rubenstein and his son among others—were indeed allowed in. And not much later, the ladder was pulled up, and the doors were locked. I had to stand and watch the aircraft return to Belgium only half-full. There they went! Myself? I was taken back to the brick-built barracks of the S.S.

I had a complete black-out. The thirty-four months of captivity, with all their horrors, passed before my eyes. I fainted. When I came round, I began to ask myself what I had actually lost in Belgium. Who would I find there? I had nobody there. And here, at least, I had a bed and was given food. I lost all my energy and relapsed into a deep depression without any hope. I simply had to wait and see what now would happen to me, wait and see what plans the authorities might now have in store for me.

Father and son Rubenstein, who were indeed allowed to travel in the airplane, had been with me in all the camps. Not Bismarckhütte, but Saccrau, Laurahütte, Blechhammer. The senior Rubenstein was one of the older people who survived the camp. Before the war he had had a kitchenware shop in the Somersstraat in Antwerp. After the war he became a schamas, a sort of sacristan, in the big synagogue in the Oostenstraat in Antwerp. His son became a leader in the youth organization Hanoar after the war. Later he went to Israel, where he became the head of the ground personnel of Sabena, in Lot.

A few days later, after the calamitous event with the airplane, a couple of impressive, well-dressed American officers came to us. They told us that, within a couple of weeks, in accordance with an agreement between the Americans and the Russians, the whole district would have to be handed over by the Americans to the Russians and cleared out. But they said that we westerners should not to be disturbed by this arrangement. We would all be repatriated in time.

This announcement was a great disappointment for the prisoners from the Eastern European countries. They cried out with horror and lowered their heads in grief. Intuitively, they felt that soon, with the Russians, they would undergo a whole new ordeal under the Russian yoke.

I, too, began to tremble. As I thought about it, I realized that within a couple of weeks the Russians would be here! I was indeed registered as a Belgian, but to which authorities could I now turn? I had nowhere to go; I had been left behind here, completely helpless.

This miserable uncertainty lasted for another ten days. Only then did they come to tell the remaining western ex-prisoners like me that a train would come and take us to the west. To the Netherlands, Belgium, France. An enormous relief—we were so longing to get away from here! Just about the whole camp was being evacuated. Before we left, we could still get a few clothes. They lay piled up outside in a heap, poor colorless rags from which we hurriedly made our choice. I was worried that these clothes were infested with lice, one of the unmentionable traumas with which I would have to live. But the feeling of finally being clothed like a civilian was wonderful, really indescribable. The clothes, when we put them on felt unusually warm and heavy.

The train which came to pick us up was a supply train of poorly covered freight wagons. And thus we, like cattle, went back to Belgium inside a wagon with straw moving in fits and starts, without the slightest kind of medical, social, or psychological guidance.

In spite of this, there was a fairly pleasant and relaxed atmosphere, with a bit of chatting. Here and there, somebody lit a cigarette. These were our first experiences discovering a regained freedom. We still had to get used to the idea that we could choose to do, or not do, whatever we pleased.

At one of the train stations, we met up with another transport, a train with American occupation troops who were traveling in the opposite direction. They were in freight wagons like ours, no more or less comfortable. When they saw us, they began to laugh. They generously shared their food with us, tins of beans (typical soldier's food). We were very grateful to them for this. The food was quite different from the rather monotonous fare that we received from the Red Cross. And we now ate the same as the Allies and, most importantly, they shared it with us! That gave us a feeling of triumph, of oneness, of brotherly solidarity.

In our train, I met an old classmate of mine, Hersh Ickovic. We had been together in class for eight years. I knew him well. In the class, we had always been somewhat competitive. I usually came first in the class at examination time, and Ickovic came second or third; but this was mitigated by the fact that he was much better at soccer than I. We had been really good friends. This reunion after three years of captivity was something truly valuable.

In the train, I also re-met a certain Tornheim, a somewhat older man who had had corset shop in the Lange Leemstraat in Antwerp. We all looked the same—thin and wasted-away, lonely, broken, but curious to know what awaited us in Belgium.

After two days and two nights, we arrived in Namen on May 20, 1945. Namen was, for us, a milestone in the liberation process. From now on, we were free from the world of the concentration camps and returned to civilization. On the basis of the identity cards which we had received in Buchenwald, we were now handed a kind of repatriation paper—official documents that later could be exchanged for a real identity card in the municipality where we wished to reside. We were also given a gift of 100 Belgian francs, upon which to survive. We did not have the slightest idea of the value of these francs, although we were soon to discover that it was very little. But from now on we were considered to be self-supporting and independent, and we had to manage as best we could.

Next, the train brought us to Brussels-South. The ex-prisoners who had been repatriated by the aircraft "Minister Van Zeeland" had been sent directly to St. Peter's Hospital, where they received a full medical examination and where they could also stay until they adjusted psychologically. But we were simply released from the train and put on the street. We were left to fend for ourselves.

The Place Roupe was not far from the South Station. I went there together with Ickovic. The Jewish community had established a kind of receiving center for ex-prisoners in this square. Here, one received vouchers, which were exchanged for a meal twice a day. This center was also a place where all the news about the concentration camps and about the Jewish war victims arrived. Here were hung lists of people being sought or those who had perished in the camps. There were Jews everywhere, hundreds and hundreds of them. That so many Jews still existed after everything—even Jews who went around in orthodox clothes—was a thing that I could not have guessed. And they were all searching for some person. With every step I made, I was approached by someone. A desperate woman carrying a photo of her children, of her parents, of her relatives. Husbands searching for their wives. "Have you not seen this one? Do you not recognize this man? Would you by any chance know if you have seen my children?" It was very painful for us. It was almost impossible to explain to them how small their chances of success were. We actually got the feeling that we were the only ones who had returned, as if everything behind us had gone up in smoke. We were truly amazed if somebody told us how he or she had been able to hide somewhere in Brussels, in Flanders, or (mostly) Wallonie during all those years of war. The thing that we did indeed notice was that the "Left" had obviously been most active in that kind of support activity.

Together with Ickovic I decided to stay on for a while in Brussels. We rented a room together to share the costs and to avoid loneliness. Other people who had not been in the concentration camps were like

First Belgian document after my repatriation (in two parts).

Sonja Zinger, Schaerbeek, 256 rue de la Post, who took care of me like a sister after the liberation.

extraterrestrial beings to us. We could not explain to them how and what we had experienced and suffered. It was as if we each of us were living on an desert island with only our memories.

After a while I met a distant relative by marriage at the Place Rouppe, where I went daily. Her name was Esther Goldfinger. A cousin of my mother was married to one of Esther's brothers. I knew Esther fairly well, from the holiday colony where I had always gone as a child. This was the Villa Altol in Kappelenbos. The first thing that Esther asked me when, to our amazement, we bumped into each other was if I had seen her husband, Abraham Rosenfeld. My answer was in the negative, almost by rote. But then she told me that, a cousin of my mother was living here in Brussels, Sonja Zinger. This was for me a piece of news that fell from heaven, truly incredible! Before the war, Sonja had lived at 188 Kroonstraat in Antwerp when we had lived at 200 Kroonstraat. We lived very close to each other, and the family had been intimate friends. When I was six, Sonja was in her early twenties, but she had been very fond of me as a child. I remember how she and her girlfriend had sometimes taken me with them to the cinema, once every four or five months—a great luxury for me! Now that I heard that she was here, I was overcome with emotion. She was still my only blood relative. Esther told me how Sonja had been able to hide in the Walloon provinces, in Charleroi-Dampremy. Sonja's family was deported, together with mine (with the Seventh Transport). We had to meet again. Sonja's brother was Herschl Zinger, the boy who had gone with my brother Samuel to Roeselare. Herschl finally ended up in London and was thus able to escape the clutches of the Nazis.

Immediately after this news about Sonja, she visited me on the Place Rouppe, and invited me to come to her house. We had a substantial hot meal and began to talk at length with each other. Once again, a desper-

Membership card of ex-prisoners from the concentration camps of Breendonk, 1946. Address: rue de la Post 256.

ate litany of questions. Had I seen her sisters? Had I seen her brother-in-law? Had I seen her father, her nephews? I could not help her. But Sonja had remained the kind-hearted person of the earlier days. She proposed that I should come and live at her place. She herself was not very rich; she had a small living room, an attic room, not even heated but it had running water. If I wished, I could pass the nights there on a camp bed.

Considering my situation, her suggestion was a gift from heaven. I had no family, no income. I existed on benefits, from one day to the next. Now I had, after fourteen days of wandering, found a hearth and a roof over my head with people who worked for their bread. They had no children. And Sonja still had the family spirit.

I tried to the best of my ability to push the memory of my concentration camp life into the background. At all cost, I had to try to integrate myself into daily civilian life. I still went each day to the Place Rouppe, but most of the people who went there seeking solace could only speak about the concentration camps, about the horrors, and about the madness of those days. They now had food and shelter, but mentally they still went on living with the terror of Nazism. The life of the concentration camps was their only topic of conversation, from the early morning until late in the evening.

The only hope that I still nourished was that Samuel, my elder brother, would still be alive. Or my father. Perhaps they had devised some means of escaping the concentration camps. But I was never presented with this happy surprise. After a short time, I saw a list in the Place Rouppe where they were mentioned as being deported and murdered. Gradually, I had to accept the fact that there was no one of my immediate family still alive except me, although I nurtured the hope for a year and a half that at least one of them would still appear.

Epilogue

Overtime, I tried to lead a normal, organized life—I had no other choice. Employment was one issue that I did not really understand. How was I to prepare for the future? How was I to learn to earn my daily crust of bread? Without being unpleasant, Sonja asked me in September 1945 when I intended to begin working at something and what my plans were. What kind of career was I thinking of? I was still uncomfortable with the idea of working—how should I go about it?

I already had been to Antwerp a few times to see the civil authorities and the police about putting in order the issue of my identity. I experienced much pain in the process of returning to Borgerhout. When I passed my parent's home, I felt like falling to my knees. Wherever I looked, Jewish life was again recovering, with little shops and businesses. But for me, this was not yet to be my lot. I was still too much in doubt. When I returned to Brussels in the evening, I experienced a feeling of relief. I had already made some friends in this city, and I knew my way around somewhat. However, I could no longer continue to be a parasite. Every fortnight, I returned to Antwerp to adjust gradually to normal living conditions and to consider my future. I became interested in the diamond industry. The same dilemma that my father had faced in the 1920s now presented itself to me. Diamond cleaving was the ideal, but this work demanded a long and very expensive period of training. Consequently, I made the choice to train as a diamond girdler.

I began to earn my first money and become self-reliant in the spring of 1946. I was exceptionally proud of this because it was a sign that I was again integrating myself into society. Daydreaming about my family was pointless—I had to face up to the situation. But I still lived in Brussels.

Sonja told me in December 1946 that she would soon leave for

America, following her brothers-in-law. It was very hard for me to adjust to her departure; I now felt that I had become an orphan. But time is a great healer, and gradually after my cousin had left, I began to understand how little sense there was in remaining in Brussels. My place of work was in Antwerp. One day, I bolstered my courage and made the move; I settled at Bloemstraat 45. This was only one door away from the place where I had lived as a child in 1930.

Every spot of this neighborhood awakened memories in me. The world of my childhood, which had been destroyed in the cruelest way, had been washed away.